Palgrave Studies on Chinese Education in a Global Perspective

Series Editors
Fred Dervin
Department of Education
University of Helsinki
Helsinki, Finland

Xiangyun Du
College of Education
Qatar University
Doha, Qatar

The transformation of China into a global superpower is often attributed to the country's robust education system and this series seeks to provide a comprehensive, in-depth understanding of the development of Chinese education on a global scale. The books in this series will analyze and problematize the reforms, innovations and transformations of Chinese education that are often misunderstood or misrepresented beyond its own borders and will examine the changes in Chinese education over the past 30 years and the issues as well as challenges that the future of Chinese education faces.

Caitríona Osborne • Danping Wang
Qi Zhang
Editors

Teaching Chinese Characters in the Digital Age

Insights on Current Trends and Future Directions

Editors
Caitríona Osborne
Irish Institute for Chinese Studies
University College Dublin
Belfield, Dublin, Ireland

Qi Zhang
School of Applied Language and
Intercultural Studies
Dublin City University
Dublin, Ireland

Danping Wang
School of Cultures, Languages and
Linguistics
University of Auckland
Auckland, New Zealand

ISSN 2945-6576   ISSN 2945-6584   (electronic)
Palgrave Studies on Chinese Education in a Global Perspective
ISBN 978-3-031-64783-3   ISBN 978-3-031-64784-0   (eBook)
https://doi.org/10.1007/978-3-031-64784-0

© The Editor(s) (if applicable) and The Author(s), under exclusive licence to Springer Nature Switzerland AG 2024

This work is subject to copyright. All rights are solely and exclusively licensed by the Publisher, whether the whole or part of the material is concerned, specifically the rights of translation, reprinting, reuse of illustrations, recitation, broadcasting, reproduction on microfilms or in any other physical way, and transmission or information storage and retrieval, electronic adaptation, computer software, or by similar or dissimilar methodology now known or hereafter developed.
The use of general descriptive names, registered names, trademarks, service marks, etc. in this publication does not imply, even in the absence of a specific statement, that such names are exempt from the relevant protective laws and regulations and therefore free for general use.
The publisher, the authors and the editors are safe to assume that the advice and information in this book are believed to be true and accurate at the date of publication. Neither the publisher nor the authors or the editors give a warranty, expressed or implied, with respect to the material contained herein or for any errors or omissions that may have been made. The publisher remains neutral with regard to jurisdictional claims in published maps and institutional affiliations.

This Palgrave Macmillan imprint is published by the registered company Springer Nature Switzerland AG.
The registered company address is: Gewerbestrasse 11, 6330 Cham, Switzerland

If disposing of this product, please recycle the paper.

Acknowledgements

The editors are particularly grateful to two funding bodies that helped get this project off the ground: UCD Global Engagement Seed Fund 2021 and the Chinese Embassy in Ireland. We are indebted to the reviewers for their time in providing invaluable feedback on an early proposal of this edited book and to Palgrave Macmillan (in particular, Cathy Scott, Sasikala Thopu and Pushpalatha Mohan) for their continued support throughout this project. We thank the contributing authors for their dedication in the form of both their chapters herein and their contributions—along with Professor George X. Zhang, Professor Li Quan, Professor Helen Shen, Professor Joel Bellassen and Professor Nathan Hill—to the 2022 online seminar series *Exploring the Present and Future of Teaching Chinese Characters Online* that inspired the creation of this book.

Praise for *Teaching Chinese Characters in the Digital Age*

"A valuable collection of reflections and research on Chinese character teaching during the global pandemic years offers a transformative glimpse into the future of Chinese character education. This groundbreaking work sparks new actions and research, heralding a digital turn in teaching Chinese characters in the new age of technology."

—*Professor Li Quan, Renmin University*

"The advance of science and technology has brought human society into the digital age. This era has put forward new requirements and standards for all aspects of Chinese language education. In the area of Chinese character instruction, we have observed major changes in teaching philosophy, instructional approaches, and curriculum design. I consider the book *Teaching Chinese Characters in the Digital Age - Insights on Current Trends and Future Directions* a timely and highly welcomed one in the field. It addresses important issues raised in the educational practice concerning how to effectively use digital tools, digital platforms, and digital resources to optimize character recognition and production; how to design multifaceted curricula to fit goals of different Chinese programs and individual needs, and how our instruction can take into consideration learners' cognitive processing of characters by using appropriate digital tools to maximise their learning outcomes. From both educators and learners' perspectives, the book also has touched on how to prepare our teachers and students for a smooth transition of Chinese character learning from a traditional paper-pen to a paperless mode – a mainstream mode of classroom learning in the digital age."

—*Professor Helen H. Shen, The University of Iowa*

"Chinese characters often mean love, or hate, or both for almost all L2 Chinese learners and many who teach Chinese as a foreign language. Not surprisingly, there is a wealth of research and publications on the topic. This book, however, signifies a milestone and is unique in a number of ways.

It focuses on exploring alternative answers to a long debated and sensitive question – the need to learn how to write characters by hand. While learning online and typing characters were initially a necessity forced upon learners and teachers during the pandemic, such practices now also represent a transformative shift in the digital age open to more innovative development.

It is a locally funded project but with international perspectives, the result of a long running project featuring collaboration and exchange both online and offline with the involvement of not only the contributors but also many others over the time of the project, with critical and theoretical reflections on the relevant empirical research and personal experience.

It combines theory with practice and offers helpful insight into the learning and teaching of Chinese characters in universities in the digital age, with emphasis on the development of methodologies and theories for character teaching. The book is, therefore, inspirational for both learners and teachers of Chinese characters, and particularly in higher education."

—*Professor George X. Zhang, Richmond American University London*

Contents

1 Introduction   1
Caitríona Osborne, Danping Wang, and Qi Zhang

Theme I   Teaching and Learning Chinese Characters Online   21

2 Chinese Character Instruction During Emergency Remote Teaching: A Review Study   23
Linda Lei and Danping Wang

3 Investigating the Student Perspective on the Present and Future of Teaching Chinese Characters Online   47
Caitríona Osborne

Theme II   Critical Perspectives Regarding Typing Chinese Characters in the CFL Classroom   79

4 The E-writing Approach to L2 Chinese Pedagogy: Educational Imperative and Empirical Evidence   81
Matthew D. Coss

5 Embodied Learning of Chinese Characters Through Typing and Handwriting in the Multimodal Virtual Space: Implications for a Digital Future   105
Qi Zhang

Theme III   Development of Methodologies and Theories for Character Teaching   133

6 Enhancing Understanding and Engagement with the Chinese Writing System in Second Language Classrooms   135
Andrew Scrimgeour

7 Visual Skill and Orthographic Decomposition in Character Learning   163
Yi Xu

8 Psycholinguistic Research Related to Chinese Character Recognition: Implications for CFL Teaching   197
Xi Fan and Ronan Reilly

Theme IV   Reflective Narrative   221

9 Reflections on Learning Chinese Characters   223
Bob Adamson

Index   239

Notes on Contributors

Bob Adamson specialises in curriculum reform, with particular focus on language policies. He has worked in schools, colleges and universities in China, the UK, France and Australia, and formerly held the UNESCO Chair at the Education University of Hong Kong. He was a member of the People's Education Press and Longman team who wrote the *Junior English for China* and *Senior English for China* textbook series used by over 400 million students. In 2013, he was awarded the title of "Kunlun Expert" by the Qinghai Provincial Government for his work in minority language education in China.

Matthew D. Coss is a PhD candidate in Second Language Studies at Michigan State University and is an experienced teacher of Spanish and Mandarin Chinese as additional languages. His research focuses on the multiple existing and potential interfaces between additional language learning research and practice, with particular focus on (task-based) language teaching and assessment, language programme design and evaluation and language teacher education. He is the co-editor of *Transforming Hanzi Pedagogy in the Digital Age: Theory, Research, and Practice* (电写时代的汉字教学—理论与实践), published by Routledge in 2024.

Xi Fan works as a Psychology Lecturer at Guangzhou Medical University in China. She completed her PhD in Cognitive Science at Maynooth

University. Her research focuses primarily on the cognitive science of reading and visual attention.

Linda Lei recently completed her PhD at the School of Cultures, Languages and Linguistics at the University of Auckland, New Zealand. She has taught Mandarin to students of various age groups and proficiency levels in New Zealand, USA and China. Her research interests are centred on literacy development in Chinese as a foreign language. Her doctoral thesis explores the character learning experiences of beginner learners of Chinese as a foreign language, examining their beliefs about character learning, strategies they employ and their character-related skills.

Caitríona Osborne is an Assistant Professor in the Irish Institute for Chinese Studies at University College Dublin. Dr Osborne collaborates with scholars in Ireland, the UK, and China in various research papers on the topic of teaching and learning Chinese and introduces her students to aspects of these effective teaching approaches in order to assist them in their learning. One such method involves the use of different colours to learn characters which she is also currently examining in further research.

Apart from research into teaching approaches, Dr Osborne has also co-authored papers on the presence of translanguaging in the classroom, the use of machine translation in the classroom, and the effects of extra-curricular language and culture activities on students' formal learning. She currently teaches Chinese as a foreign language to beginner learners, while she also teaches the Chinese teaching methodology modules associated with the Professional Diploma and MA in Teaching Chinese Language and Culture at University College Dublin.

She is the media coordinator of the Irish Association of Applied Linguistics and is the assistant editor of the *Chinese as a Second Language Research* journal.

In 2022, Dr Osborne was awarded a college-level Teaching Excellence Award for her contribution to educational excellence in UCD.

Ronan Reilly is a Professor of Computer Science at Maynooth University. He obtained his primary and PhD degrees in the fields of psychology and computer science at University College Dublin and was a post-doctoral fellow in the Beckman Institute, University of Illinois at Urbana-

Champaign, USA. Professor Reilly's research interests are primarily in the areas of cognitive science and artificial intelligence. Since his PhD, he has been interested in studying language understanding and reading. His background in both psychology and computer science has allowed him to exploit computational modelling as a tool for theory development.

Andrew Scrimgeour is an Adjunct Research Fellow at the University of South Australia. He has been involved in Chinese teaching since the early 1980s and continues to undertake research into literacy development, learner diversity, curriculum design and teacher training for Chinese language learning in schools. He co-authored *Teaching Chinese as a Second Language: The Way of the Learner* with Dr Jane Orton in 2019.

Danping Wang is a Senior Lecturer and programme leader of Chinese at the University of Auckland, New Zealand. She has a strong track record in obtaining and completing major external research funding, including a UGC grant in Hong Kong and the Marsden Fund grant from the Royal Society of New Zealand. She was awarded the Research Excellence Award by the Faculty of Arts in 2020 for her commitment to advancing the theoretical development of multilingualism. In 2023, she was awarded the Dean's Award for Teaching Excellence, being the Overall Winner across all categories by the Faculty of Arts and honoured with the Sustained Excellence Award in Teaching by the University of Auckland for her contribution to transformative and relational teaching approach.

Danping's research focuses on addressing critical issues in foreign language education, particularly in Chinese language teaching. Her research interests include curriculum development, policy analysis, integration of technology and teacher education within the field. She actively contributes as an editorial board member for a number of impactful journals and has edited several special issues in journals such as *Applied Linguistics Review*, *International Journal of Computer-Assistant Language Teaching and Learning*, *Global Chinese* and *International Journal of Chinese Language Teaching*.

Yi Xu, PhD in Second Language Acquisition & Teaching, is a Professor in Chinese Language Acquisition at the University of Pittsburgh. She served as the former President of the Chinese Language Teachers

Association, US, and has published extensively in journals including *Foreign Language Annals, The Modern Language Journal, System, Language Teaching Research, Chinese Language Teaching in the World,* etc. She specializes in linguistic perspectives of Chinese as a foreign language, including learners' reading acquisition, character and vocabulary learning and grammatical development. Her recent projects include world language teachers' experiences and perceptions of the impact of remote language teaching.

Qi Zhang is an Assistant Professor in the School of Applied Language and Intercultural Studies at Dublin City University. She received her BA in Chinese Language and Literature at Sun Yat-sen University, PR China, MA in Translation at Durham University and PhD in Linguistics at Newcastle University. She joined Dublin City University in 2011 as the coordinator for Chinese. She is currently a member of CTTS (Centre for Translation and Textual Studies), a committee member of IRAAL (Irish Association of Applied Linguistics) and APTIS (Association of Programmes in Translation and Interpreting UK and Ireland).

She is the external advisor for the Teaching Council for Mandarin Chinese in Ireland. Her teaching ranges from semi-specialised translation to language and cultural studies. She has authored a number of refereed articles and book chapters on Chinese language education, including teaching and learning Chinese as a foreign language, language attitudes, translation pedagogy and Chinese language study among ethnic minorities.

List of Figures

Fig. 3.1	Overview of research process	55
Fig. 3.2	Participant profile (n = 35)	57
Fig. 3.3	Participants' general experience of learning CFL online	58
Fig. 3.4	Participants' experience of learning CFL online in relation to character learning (n = 41)	59
Fig. 3.5	Skills being supported during independent learning time through online resources (n = 34)	60
Fig. 3.6	Items assisting character learning	62
Fig. 3.7	Constraints in the online space when learning Chinese characters	63
Fig. 3.8	Participant ideas on software/technology that could meet their character learning needs (n = 16)	65
Fig. 3.9	Likert-scale questions relating to handwriting Chinese characters (n = 37)	66
Fig. 3.10	Likert-scale questions relating to typing Chinese characters (n = 37)	67
Fig. 3.11	Assessment mode completed online/at-distance (n = 35)	68
Fig. 3.12	Assessment exercises completed online/at-distance (n = 35)	69
Fig. 5.1	Strategies for learning Chinese characters online	113
Fig. 5.2	Learner perceptions of handwriting	116
Fig. 5.3	Learner perceptions of typing	118
Fig. 5.4	Teachers' identification of student needs for character acquisition	120

Fig. 5.5	Teaching style in relation to writing modalities	121
Fig. 5.6	Teaching methods in relation to writing modalities	123
Fig. 5.7	Schematic representation of the multimodal encoding process underlying typing and handwriting. (Adapted from Zhang and Reilly 2015)	124
Fig. 5.8	Dual-modal processing in learning Chinese characters	126
Fig. 7.1	One pair of pattern discrimination and location memory stimuli	169
Fig. 7.2	12 Configurations of compound characters	182
Fig. 9.1	Routes to assist students in comprehending and producing Chinese characters	233
Fig. 9.2	Continua for teacher decision-making	237

List of Tables

Table 2.1	An overview of the reviewed studies (n = 20)	28
Table 5.1	Strengths and limitations of two writing modalities	108
Table 5.2	Overall learner perceptions of handwriting	115
Table 5.3	Overall learner perceptions of typing	118
Table 6.1	Comparison of HSK1 300 characters included in each textbook	150
Table 6.2	families of related components	155
Table 7.1	Correlations between visual skills and participants' gain scores in character learning	171
Table 7.2	Participants' responses to "chunking" survey questions	177
Table 7.3	Participants' chunking performance on different characters and configurations	183
Table 7.4	Participants' error samples in low-accuracy chunking characters	187
Table 8.1	Summary of the impact of orthographic features on Chinese character cognition research	213

1

Introduction

Caitríona Osborne, Danping Wang, and Qi Zhang

Introduction

If you have opened this book, you probably have a hand in Chinese as a foreign language (henceforth CFL) to some capacity, most likely with an invested interest in teaching and learning Chinese characters. You may be a teacher, or a student, hoping to seek clarity on how characters should be approached in formal learning in the current digital age. Perhaps you are a researcher, looking to gain an overview of the seemingly opposing schools of thought: handwriting versus typing. You might even have a preconceived idea of the place of characters in teaching and learning CFL, and maybe you have come to this book to seek affirmation.

This book is not an attempt to persuade or dissuade you of any approaches mentioned within the chapters. Having gained a general insight into aspects of teaching CFL online in recent years, this book distinctively looks to the future of teaching Chinese characters in the current digital era (Wang and Zhao 2020). The book examines this through cutting-edge research from the perspectives of teaching methodologies, critical issues and the development of theories in collating global studies from leading experts. You will see in the pages that follow an interweaving of approaches and priorities among different authors in in-depth discussions which, it is intended, allow you to consider deeply your own views and habits when it comes to Chinese characters. Through absorbing the knowledge and expertise of the authors within this book and applying it to practice, it is envisioned that the experience of both teaching and learning CFL can be enhanced. Rather than opposing opinions creating noise in the field and exposing the weaknesses of certain approaches, the goal of this book is for researchers and practitioners to instead uncover the strengths of such, thus allowing harmony to exist between dichotomous opinions.

This introduction will frame the rationale for this book and address the latest discussions and trends related to teaching Chinese characters. It will document the three main themes of the book and provide a synopsis of each chapter before commenting on future research trends in the field.

The Road to This Edited Book

The journey to this edited book began with funding received from University College Dublin's Global Engagement Seed Fund and the Chinese Embassy in Ireland to explore the handling of teaching Chinese characters in the CFL university classroom during the current digital era. As this book will detail, the immediate and unprecedented switch to remote learning as a result of COVID-19 meant that instructors worldwide had to rapidly re-design their courses for an online environment. Transferring Chinese language courses online caused major disruption as instructors tackled the obstacle of teaching Chinese characters while ensuring that students could still fulfil their learning outcomes (e.g. Wang and East 2020; Zhang 2020). Certainly, Chinese characters are a main difficulty for CFL learners, and in the era of remote learning the teaching of such becomes even more complicated when the use of technology is so prevalent. Now that we are no longer in an emergency period of remote teaching, it is time to uncover and share learnings to support practitioners and students. This book will address such through empirical research and documentation of practices and approaches from both researchers and practitioners in the chapters that follow. Despite the long-standing tradition for scholars based in China to publish research on Chinese character teaching in Chinese, this book breaks new ground by featuring research from scholars outside of China. While the aim is to disseminate research and practices, it is also envisioned that this book will inspire future collaborations and research to the field from other researchers and practitioners around the world.

In 2021, Dr Caitríona Osborne received funding from the Global Engagement Seed Fund under the strand of "Building Global Partnerships" and thereby initiated a new research partnership with Dr Danping Wang at the University of Auckland and Dr Qi Zhang from Dublin City University. The expertise of Dr Wang was particularly beneficial as New Zealand has already successfully introduced Chinese to the school curriculum, a task that Ireland is currently in the early stages of. Dr Wang had also recently conducted initial research on the experience of beginner learners of Chinese in the era of emergency remote teaching (ERT), while Dr Zhang had investigated the experience of Chinese language teachers during this time. Dr Osborne is an active researcher in the field of teaching and learning Chinese with a particular focus on Chinese characters and has experience researching innovative methods to improve the learner experience. This international collaboration enabled best practice for teaching CFL in the current digital era to be sought through empirical research.

The funded project examines the handling of teaching Chinese characters in the CFL university classroom during the current digital era and encompasses three perspectives: teaching methods, learning strategies and curriculum design. The data collected for the project involved surveys and follow-up interviews with teachers and students to examine curriculum and assessment adaptations, specifically in relation to teaching characters (see Chaps. 3 and 5 for presentation of these results). The goal of collecting this data was, firstly, to capture the learner and instructor experience, while analysis of such was intended to provide recommendations for online CFL course curricula.

Recognising the value and need for a collaborative approach to this issue, the three project leaders and editors of this book organised a 10-week online seminar series in autumn 2022 to allow findings to be shared from this project while also providing a platform for other specialised researchers in the area to disseminate their own findings. Keynote speakers from Ireland, China, the UK, France, the USA and Australia delivered talks on emerging topics in the field of teaching CFL with a focus on character teaching and learning online. Topics ranged from a history of teaching Chinese characters in Europe, student and teacher perspectives, teaching resources, literacy skills and typing, to name but a few (Eventbrite 2024). This seminar series attracted an audience of over 400 researchers, practitioners and students, and from this the project leaders were compelled to compile this edited book to further contribute to knowledge sharing and collaboration in the field.

The Themes of This Book

This edited book comprises eight further chapters under three distinct themes that reflect areas of cutting-edge research in the field of CFL with a distinct focus on implications for teaching and learning Chinese characters. They are: (I) teaching and learning Chinese characters online, (II) critical perspectives regarding typing Chinese characters in the CFL classroom and (III) development of methodologies and theories for character teaching. The detailed content of the chapters can be found in the following sections, while it is worth noting that as a whole, the book aims to advance theories in teaching methodologies, clarify terminology within the field of CFL and interrogate policies from both the student and teacher perspectives in relation to teaching Chinese. In short, the book collates global studies from leading experts with the ultimate aim of enhancing the experience of teaching and learning CFL.

Theme I: Teaching and Learning Chinese Characters Online

This first theme has garnered attention in recent years, particularly through the lens of the COVID-19 pandemic. Studies published since the emergence of COVID-19 have shed light on the professional and emotional experiences of teachers and discuss the use of technology after the pandemic (e.g. Wang 2023; Zhang 2022), while the resilience of teachers during this time has been more recently explored (e.g. Lu and Hua 2024). From the learner's perspective, their experience of learning online versus in person has been documented (e.g. Qing and Diamantidaki 2020; Wang et al. 2022), while their emotional well-being has also been reported on (Wang and Jiang 2022). Key findings from these indicate that while technology is not expected to replace teachers, it is envisioned that this will become a key skill in the future. Yet, despite the potential opportunities coming to light in this area, students still report that the online experience is incomparable to face-to-face teaching. Theme I therefore takes a closer look at this topic through a deep dive into the student perspective (in Chap. 3) and the main issues emerging when it comes to the handling of Chinese character instruction from 2020 to 2023 (see Chap. 2).

Of course, attention on teaching and learning Chinese characters existed in the literature prior to the global catalyst of COVID-19, with studies on innovative teaching methods and approaches (e.g. Osborne et al. 2022; Xu and Padilla 2013), theory building (e.g. Guan et al. 2011; Knell and West 2017), learner strategies (e.g. Everson 1998; Shen 2005) and indeed the role of technology (e.g. Allen 2008; Hsiao and Broeder 2014). With our communication habits evolving to utilise technology more, thereby relying on handwriting less, it is easy to see how and why there exist such staunch advocates of bringing new technology trends to the CFL classroom. For example, as of January 2024, there are over five billion users of social media worldwide, while in China, WeChat (a communications app) sees over one billion monthly active users (Datareportal 2024). In a review of research in the area of technology-assisted teaching and learning of CFL, Lyu and Qi (2020) note that the most common topic emerging was in relation to teacher training, and these studies advocated for a collaborative approach among teachers, policyholders, technology experts and researchers in developing effective teacher training programmes and teaching technology. Lyu and Qi's (2020) review also highlighted numerous studies utilising student feedback to enhance their teaching. In a meta-analysis specifically related to mobile-assisted learning of CFL, three studies documented the affordances of such (Zhou 2020). These included accessibility, authentic materials, access to native speakers and increased motivation among learners (ibid.), which also echo Lyu and Qi's (2020) findings. Chapters 4 and 5 in this book delve into two topics on typing Chinese characters in the CFL classroom, with the next section in this chapter providing more background to this theme.

On the other hand, when it comes to handwriting Chinese characters, a solid argument exists that handwriting characters also assists the reading ability of CFL learners (Cao et al. 2013; Chang et al. 2014; Kim et al. 2020; Tan et al. 2005). Differing from an alphabetic language, the formation of Chinese characters can be based on sound, meaning or symbols (see Yin 2016). However, this information is difficult for a learner to access based on a lack of grapheme-phoneme correspondence in Chinese (Chen and Pasquarella 2017). Naturally, as teaching CFL as a discipline stemmed from China in the 1950s (Zhu 2010), teaching and learning Chinese characters worldwide contains elements of memorisation strategies (e.g. Osborne et al. 2018) which are prevalent in the Chinese education system (Xu 2022). This approach has caused a stir in the research with some researchers, critiquing its lack of creativity in the classroom (see Bhattacharya 2022). Despite these debates, handwriting and rote memorisation are seen to be popular among CFL students worldwide, as Chap. 3 will report on.

Summarising the main findings from the literature in recent years, Chap. 2 reviews studies on Chinese character instruction during ERT published in 2020–2023. Dr Linda Lei and Dr Danping Wang identify six key concepts reported on in the literature and demonstrate the positives and negatives felt by the field collectively. Indeed, the authors acknowledge and address the ongoing dilemma of teaching and learning handwriting Chinese characters in the current digital age. However, rather than dwelling on any negatives, the authors see the opportunity that learning online has brought and encourage instructors to include technology-enhanced learning in their classrooms, thus strengthening the longevity of Chinese-language programmes worldwide.

In Chap. 3, Dr Caitríona Osborne presents the first set of data collected by the funded project mentioned previously. In this chapter, the author documents the student perspective of learning Chinese online with particular reference to the characters. From student questionnaires and interviews gathered from six English-speaking countries worldwide, the chapter provides technological and pedagogical recommendations for current and future online courses stemming directly from the student voice. While it is imperative that research involving practitioners and curriculum developments is carried out, the student voice cannot be ignored. This chapter enables readers to see, verbatim, student opinions on a range of topics in both the online and face-to-face classroom.

It is intended that through these two chapters, practitioners and researchers will be able to future-proof their curricula by considering both the key concepts highlighted by Lei and Wang and the student voice presented by Osborne.

Theme II: Critical Perspectives Regarding Typing Chinese Characters in the CFL Classroom

The second theme of the book details a major topic in teaching and learning CFL online that has been touched on briefly in the previous section. Indeed, typing in CFL teaching and learning certainly sparks heated debates in the sphere with sometimes extreme views being published, such as advocating for eliminating handwriting altogether (e.g. Allen 2008). Previously, there have also been explorations to delay character instruction (e.g. Osborne 2018; Packard 1990) in order to ease students into their learning; however, this approach was seen to improve students' speaking skills rather than have any effect on long-term character learning. Again, the global catalyst of COVID-19 saw typing being heavily relied on for teaching and assessment in the online space (see Chaps. 2 and 3). Now, after the pandemic, we can begin to uncover the outcomes of such emergency implementation of typing and decipher the possible affordances for future curricula.

Those reading this book who have experience of teaching Chinese characters will be all too familiar with students themselves questioning the need to learn how to write characters by hand. One might explain the benefits of writing on reading (see previous section); however, this explanation may not be satisfactory for some students depending on how (and indeed if) they intend to use the language after completing a given course and more so when the prevalence of technology use is considered. Certainly, if primary communication is through typing/other digital means, then it may make sense that typing is the focus if communication is the goal. Interestingly, research is now emerging that states a typing-only approach may see learners performing as well as those learning only through handwriting where reading comprehension is concerned (Zhang 2021). However, in a review of comparison studies involving handwriting and typing from 2009 to 2019, Lyu et al. (2021) found that the studies demonstrated typing had a greater effect on Chinese learners' phonology recognition and phonology-orthography mapping compared to handwriting, while handwriting showed benefits to orthography recognition and orthography-semantic mapping at character and lexical levels. Interestingly, these studies presented mixed reviews when it came to the effects of typing on writing performance (ibid.).

Adding the catalyst of COVID-19 into the mix that saw a mass migration of courses to the online space, research needs to be teased out in this area so that instructors can make informed choices when it comes to introducing typing to their classrooms. The studies reported in the chapters of Theme II shed light on the application of typing Chinese characters to the CFL classroom with the aim of addressing any ambiguities associated with this approach. Chapter 4 goes straight to the source in presenting the innovative e-writing approach. Proposed by Matt Coss, this approach advocates for a focus on typing first before handwriting.

While handwriting still has its place in the classroom, the author's proposal places typing to the fore. Through this chapter, it is intended that researchers and practitioners can understand what encompasses the e-writing approach and determine its usefulness for their own situations. Equipped with this knowledge, practitioners can be empowered to incorporate this approach—or elements of it—into their own CFL classroom to enhance their teaching and therefore the learner experience. As Coss will highlight, Chu et al. (2024) provide the first comprehensive introduction to the e-writing approach.

Secondly, in Chap. 5, Dr Qi Zhang presents the second set of data collected by the funded project mentioned previously. Here, the affordances of typing and handwriting when learning Chinese characters are examined from the perspectives of students and teachers. The chapter aims to iron out student and teacher perceptions of typing in the CFL classroom with data gathered from six English-speaking countries worldwide. Specifically, the chapter highlights the application of embodiment as a theoretical framework in both writing modalities during the learning process. In doing so, the author proposes the use of both typing and handwriting to assist in Chinese character acquisition.

Through Chaps. 4 and 5, it is intended that practitioners can be empowered to make informed choices, while researchers can identify scope for future studies so that more can be understood on the relationship between handwriting and typing, and indeed the affordances and/or implications of typing in the CFL classroom. The research mentioned in this section, and indeed these two chapters, highlight further how one approach to teaching Chinese characters is not necessarily better than the other. Chapters 4 and 5 demonstrate the affordances of both approaches, enabling the reader to design their curriculum according to student needs.

Theme III: Development of Methodologies and Theories for Character Teaching

The final theme of this edited book focuses on the big picture of developing methodologies and theories in teaching Chinese characters. Through detailing the theories of various approaches, the chapters within this section empower the reader to consider what the priorities are for a CFL curriculum according to their own situation rather than following the status quo of the latest trend. Chapters 6, 7 and 8 enable the reader to understand key challenges and explore different approaches from experts worldwide. Coupled with the knowledge gained in the previous two themes, it is intended that the final chapters in this book can provide a basis for future CFL curricula to be developed in the digital era. Given the criticisms associated with rote learning—an approach that seems to traditionally dominate CFL teaching and learning (see Theme I)—it is unsurprising that researchers are drawn to explore new and innovative methodologies for teaching CFL. Of course, considering that the writing system is one of the main obstacles for learners, it is even less surprising that studies explore the effectiveness of both traditional and original approaches to teaching Chinese characters (see Osborne 2018; Zhang 2024).

In addition to rote learning, this introduction has already touched on other approaches to teaching and learning characters, mainly centring on utilising technology. With the drive for exploring the affordances of technology in the CFL classroom only exacerbated by COVID-19, the years 2020–2023 saw a sharp increase in studies surrounding the difficulties of teaching and learning CFL online and how best to cope with moving to at-distance learning (e.g. Wang and East 2022; Zhang 2022; Zhang 2020). While this exploration is welcomed and certainly required, it is important not to let technology lead the way, but rather use it as a tool to reach different goals in the classroom (Wang and East 2020). It is perhaps easy to become entrenched in the technology-related research that is emerging lately. However, the chapters within Theme III aim to bring the attention back to key literacy challenges when teaching Chinese, this time through the lens of the current digital age.

Chapter 6 thereby addresses the key challenges in building literacy skills in novice CFL learners and identifies issues in the teaching of Chinese characters in the CFL classroom. After a critique of current teaching resources, Andrew Scrimgeour recommends a conceptual and systematic approach to building reading and writing skills and provides examples of resources and techniques for this aim. He speaks about how interactive technology could assist CFL learners from the very beginning of their journey, which could, in turn, positively influence their literacy skills.

In Chap. 7, Prof Yi Xu explores the role of visual skills in facilitating character learning. Specifically, through a student and teacher survey, perceptions of chunking as a character learning strategy are reported on. In addition, the author presents data from an exploratory study investigating student performance in visual chunking. The chapter demonstrates how students can utilise the perceptual aspect of orthographic awareness to advance character learning, and it highlights the usefulness of such an approach in the current digital age.

In addition to the work and research conducted by scholars from English-speaking countries, Chap. 8 presents a joint study by researchers from China and Ireland to synthesise key psycholinguistic findings in relation to character and word recognition. Dr Xi Fan and Dr Ronan Reilly touch on topics such as the effects of visual complexity, superiority of radicals in characters and words and radical/character transposition on native Chinese and CFL speakers. One of the goals of this chapter is to strengthen teachers' knowledge in this area, thereby allowing them to bridge the empirical research between language practitioners and psycholinguists.

Within these chapters, an overview of some major challenges is provided with practical advice on how students can be supported, and indeed, the role that technology can play in this support. In this way, the focus is not on new technologies, but rather on how practitioners can utilise such to specifically address the challenges highlighted.

The last chapter of this book reveals Prof Bob Adamson's reflections on his attempts to learn Chinese characters throughout different stages of his life. Through a brief reflective narrative of a personal learning experience, he encapsulates the pedagogical approaches described in the chapters and argues for a principled pragmatic pedagogy based on students' needs, interests and abilities. Thus, Adamson's journey is documented with an interweaving of specialised knowledge that enables the reader to comprehend the experience of a CFL learner throughout the various stages. This invaluable chapter allows researchers and practitioners to step into the mind of a CFL learner who also happens to be an expert in curriculum studies and, in turn, encourages the application of new learnings to the classroom. For example, introducing more e-writing tools could help to empower students to embrace digital communication in Chinese and spend less time chasing perfect handwriting skills, depending on the individual classroom goals.

Key Concepts

There are a number of key concepts seen throughout this edited book. It should be noted that throughout the chapters, authors will use certain terms as standard to their region. This list aims to eliminate any misunderstandings by providing clear definitions.

- *Chinese as a foreign language (CFL) or Chinese as a second language (CSL):* Used according to the authors' context and situation in this book. As Ringbom and Akademi (1980, p. 1) describe:
  In a second-language acquisition situation, the language is spoken in the immediate environment of the learner, who has good opportunities to use the language by participating in natural communication situations. In a foreign-language learning situation, the language is not spoken in the learner's immediate environment, although mass media may provide opportunities for practicing receptive skills. The learner has little or no opportunity to use the language in natural communication situations.
  Some authors may also use *Chinese as an additional language (CAL)* or *L2 Chinese* depending on preference.
- *Chinese character:* In basic terms, Chinese characters are the written form of Chinese. Chinese characters are also referred to as 汉字 or Hanzi in various studies. A character is composed of lines (or strokes) that form shapes or components that may provide information on pronunciation or meaning (Hu 2020, p. 225). Hu elaborates: "learning characters is underpinned by a triangle connecting their shape, pronunciation, and meaning" (ibid.). These three elements—shape (形 in Chinese), pronunciation (音 in Chinese) and meaning (义 in Chinese)—of a Chinese character may be named differently, including

"grapheme" for shape, "phoneme" or "sound" for pronunciation and "morpheme" for meaning.
- *Emergency remote teaching (ERT):* As defined by Hodges et al. (2020), this refers to a:
  temporary shift of instructional delivery to an alternate delivery mode due to crisis circumstances. It involves the use of fully remote teaching solutions for instruction or education that would otherwise be delivered face-to-face or as blended or hybrid courses and that will return to that format once the crisis or emergency has abated.

  When *online learning* or *at-distance learning* is mentioned in the chapters, it refers to experiences that are planned to be online from the outset and designed particularly for this purpose.
- *Writing:* This term can refer to individual character composition (e.g. Guan et al. 2013) or text composition, depending on the context of each chapter.

Looking to the Future

The following sub-sections demonstrate the future directions concerning the teaching and learning of Chinese characters as outlined in the chapters of this edited book. Two major aspects will be discussed in each section of (1) technology and (2) curriculum design. The recommendations listed throughout the chapters in this book serve as a starting point for redeveloping curricula and redesigning the classroom set-up to support and enhance student learning in the digital age. Therefore, the experts in this book call for further research and documentation of such in order to advance the new concepts and suggestions herein. Student and practitioner voices, as well as practical application of redeveloped curricula, are crucial in advancing the field and in supporting CFL students appropriately in the digital age.

Curriculum Design

As this chapter and others within the book highlight, the catalyst of the COVID-19 pandemic forced a restructure and redesign of CFL modules worldwide. This unprecedented and unique situation—while stressful for both students and teachers at the time—forced practitioners to rapidly prioritise learning outcomes based on their individual situations. Given this, as Chap. 3 demonstrates, students had vastly different experiences around the world. However, through documenting these curricula changes, practitioners can now take time to consider any redesign they deem appropriate to undertake, rather than hastily implementing changes as in the period of ERT.

Theme III of this edited book is particularly relevant to this redesigning of curricula. Chapter 6 calls for an approach to introducing characters that does not necessarily rely on popular textbooks, thus asking practitioners and researchers to carefully consider what characters are taught and when. Indeed, Chap. 8 comments on the factors that influence this decision-making and encourage communication between researcher and practitioner. Chapters 4 and 5 in Theme II are also particularly relevant to curriculum redesign in addressing the approach to typing in the CFL classroom. While Chap. 5 highlights the benefits and affordances of typing, Chap. 4 also describes how handwriting and typing can exist in harmony in the CFL classroom and calls for more research to document experiences of an innovative approach involving both handwriting and typing Chinese characters.

Technology

In looking to the future of what has been learned during ERT, the chapters in this book demonstrate the importance of integrating technology-assisted teaching into curricula, being innovative in the design of teaching materials and the accessibility of online resources (e.g. Chaps. 2 and 3 in Theme I). In Chap. 3, features of a proposed application are suggested based on students' experiences of learning Chinese online, while in Chap. 6, a specific resource is described with the aim of supporting initial literacy development. Chapter 7 describes an application that is already published online that allows students to delve into the etymology of characters to advance their orthographic awareness. Certainly, through adopting the suggested technology and applications into classrooms worldwide, the affordances and limitations of such can be deciphered through empirical studies.

It is apparent that researchers, practitioners and technologists should communicate with each other in order to decipher the needs of CFL learners, the practicality of any proposed applications and indeed the possibility of developing such. Further research involving all three voices could begin to address this gap and move closer to tangible outcomes designed specifically for the CFL classroom in the current digital age. Certainly, the testing of such should include the student voice in order to enhance their experience.

A Final Word

In summary, the COVID-19 pandemic succeeded in expediting the teaching of Chinese to an online/at-distance model at a time when skills, technology and best practice guidelines were still being explored and debated in the literature, as the chapters of this book will attest to. Prior to the pandemic, the parameters for involving technology in the CFL classroom were relatively free and could depend on instructors' preferences, skills and/or goals for their classroom. From the instructor's perspective, criteria such as ensuring learning outcomes, supporting students holistically and the technological ability of both them and their students were sure to greatly influence the rapid re-design of their modules brought about by COVID-19. With this forced catalyst, students were bound to be confronted with a variety of different teaching approaches spurring a mix of positive and negative experiences.

This edited book makes reference to research conducted during the emergency period when rapid decisions needed to be made in the switch to fully remote learning. From these studies, it can be seen that the different goals of the instructors affected their approach to teaching and assessment, from specific learning outcomes to ensuring student well-being. At a time when COVID-19 is thankfully no longer causing widespread lockdowns, we can now begin to uncover the sustained approaches to teaching, learning and assessment in the CFL classroom during the digital age, particularly when it comes to Chinese characters.

Specifically, this book contributes a number of practical recommendations that aim to inspire both researchers and practitioners. Firstly, it provides an overview of the ERT situation and information on the CFL learner's trajectory that allow us to take stock of research so far and notice future research opportunities and gaps that need to be addressed. For example, it is imperative that CFL learners' processing of characters is explored and understood further to fine-tune teaching styles and approaches. Secondly, the use of technology in the classroom to enhance teaching and learning and to aid student retention is strongly advocated. There is a clear need for online resources to be developed to support student learning in the digital age. In terms of the learning process, applications supporting orthographic awareness, student-teacher communication and opportunities to handwrite are suggested. Meanwhile, advanced assessment features that could diminish instances of academic dishonesty whereby online exams are unavoidable are also encouraged. Incorporating technology as an approach to teaching Chinese characters, such as typing and the e-writing approach, is another way to ensure that future courses are well prepared for the digital future.

This book is a vital resource that will enable instructors and researchers to take stock of current practices and explore cutting-edge research, thereby helping to support their own students in the CFL classroom. It is further intended that more empirical studies will stem from the themes highlighted in this book, including in regions other than the countries reported on herein, thus advancing research in the field.

References

Allen, Joseph R. 2008. Why Learning to Write Chinese is a Waste of Time: A Modest Proposal. *Foreign Language Annals* 41 (2): 237–251. https://doi.org/10.1111/j.1944-9720.2008.tb03291.x.

Bhattacharya, Usree. 2022. "I am a Parrot": Literacy Ideologies and Rote Learning. *Journal of Literacy Research* 54 (2): 113–136. https://doi.org/10.1177/1086296X221098065.

Cao, Fan, Ben Rickles, Marianne Vu, Ziheng Zhu, Derek Ho Lung Chan, Lindsay N. Harris, Joseph Stafura, Yi Xu, and Charles A. Perfetti. 2013. Early Stage Visual-Orthographic Processes Predict Long-Term Retention of Word Form and Meaning: A Visual Encoding Training Study. *Journal of Neurolinguistics* 26 (4): 440–461. https://doi.org/10.1016/j.jneuroling.2013.01.003.

Chang, Li-Yun, Yi Xu, Charles A. Perfetti, Juan Zhang, and Hsueh-Chih Chen. 2014. Supporting Orthographic Learning at the Beginning Stage of Learning to Read Chinese as a Second Language. *International Journal of Disability, Development and Education* 61 (3): 288–305. https://doi.org/10.1080/1034912X.2014.934016.

Chen, Xi, and Adrian Pasquarella. 2017. Learning to Read Chinese. In *Learning to Read across Languages and Writing Systems*, ed. Ludo Verhoeven and Charles Perfetti, 1–30. Cambridge: Cambridge University Press.

Chu, Chengzhi, Matthew D. Coss, and Phyllis Ni Zhang, eds. 2024. *Transforming Hanzi Pedagogy in the Digital Age: Theory, Research, and Practice [电写时代的汉字教学——理论与实践]*. Routledge.

Datareportal. 2024. Digital 2024: Global Overview Report. Accessed February 20, 2024. https://datareportal.com/reports/digital-2024-global-overview-report

Eventbrite. 2024. Exploring the Present and Future of Teaching Chinese Characters Online. Accessed March 12, 2024. https://www.eventbrite.ie/e/exploring-the-present-and-future-of-teaching-chinese-characters-online-tickets-391690846867

Everson, Michael E. 1998. Word Recognition Among Learners of Chinese as a Foreign Language: Investigating the Relationship Between Naming and Knowing. *Modern Language Journal* 82 (2): 194–204. https://doi.org/10.1111/j.1540-4781.1998.tb01192.x.

Guan, Connie Qun, Ying Liu, Derek Ho Leung Chan, Feifei Ye, and Charles A. Perfetti. 2011. Writing Strengthens Orthography and Alphabetic-Coding Strengthens Phonology in Learning to Read Chinese. *Journal of Educational Psychology* 103 (3): 509–522. https://doi.org/10.1037/a0023730.

Guan, Connie Qun, Feifei Ye, Richard K. Wagner, and Wanjin Meng. 2013. Developmental and Individual Differences in Chinese Writing. *Reading and Writing* 26 (6): 1031–1056. https://doi.org/10.1007/s11145-012-9405-4.

Hodges, Charles, Stephanie Moore, Barb Lockee, Torrey Trust, and Aaron Bond. 2020. The Difference Between Emergency Remote Teaching and Online Learning. *EDUCAUSE Review*, March 27, 2020. https://

er.educause.edu/articles/2020/3/the-difference-between-emergency-remote-teaching-and-online-learning

Hsiao, Ya Ping (Amy), and Peter Broeder. 2014. Let's Tweet in Chinese! Exploring How Learners of Chinese as a Foreign Language Self-Direct in their Use of Microblogging to Learn Chinese. *Journal of the European Confederation of Language Centres in Higher Education (CERCLES)* 4 (2): 469–488. https://doi.org/10.1515/cercles-2014-0024.

Hu, Bo. 2020. Teaching Chinese characters: What We Know and What We Can Do. In *The Routledge Handbook of Chinese Language Teaching*, ed. Chris Shei, Monica McLellan Zikpi, and Der-Lin Chao, 225–237. Oxon and New York: Routledge.

Kim, Young-Suk Grace, Qian Guo, Yan Liu, Yan Peng, and Li Yang. 2020. Multiple Pathways by Which Compounding Morphological Awareness is Related to Reading Comprehension: Evidence from Chinese Second Graders. *Reading Research Quarterly* 55 (2): 193–212. https://doi.org/10.1002/rrq.262.

Knell, Ellen, and Hai-I (Nancy) West. 2017. To Delay or Not to Delay: The Timing of Chinese Character Instruction for Secondary Learners. *Foreign Language Annals* 50 (3): 519–532. https://doi.org/10.1111/flan.12281.

Lu, Xiuchuan, and Zhu Hua. 2024. Teacher Resilience and Triple Crises: Confucius Institute Teachers' Lived Experiences during the COVID-19 Pandemic. *Applied Linguistics Review* 15 (1): 335–354. https://doi.org/10.1515/applirev-2021-0193.

Lyu, Boning, and Xuedan Qi. 2020. A Review of Research on Technology-Assisted Teaching and Learning of Chinese as a Second or Foreign Language from 2008 to 2018. *Frontiers of Education in China* 15: 142–163. https://doi.org/10.1007/s11516-020-0006-8.

Lyu, Boning, Chun Lai, Chin-Hsi Lin, and Yang Gong. 2021. Comparison studies of typing and handwriting in Chinese language learning: A synthetic review. *International Journal of Educational Research* 106: 101740.

Osborne, Caitríona. 2018. Examining Character Recognition and Recall Skills of CFL Beginner Learners Under Four Different Approaches. *TEANGA, the Journal of the Irish Association for Applied Linguistics* 25: 52–73. https://doi.org/10.35903/teanga.v25i0.49.

Osborne, Caitríona, Qi Zhang, and George Xinsheng Zhang. 2018. Which is More Effective in Introducing Chinese Characters? An Investigative Study of Four Methods Used to Teach CFL Beginners. *The Language Learning Journal* 48 (4): 385–401. https://doi.org/10.1080/09571736.2017.1393838.

Osborne, Caitríona, Qi Zhang, and Bob Adamson. 2022. The Next Steps for Teaching Characters in CFL: Investigating the Effects of Four Character-Teaching Methods on Beginner Learners. *International Journal of Chinese Language Education* 11: 45–82. https://doras.dcu.ie/27617/1/IJCLE_No.11_Jun22_03.pdf.

Packard, Jerome L. 1990. Effects of Time Lag in the Introduction of Characters into the Chinese Language Curriculum. *The Modern Language Journal* 74 (ii): 167–175. http://languagelog.ldc.upenn.edu/~bgzimmer/Packard1990.pdf.

Qing, Li, and Fotini Diamantidaki. 2020. Evaluating Mandarin Language Students' Online Experience during COVID-19: A Case Study from London. *Journal of Education, Innovation and Communication* 2 (2): 56–79. https://doi.org/10.34097/jeicom-2-Dec2020-4.

Ringbom, Hakan, and Abo Akademi. 1980. On the Distinction between Second-Language Acquisition and Foreign-Language Learning. *Papers in Language Learning and Language Acquisition..* https://files.eric.ed.gov/fulltext/ED269973.pdf.

Shen, Helen H. 2005. An Investigation of Chinese-Character Learning Strategies among Non-Native Speakers of Chinese. *Department of Asian Languages and Literature* 33 (1): 49–68. https://doi.org/10.1016/j.system.2004.11.001.

Tan, Li Hai, John A. Spinks, Guinevere F. Eden, Charles A. Perfetti, and Wai Ting Siok. 2005. Reading Depends on Writing, in Chinese. *Proceedings of the National Academy of Sciences of the United States of America* 102 (24): 8781–8785. https://doi.org/10.1073/pnas.0503523102.

Wang, Lih-Ching Chen. 2023. Experiences of Chinese-as-a-Foreign-Language Teachers in Implementation of Emergency Remote Teaching during the COVID-19 Pandemic. *International Journal of Instruction* 16 (4): 1099–1120. https://doi.org/10.29333/iji.2023.16460a.

Wang, Danping, and Martin East. 2020. Constructing an Emergency Chinese Curriculum during the Pandemic: A New Zealand Experience. *International Journal of Chinese Language Teaching* 1 (1): 1–19. https://doi.org/10.46451/ijclt.2020.06.01.

Wang, Qing, and Yuhong Jiang. 2022. A Positive Psychology Perspective on Positive Emotion and Foreign Language Enjoyment among Chinese as a Second Language Learners Attending Virtual Online Classes in the Emergency Remote Teaching Context amid the COVID-19 Pandemic. *Frontiers in Psychology* 12. https://doi.org/10.3389/fpsyg.2021.798650.

Wang, Danping, and Zhao Yang. 2020. Introduction to the Special Issue. *International Journal of Chinese Language Teaching* 1 (1): I–V. https://doi.org/10.46451/ijclt.2020.06.06.

Wang, Yanlin, Hong Zhan, and Shijuan Liu. 2022. A Comparative Study of Perceptions and Experiences of Online Chinese Language Learners in China and the United States during the COVID-19 Pandemic. *Journal of China Computer-Assisted Language Learning* 2 (1): 69–99. https://doi.org/10.1515/jccall-2022-0009.

Xu, Jinqi. 2022. Memorisation is Not Rote Learning: Rethinking Memorisation as an Embodied Practice for Chinese Students. *Journal of Multilingual and Multicultural Development.* https://doi.org/10.1080/01434632.2022.2134878.

Xu, Xiaoqiu, and Amado M. Padilla. 2013. Using Meaningful Interpretation and Chunking to Enhance Memory: The Case of Chinese Character Learning. *Foreign Language Annals* 46 (3): 402–422. https://doi.org/10.1111/flan.12039.

Yin, John Jing-Hua. 2016. Chinese Characters. In *The Routledge Encyclopedia of the Chinese Language*, ed. Sin-Wai Chan, Florence Li Wing Yee, and James W. Minett, 51–63. Oxon, UK: Routledge.

Zhang, Qi. 2020. Narrative Inquiry into Online Teaching of Chinese Characters during the Pandemic. *International Journal of Chinese Language Teaching* 1 (1): 20–34. https://doi.org/10.46451/ijclt.2020.06.02.

Zhang, Phyllis Ni. 2021. Typing to Replace Handwriting: Effectiveness of the Typing-Primary Approach for L2 Chinese Beginners. *Journal of Technology and Chinese Language Teaching* 12 (2): 1–28. http://www.tclt.us/journal/2021v12n2/zhangn.pdf.

Zhang, George Xinsheng. 2022. Online Chinese Language Teaching Now and Post-COVID-19: Challenges and Opportunities from the Experience and Perspective of a UK Teacher. In *Frontiers of L2 Chinese Language Education: A Global Perspective*, ed. Yanyin Zhang and Xiaoping Gao, 156–169. Oxon and New York: Routledge.

Zhang, Shenglan. 2024. Effective Character Teaching Methods for L1 English Chinese-as-a-Foreign-Language Learners: A Review of Empirical Research. *Chinese as a Second Language, the Journal of the Chinese Language Teachers Association, USA.* https://doi.org/10.1075/csl.00033.zha.

Zhou, W. 2020. Mobile Assisted Chinese Learning as a Foreign Language: An Overview of Publications between 2007 and 2019. *Frontiers of Education in China* 15: 164–181. https://doi.org/10.1007/s11516-020-0007-7.

Zhu, Zhiping. 2010. A Historical Perspective of Teaching Chinese as a Second Language. In *Teaching and learning Chinese: Issues and Perspectives*, ed. Jinfa Cai, Jianguo Chen, and Chuang Wang, 33–69. New York, NY: Continuum International Publishing Group.

Theme I

Teaching and Learning Chinese Characters Online

2

Chinese Character Instruction During Emergency Remote Teaching: A Review Study

Linda Lei and Danping Wang

Introduction

The pandemic has posed unprecedented challenges to language education, forcing educational institutions worldwide to swiftly adopt emergency remote teaching (ERT). This rapid shift to online instruction has introduced new challenges and opportunities in the teaching and learning of Chinese as a second language (CSL) (Cui 2020; Liu 2022b; Tao and Gao 2022; Wang and Zhao 2020), particularly concerning teaching and learning Chinese characters (Zhang 2020b). Although scholars have begun exploring the rationale, resources and methods for teaching Chinese characters digitally (Zhang 2021a; Zhang and Min 2019), it wasn't until COVID-19 that the majority of Chinese teaching professionals and students worldwide found themselves in urgent need of

---

L. Lei (✉) • D. Wang
School of Cultures, Languages and Linguistics, University of Auckland, Auckland, New Zealand
e-mail: linda.lei@auckland.ac.nz; danping.wang@auckland.ac.nz

policy guidance and digital solutions to address or compensate for the limitations of the traditional pen-and-paper approach in the online classroom setting (Ma 2022; Qu 2021; Wang and East 2020; Zahradnikova 2022).

In addition to both teachers and students being unprepared for the abrupt shift in the mode of delivery (Gao 2020; Zhang 2020b), a more significant challenge in teaching Chinese online is intricately intertwined with the unique nature of the Chinese writing system. The Chinese writing system is both nonalphabetic and logographic. The distinctiveness of this writing system necessitates motor movements, such as handwriting exercises, when learning to read and write Chinese characters (Zhang et al. 2022). The concern arises from the limitations of the online environment in providing opportunities for learners to solidify their grapheme–morpheme mapping capacity, which is found to be essential for character recognition and retention for developing Chinese literacy, as indicated in numerous previous studies (e.g., Lei and Wang 2023; Liu et al. 2007; Zhang and Xing 2023; Zhang 2020b; Zhou and Marslen-Wilson 1999; Zhou and McBride 2018). In recent years, however, an increasing number of articles have been published in response to the rapid development of technology and the growing preferences for digital communication using typing instead of handwriting (He 2021; Zhang and Lu 2014; Zhang and Min 2019). A more comprehensive and updated understanding of the advantages and disadvantages of handwriting and typing would be crucial for teachers and curriculum developers in advancing Chinese character instruction (Li 2022; Lyu et al. 2021).

Since the beginning of the COVID-19 pandemic, there has been a significant increase in the publication of studies addressing the challenges and critical issues related to Chinese character instruction. Situated in diverse contexts with various research objectives, these studies offer valuable first-hand experiences of navigating digital solutions to maintain handwriting as the teaching norm and exploring the effectiveness of implementing typing throughout the entire course or programme. These studies are laying the foundation for more profound changes in Chinese character instruction (Bond et al. 2021; Jin et al. 2022; Tao and Gao 2022; Liu 2022b). In this regard, the pandemic experience is believed to serve as a catalyst for a global-scale digital transformation in

Chinese-language teaching (Wang and Zhao 2020). Furthermore, these emerging studies contain empirical evidence regarding the attitudes, experiences and reflections of teachers and students during the critical period of adapting to online Chinese-language learning. Mapping out these publications will help teachers, researchers and curriculum developers gain new insights that can be invaluable for developing more sustainable approaches to teaching Chinese characters in the post-COVID context.

To this end, this mapping review was conducted to collate and describe the most salient topics that emerged from publications related to Chinese character instruction during the pandemic years. Specifically, the study seeks to answer two research questions: What is the status quo of the publications on Chinese character instruction during emergency remote teaching? What are the focal research areas of these publications?

Methodology

This study followed the standard steps of a systematic review (Gough and Richardson 2018; Macaro 2019). It began with scoping searches to find literature that matched our research goal, which is to understand Chinese character instruction during the pandemic years. We then set inclusion and exclusion criteria to choose articles, looking at titles, abstracts and full texts. After selecting the literature, our first step was to provide a brief statistical analysis of the publication details from the chosen papers. This helped us gain an overview of the existing research landscape. Next, we used thematic analysis (Guest et al. 2014; Lin et al. 2022; Ma 2022; Neuendorf 2018; Wang and East 2023; Wang and Jiang 2022) to explore the content of the publications and identify key themes and their implications for future research in Chinese character instruction.

Literature Search

To identify relevant studies for inclusion in this study, we conducted keyword searches in four databases: the Educational Resources Information

Center (ERIC) database, Linguistics & Language Behaviour Abstracts (LLBA), Scopus and Web of Science (WoS). ERIC and LLBA are renowned for their focus on education and linguistics respectively (In'Nami and Koizumi 2010; Zhang 2021b), making them valuable resources for studies related to Chinese-language instruction. Scopus and WoS were selected for their extensive coverage (Li 2020), ensuring a comprehensive exploration of research contributing to our understanding of teaching Chinese characters online.

Given the study's focus on Chinese character teaching and learning during the COVID-19 pandemic, we restricted our search to publications after January 2020. In early May 2023, the UN World Health Organisation declared the end to COVID-19 as a global health emergency. Thus, the search period was set as the end of May 2023 in this review. The search string used included terms such as "Chinese character(s)" in conjunction with "emergency remote teaching", "COVID", or "pandemic". Additionally, we meticulously reviewed the reference sections of each article to identify any additional relevant literature to include in this review study. After removing duplicates, our search yielded 58 studies published as journal articles and book chapters.

Literature Selection

Following the literature search, we applied inclusion and exclusion criteria to further refine the selection of publications relevant to this study. Three criteria guided our literature selection process. First, we included only empirical research based on observable and measurable evidence or data. Second, we focused on research related to the teaching or learning of Chinese to speakers of other languages. Third, we included research that contained a specific section on, or was entirely focused on, Chinese character teaching.

With these criteria in mind, we began by carefully reviewing titles, abstracts and keywords, and sometimes the entire papers, to gain a comprehensive understanding of each study. Next, we examined the methodology sections to ensure that the publications represented empirical studies conducted within a specific educational context. Moreover, we verified that the participants were engaged in the teaching and learning of Chinese as a second, foreign or additional language. Research related to the teaching and learning of Chinese by native speakers of Chinese was excluded. Finally, we thoroughly reviewed the entire papers to confirm whether the impact of the pandemic was incorporated as the main background of the study. In the end, our review identified 20 publications that met these criteria.

Findings

Existing Publications

The selected papers were categorised into eight subcategories, as shown in Table 2.1. In the following sections, we will provide a brief description of each subcategory, highlight significant trends and offer potential interpretations of the findings.

As shown, the Chinese teaching research community responded swiftly to the challenges of teaching Chinese characters in the context of ERT. Four papers specifically addressed the emergent challenges of online Chinese education in individual Chinese programmes in Australia (Gao 2020), Ireland (Zhang 2020b), the UK (Zhao et al. 2020) and the USA (Xu et al. 2020). These four papers are part of a special issue edited by Wang and Zhao (2020), titled *A Digital Future of Chinese Language Teaching*. Notably, with four contributions in a special issue comprising six articles, the teaching of Chinese characters has indeed emerged as one of the most challenging issues for Chinese teaching professionals.

Over the past four years, there has been an uneven distribution in the number of published studies, with 2022 seeing the highest number of publications. This surge in publications can be partially attributed to S. Liu's (2022b) edited volume named *Teaching the Chinese Language Remotely*, which features numerous studies from diverse contexts. In this book, five chapters focus specifically on teaching Chinese online during ERT. It is worth noting that, apart from the five chapters in Liu's book, most of the publications included in this review are journal articles.

Table 2.1 An overview of the reviewed studies (n = 20)

No.	Subcategory	Details	Number of studies
1	Year of publication	2020	4
		2021	3
		2022	10
		2023	3
2	Type of publication	Journal article	14
		Book chapter	6
3	Research design	Quantitative	1
		Qualitative	9
		Mixed	10
4	Research instrument	Questionnaire	14
		Interview	10
		Reflective narrative	8
		Test	4
		Observation	2
5	Participant	Students	8
		Teachers	6
		Students and teachers	6
6	Level of the course	Beginners only	6
		Beginning to intermediate	4
		Intermediate to advanced	2
		All levels	1
		Not specified	1
7	Education organisation	University	16
		School	3
		Confucius Institute	1
8	Location	Asia	5
		Oceania	5
		Europe	4
		North America	4
		Africa	2

Note. For Subcategory 4, the total number of studies exceeds 20 because most studies used more than one instrument. For Subcategory 6, the total number of studies is 14 because this subcategory only examined 14 studies that had student participants

Most of the research employed qualitative analysis (n = 9) or mixed methods (n = 10) designs, with only one study using a purely quantitative approach. Most studies used questionnaires (n = 14) to collect both quantitative and qualitative data. Ten papers included interviews to delve into the issues in greater depth. Among these, two papers employed focus-group interviews to stimulate group discussions (Han et al. 2023; Wang and East 2020). Reflective narratives were also more commonly employed as a means to capture teachers' personal perspectives and insights into teaching Chinese in the context of ERT (Han et al. 2023; Jiang 2022; Zhang 2020a; Zhao et al. 2020; Jin and Liu 2023). Four studies utilised tests to measure student learning achievements after applying the digital solutions in their courses (Lin et al. 2022; Ma 2022; Wang and East 2023; Wang and Jiang 2022). Another two papers presented valuable observations from the classroom for students' engagement, participation and learning progress when navigating new tools and apps as digital solutions (Han et al. 2023; Lin et al. 2022).

In terms of participants, the published articles paid attention to the changes brought about by the pandemic for both students and teachers. Most of the studies focusing on students examined the learning experiences of beginning-level (n = 6) and beginning-to-intermediate-level students (n = 4). The focus on student proficiency levels reflects teachers' and researchers' concerns about students' long-term engagement and continuation with Chinese learning. Furthermore, there was a substantial contrast in the education organisations of these participants and teachers. Most studies (n = 16) focused on higher education, with only three examining character learning in schools or community schools (Han et al. 2023; Lin et al. 2022; Jin and Liu 2023), and another study (Too 2022) surveying the learning experiences of students in a Confucius Institute at the University of Mauritius in Africa. Finally, these studies were conducted in 13 different countries across five continents. Asia and Oceania contributed the highest number of studies.

Focal Research Areas

The selected publications highlighted six main themes, which will be analysed in the following sections using specific cases from each publication for a detailed examination.

Navigating Digital Solutions

All selected publications mentioned the exploration of digital solutions in response to the sudden shift to online teaching. These solutions aim to maintain or maximise opportunities for handwriting learning as an extension of classroom instruction. Our analysis reveals that these studies emphasise the fundamental role of handwriting in Chinese character instruction, highlighting its importance in consolidating motor memory for character learning.

The documented digital solutions mainly pertain to pedagogical delivery. While most teaching shifted to online platforms such as Zoom or Microsoft Teams, teachers explored new technology, digital tools and apps to integrate with their primary teaching platforms for Chinese character instruction. Some studies mentioned that teachers used built-in features such as the whiteboard and screen sharing on Zoom to enhance visual effects and real-time feedback when teaching Chinese characters (Xu et al. 2021; Zhang 2020b). Moreover, visual aids, including images, graphs and animations, were widely employed by teachers to help students understand the meaning of characters and assist in character recognition and memorisation. This was especially beneficial for pictographic characters and those with weak semantic or phonetic cues (Gao 2020).

In addition, online stroke-order animation apps (e.g., Skritter) or websites became one of the few popular tools for online character teaching. For example, Y. Wang and Xu (2020) reported that 80% of instructors used animations to demonstrate new Chinese characters stroke by stroke, a method of character instruction normally performed by teachers writing on the whiteboard in the classroom. However, the study conducted by Q. Zhang (2020b) showed that some teachers were concerned that using stroke animation during online teaching would be time-consuming and also limit interactions. For example, instructors in Q. Zhang's (2020b) study complained that displaying stroke-order animations required more time compared to directly writing them on a whiteboard. Another instructor voiced their concerns regarding the inability to monitor students' character-writing performance and offer immediate feedback.

Overall, existing studies demonstrated that the applied digital solutions offered teachers immediate technological support to continue their daily instruction and provided students with a more interactive, real-time and innovative learning experience during ERT. When faced with another crisis that necessitates a shift to online teaching, it is expected that the search for digital solutions will occur again, but with relative ease, as teachers have already gained experience. However, it is worth noting that, to date, there is no well-known and affordable digital technology, device or software specifically designed for teaching Chinese characters.

Adjusting Assessments

Another important aspect relates to adjusting assessment mode and design. First, typing has replaced handwriting as the primary method for students to produce writing output, though some studies reported that students were instructed to take a screenshot of their handwritten homework (Ma 2022; Too 2022). While typing skills were not widely taught in the contexts of the reviewed publications, they did provide teachers and students with the much-desired freedom and flexibility in writing assessments. For example, rather than serving as a temporary solution, using Pinyin to type on keyboards has become not only an accepted method but also the preferred one for official writing assessments (Jiang 2022; Wang and East 2020, 2023; Xu et al. 2020). On the other hand, some courses maintained the traditional handwriting assessments and required students to submit images of their assignments or exam papers through online course management systems (Ma 2022; Too 2022; Zahradnikova 2022). These justifications aimed to reduce the challenges associated with assessing character writing and alleviate students' stress and anxiety (Xu et al. 2020). As noted by D. Wang and East (2020), the transition from handwriting to typing in formal assessments has significantly reduced students' deep fear of learning and remembering Chinese characters in high-stake examination conditions. The shift of assessment mode from handwriting to typing may help "unlock the potential for the Chinese language to become a global language" (p. 12).

In terms of assessment design, these studies included various strategies for modifying the components and designs of tests related to Chinese characters. For example, in Xu et al.'s study (2020), most college-level instructors reported that the frequency of handwriting assessments had significantly reduced since early 2020, especially in upper-level courses where longer pieces of writing were required. This reduction primarily resulted from the practicality of assessing students online. In Gao's (2020) research, summative assessments, such as dictation and written tests, were replaced with formative assessments, including handwritten assignments and typing exercises in quizzes. In other studies (Wang and East 2020; Zhang 2020b), handwriting assessments were eliminated, and more diverse assessment methods were developed for evaluating students' reading and writing skills through typing.

Furthermore, ERT has granted teachers and programme leaders unprecedented freedom to explore creative assessment strategies that may not have been considered or even permitted in conventional teaching conditions prior to the pandemic. For instance, in a New Zealand university, as reported by Wang and East (2023), a translanguaging approach has been integrated into the assessment of Chinese writing. This unique assessment design allows students to use multimodal texts when completing writing tasks. Survey results demonstrated the effectiveness of translanguaging in engaging novice learners in meaningful writing exercises. This innovation could open new possibilities for teaching and assessing CSL students' digital literacy.

Teachers' Attitudes

Teachers had a wide range of attitudes towards handwriting and typing when it came to teaching Chinese characters online. While many acknowledged the potential benefits of using typing to improve learning efficiency, they also recognised the accompanying difficulties and challenges in legitimising typing in the Chinese curriculum, such as the limited monitoring of student's handwriting and the lack of immediate feedback. Additionally, they emphasised the importance of receiving adequate training and support to enhance their online teaching skills.

Existing studies have demonstrated that Chinese teachers exhibited great resilience during the pandemic and a strong adaptability to embrace changes while actively navigating digital solutions to maintain the normalcy of their day-to-day teaching. In D. Wang and East's (2020) study, teachers showed positive responses in adopting various changes to ensure their students' learning experiences were not compromised in the online classroom. Additionally, when proper teaching tools were unavailable, teachers resorted to demonstrating character writing in front of the camera and providing more instant feedback on students' handwriting. Other studies found that teachers emphasised experiential learning during ERT, as this approach helped students better perceive Chinese writing as relevant and interesting (Chen 2022; Lin et al. 2022; Wang and East 2020). Teachers also provided additional support to students outside of teaching hours, such as one-on-one sessions on Zoom to answer questions about effective ways to learn Chinese characters.

During this time, teachers expressed concerns about their workload and wellbeing. Many felt the frustration of a sudden transition to online teaching without enough time to plan and prepare their courses (Lin 2022; Xu et al. 2020). They constantly found themselves in survival mode, unable to fully explore the potential of software platforms for character teaching due to time constraints and technology limitations (Zhang 2020b). Tracking students' learning progress, monitoring their handwriting—such as the stroke order—and providing timely feedback were additional challenges they faced (Zhang 2020b). They felt that the lack of technology support and immediate interactions made effective character instruction almost impossible. To cope, teachers had to resort to self-initiated, more time-consuming methods that lacked real-time or whole-group monitoring, such as breakout rooms and individual consultation sessions, especially for additional Chinese character instruction (Jiang 2022).

Teachers stressed the importance of receiving professional training and support to improve the teaching of Chinese characters online. They also emphasised the value of practical online technology training tailored to language-specific needs, as well as the importance of engaging in webinars, virtual forums, peer mentoring and observation demonstrations

(Gao 2020). Furthermore, teachers highlighted the favourable outcomes associated with prior training in online Chinese-language instruction and character pedagogy (Xu et al. 2020).

Teachers' Acceptance of Technology

Although most teachers showed a willingness to adopt various digital solutions to enhance students' learning experience during ERT, their professional knowledge, beliefs and inclination to incorporate and utilise technological tools, resources and innovations in their character teaching practices are still underexplored (Liu et al. 2018; Xu et al. 2020, 2021). One widely recognised and frequently cited model for understanding technology acceptance is the technology acceptance model (TAM) (Davis 1986). The TAM posits that perceived usefulness and perceived ease of use are key determinants of an individual's intention to use technology. Perceived usefulness refers to "the degree to which an individual believes that using a particular system would enhance his or her job performance" (Davis 1986, p. 82). As for perceived ease of use, Davis (1986) defined it as "the degree to which an individual believes that using a particular system would be free of physical and mental effort" (p. 82), while Albirini (2006) operationalised it as computer competence. Subsequent research has extended and adapted the TAM to various educational contexts, including online teaching and learning (Liu et al. 2018; Xu et al. 2020, 2021).

In the context of teaching Chinese characters online, teachers' acceptance of technology would encompass their views on the usefulness of technology for character instruction and their confidence in using digital tools, which jointly shapes their approach to online teaching. One major obstacle to teaching Chinese characters online is the lack of technology affordances for handwriting and prompt interactions. Most papers reported that teachers found it challenging to use a mouse for writing characters, and the software, devices and platforms they commonly used did not offer practical tools for "drawing" characters (Qu 2021; Zhang 2020b). This limitation in technology affordances hinders effective character instruction online. Technological and time limitations often result in a lack of comprehensive character teaching content in online classes. Existing resources may serve for demonstration purposes but may not facilitate effective teaching or monitoring of handwriting (Xu et al. 2021). However, it is also noted that the perceived value of technology may be less important when character knowledge building is a primary objective, focusing instead on integrating character instruction effectively, especially for beginner-level instructors (Xu et al. 2020).

Teachers' confidence in online teaching varied depending on their familiarity with effective tools and their ability to guide students in character reading online. This confidence was also influenced by the perceived readiness of students and the level of support teachers received from their institution and colleagues. The shift to remote work may result in limited access to immediate IT support, constraining CFL teachers' ability to gain full awareness and competence in technology affordances (Zahradnikova 2022). The reviewed publications revealed that many instructors lacked confidence in conducting handwriting instruction and assessing students' progress due to limitations in the online environment and suitable tools. The online setting makes evaluating students' ability to reproduce character forms in handwriting particularly challenging. However, some instructors reported that their confidence in online teaching had grown through experience and gaining proficiency in using basic online teaching functions (Xu et al. 2021).

Students' Feedback

The studies found that students' overall feedback on online character teaching was generally positive. While students faced challenges related to technology, time constraints and mental health during the pandemic, they were generally satisfied with teachers' prompt adaptation of their teaching strategies, assessment methods and extra support for individual students. In Gao's (2020) survey on 40 students in an Australian university, a majority of participants (64%) expressed satisfaction with the teaching methods, evaluation procedures and their own learning progress. Approximately 21% of the respondents expressed their dissatisfaction with remote instruction, while 15%—primarily those new to face-to-face Chinese instruction—remained uncertain due to their limited experience (Gao 2020). Based on the students' feedback on transitioning between online and in-person classes, Zhao et al. (2020) found that students who experienced both in-person and online delivery preferred in-person but appreciated online as a replacement. Additionally, digital materials facilitated students' autonomy in developing Chinese-language skills, such as learning polyphonic characters by oneself through referring to the scripts of listening materials (Chen 2021).

Nonetheless, various challenges, including oral interactions, mental health and wellbeing, technology and physical constraints, subject demands and workloads and uncertainty are worth mentioning (Gao 2020). For example, in Gao's (2020) study, students found it time-consuming to conduct peer or group work and receive tailored feedback from teachers in virtual classrooms, especially in large classes. Students also faced challenges due to technological constraints, such as limited access to touch screens or tablets for writing characters. The lack of access to the same technology as the teacher hindered effective monitoring of students' character learning (Wang and East 2020; Zhang 2020b). These challenges affected their performance and the effectiveness of their learning strategies. Practice using character sheets rather than rote memorisation helped them "infer 'rules' governing characters" (Gao 2020; p. 92). However, repeated practice was still widely aopted and was seen as essential and effective in deveoping character writing and reading skills.

Embracing the New Normal

Existing studies have offered valuable insights for educators and curriculum developers, serving as a compass for the reimagining and enhancement of Chinese character teaching, leveraging the experiences and opportunities garnered through extensive online instruction. In addition to pinpointing the challenges, these studies have collectively promoted an optimistic outlook for the future of Chinese-language teaching, urging teaching professionals to embrace the "new normal" (Wang and East 2020).

First, online character instruction offers opportunities for students to engage with Chinese characters in a more interactive and dynamic manner. Zhao et al. (2020) highlighted that the use of digital and multimedia resources and online games fosters active participation in character recognition activities, making the learning process more engaging and enjoyable. In addition, a broad range of activities are available to enhance students' Chinese character learning, which includes online quizzes, games, and trackpad handwriting tools that offer multiple avenues for students to practise and reinforce their character recognition and handwriting skills. The interactive nature of these activities not only keeps students engaged but also accommodates different learning styles, making it a more inclusive approach to teaching Chinese characters (Xu et al. 2020).

Moreover, online character teaching involves a wealth of multimodal resources to support students' Chinese character learning, expanding the learning space and content available to students. This enables the inclusion of additional information that may not be feasible in traditional face-to-face settings (Wang and East 2020). These resources encompass digital-input methods, online dictionaries, stroke-order animations and enhanced textual explanations (Zhang 2020b). Multimodal teaching methods such as learning, picture book translating project and finger dancing with poetry reciting can be adopted to refine students' linguistic repertoires (Jin and Liu 2023). The availability of such diverse learning materials and opportunities empowers students to access more real-life resources, contributing to a more profound understanding and mastery of Chinese characters encompassing not only the characters themselves but also their meaningful use (Ma 2022). The digitisation of these resources aligns with the current technological era, making character learning more accessible and customised to students' needs. This expanded learning environment allows for the integration of a broader array of supplementary materials, enriching the educational process (Ma 2022; Wang et al. 2022).

The reviewed publications indicated that teaching Chinese characters online fostered an open space for instructors to explore and build confidence in using technology. According to Xu et al. (2021), instructors enhanced their technological skills by creating or adapting online materials, designing online activities and effectively assessing students' handwriting abilities. This process empowered educators to become more proficient in integrating technology into their teaching practice, ultimately elevating the quality of character instruction. With online teaching becoming the new normal (Wang and East 2020; Xu et al. 2020; Zhang 2020b), taking advantage of these benefits can significantly contribute to the improvement of Chinese character instruction as a whole. Additionally, it is crucial to provide regular professional training to empower and facilitate more teachers to embrace the new normal in Chinese character teaching. Creating a sense of community and trust among students and teachers is essential for the successful exploration and implementation of innovation (Ma 2022).

Several innovative pedagogies have been recommended in existing publications to help teachers better prepare to embrace the new normal by making small changes to their teaching approaches. One approach is to curate and share a wide range of online learning materials with students to enable them to explore and familiarise themselves with these resources. For instance, www.archchinese.com allows students to input Chinese characters and view animated stroke-by-stroke demonstrations (Qu 2021). Teachers should also encourage the early use of mobile apps like Pleco and support students to engage in mobile-assisted learning. Secondly, teachers should acquire and use a variety of game-based activity apps or platforms to make digital learning more engaging, enjoyable and accessible. These could include online videos demonstrating character etymology and websites that illustrate character structures (Gao 2020; Xu et al. 2021). Students should learn in an interactive environment where they can make sense of their learning. These pedagogical recommendations and tools not only promote autonomous character learning but also provide opportunities for interactions between students and technology, as well as among students themselves.

Conclusion

In this review, we have gathered, analysed and provided an overview of 20 empirical studies on Chinese character instruction published during the pandemic years from 2020 to 2023. From our analysis, we have identified six primary areas of focus in these publications. These topics collectively paint a holistic picture of the various challenges faced by teachers and students, their solutions and feedback and the innovative approaches implemented that make a difference in student learning in the context of massive online education during ERT. These studies underscore the intricate nature of Chinese character teaching as a multifaceted professional practice, emphasising that our research focus should transcend a simplistic technical debate focused solely on the comparative effectiveness of handwriting versus typing. Additionally, it is anticipated that there will be a gradual shift towards favouring typing as the primary teaching approach in Chinese-language instruction as a new normal in response to the digital age.

The COVID-19 pandemic ignited a wave of creativity in the realm of Chinese character instruction, pushing beyond conventional discussions about tools and materials to explore fresh teaching methodologies and curriculum design, thus unlocking the full potential of Chinese-language learning in the digital age (Wang and East 2020). This underscores the imperative for flexibility and innovation in online Chinese character teaching and learning, and for educators and researchers to embark on initiatives that embrace new approaches and employ innovative technology and materials. Even as traditional classroom teaching resumes, it is strongly recommended that educators and programme coordinators integrate technology-assisted teaching into their curriculum designs, ensuring that Chinese character instruction effectively addresses the challenges of improving enrolment, retention and student engagement in our Chinese-language programmes. While handwriting remains integral to character recognition and remains a core part of our instruction, curriculum adjustments and reforms should be made to fundamentally rethink the goals of Chinese character learning in the digital future. In conclusion, as we continue to learn and maintain an open-minded approach to new ideas in Chinese character instruction, the experiences gained during the pandemic years will undoubtedly shape the future of Chinese character teaching.

Limitation

One limitation of the present review is its predominant focus on research papers published in English, which may have led to the omission of valuable insights from Chinese-language publications. For instance, S. Liu's (2022a) book offers a valuable compilation of practical teaching experiences, written in Chinese, from 21 groups of authors across ten different countries during the pandemic. The exclusion of these Chinese-language articles may limit the comprehensive exploration of diverse pedagogical approaches and cultural considerations in different contexts. In future research, efforts could be made to address this limitation by incorporating Chinese-language publications, thus providing a broader perspective on the challenges and transformations in Chinese character instruction during the COVID-19 pandemic.

Competing interests The author has no conflicts of interest to declare that are relevant to the content of this chapter.

References[1]

Albirini, Abdulkafi. 2006. Teachers' Attitudes toward Information and Communication Technologies: The Case of Syrian EFL Teachers. *Computers & Education* 47 (4): 373–398. https://doi.org/10.1016/j.compedu.2004.10.013.

Bond, Melissa, Svenja Bedenlier, Victoria I. Marín, and Marion Händel. 2021. Emergency Remote Teaching in Higher Education: Mapping the First Global Online Semester. *International Journal of Educational Technology. Higher Education* 18 (1): NA. http://dx.doi.org.ezproxy.auckland.ac.nz/10.1186/s41239-021-00282-x.

---

[1] References with * are the reviewed articles

*Chen, Mengtian. 2022. Digital Affordances and Teacher Agency in the Context of Teaching Chinese as a Second Language during COVID-19. *System* 105: 1–13. https://doi.org/10.1016/j.system.2021.102710

*Chen, Chen. 2021. Using Scaffolding Materials to Facilitate Autonomous Online Chinese as a Foreign Language Learning: A Study during the Covid-19 Pandemic. *SAGE Open* 11(3): 1–12. https://doi.org/10.1177/21582440211040131

Cui, Xiliang. 2020. Chinese Teaching against the Background of Global Public Health Emergency [全球突发公共卫生事件背景下的汉语教学]. *Chinese Teaching in the World [世界汉语教学]* 34 (3): 291–99. https://doi.org/10.13724/j.cnki.ctiw.2020.03.001

Davis, Fred D. 1986. A Technology Acceptance Model for Empirically Testing New End-User Information Systems: Theory and Results. PhD diss., Massachusetts Institute of Technology.

*Gao, Xiaoping. 2020. Australian Students' Perceptions of the Challenges and Strategies for Learning Chinese Characters in Emergency Online Teaching. *International Journal of Chinese Language Teaching* 1(1): 83–98. https://doi.org/10.46451/ijclt.2020.06.04

Gough, David, and Michelle Richardson. 2018. Systematic Reviews. In *Advanced Research Methods for Applied Psychology*, ed. Paula Brough, 63–75. London: Routledge.

Guest, Greg, Kathleen MacQueen, and Emily Namey. 2014. *Applied Thematic Analysis*. Thousand Oaks, California: SAGE Publications, Inc. https://doi.org/10.4135/9781483384436.

*Han, Jinghe, Qiaoyun Liu, and Ruiyan Sun. 2023. A Multimodal Approach to Teaching Chinese as a Foreign Language (CFL) in the Digital World. *International Journal of Computer-Assisted Language Learning and Teaching* 13 (1): 1–16. https://doi.org/10.4018/IJCALLT.322026

He, Wayne Wenchao. 2021. Innovative Excellence: A Case Study of a Chinese Language Flagship Program. In *Frontiers of L2 Chinese Language Education: A Global Perspective*, ed. Yanyin Zhang and Xiaoping Gao, 8–29. London: Routledge. https://doi.org/10.4324/9781003169895-2.

In'Nami, Yo, and Rie Koizumi. 2010. Database Selection Guidelines for Meta-Analysis in Applied Linguistics. *TESOL Quarterly* 44 (1): 169–184.

*Jiang, Wenying. 2022. Remote Chinese Language Teaching at the University of Queensland during the COVID-19 Pandemic: A Reflection from Australia. In *Teaching the Chinese Language Remotely: Global Cases and Perspectives*, ed. Shijuan Liu, 167–180. Cham: Springer. https://doi.org/10.1007/978-3-030-87055-3_7

*Jin, Jing, and Yina Liu. 2023. Towards a Critical Translanguaging Biliteracy Pedagogy: The 'aha Moment' Stories of Two Mandarin Chinese Teachers in Canada. *Literacy* 57 (2): 171–184. https://doi.org/10.1111/lit.12323

Jin, Li, Elizabeth Deifell, and Katie Angus. 2022. Emergency Remote Language Teaching and Learning in Disruptive Times. *CALICO Journal* 39 (1): i–x. https://doi.org/10.1558/cj.20858.

Lei, Linda, and Danping Wang. 2023. Novice Chinese Learners' Character Learning Strategies and Character Skills: A Think-Aloud Study. In *Teaching Chinese in the Anglophone World: Perspectives from New Zealand*, ed. Danping Wang and Martin East, 243–258. Cham: Springer. https://doi.org/10.1007/978-3-031-35475-5_16.

Li, Michael. 2020. A Systematic Review of the Research on Chinese Character Teaching and Learning. *Frontiers of Education in China* 15 (1): 39–72. https://doi.org/10.1007/s11516-020-0003-y.

Li, Liu. 2022. Impact of Typing vs Handwriting on CFL Students' Character Learning. In *Reading in Chinese as an Additional Language: Learners' Development, Instruction, and Assessment*, ed. Liu Li and Dongbo Zhang, 43–60. London: Routledge. https://doi.org/10.4324/9781003029038-5.

*Lin, Chin-hui. 2022. Emergency Remote Chinese Language Learning at a German University: Student Perceptions. In *Teaching the Chinese Language Remotely: Global Cases and Perspectives*, ed. Shijuan Liu, 57–83. Cham: Springer. https://doi.org/10.1007/978-3-030-87055-3_3

*Lin, Yao-San, Jie Ni Lim, and Yung-Sen Wu. 2022. Developing and Applying a Chinese Character Learning Game App to Enhance Primary School Students' Abilities in Identifying and Using Characters. *Education Sciences* 12 (189): 1–14. https://doi.org/10.3390/educsci12030189

Liu, Shijuan, ed. 2022a. *Online Chinese Teaching and Learning in 2020 [2020 中文线上教学]*. National Foreign Language Resource Center, University of Hawai'i.

———, ed. 2022b. *Teaching the Chinese Language Remotely: Global Cases and Perspectives*. Cham: Springer. https://doi.org/10.1007/978-3-030-87055-3.

Liu, Ying, Min Wang, and Charles A. Perfetti. 2007. Threshold-Style Processing of Chinese Characters for Adult Second-Language Learners. *Memory & Cognition* 35 (3): 471–480. https://doi.org/10.3758/BF03193287.

Liu, Haixia, Chin-Hsi Lin, Dongbo Zhang, and Binbin Zheng. 2018. Chinese Language Teachers' Perceptions of Technology and Instructional Use of Technology: A Path Analysis. *Journal of Educational Computing Research* 56 (3): 396–414. https://doi.org/10.1177/0735633117708313.

Lyu, Boning, Chun Lai, Chin-Hsi Lin, and Yang Gong. 2021. Comparison Studies of Typing and Handwriting in Chinese Language Learning: A Synthetic Review. *International Journal of Educational Research* 106: 1–15. https://doi.org/10.1016/j.ijer.2021.101740.

*Ma, Yue. 2022. A Blessing in Disguise: The Emergency Remote Teaching of Chinese in University of Cape Town in South Africa. In *Teaching the Chinese Language Remotely: Global Cases and Perspectives*, ed. Shijuan Liu, 111–134. Cham: Springer. https://doi.org/10.1007/978-3-030-87055-3_5

Macaro, Ernesto. 2019. Systematic Reviews in Applied Linguistics. In *The Routledge Handbook of Research Methods in Applied Linguistics*, ed. Jim Mckinley and Heath Rose, 230–239. London: Routledge.

Neuendorf, Kimberly A. 2018. Content Analysis and Thematic Analysis. In *Advanced Research Methods for Applied Psychology*, ed. Paula Brough, 211–223. London: Routledge.

*Qu, Yanfeng. 2021. Student Engagement and Pedagogical Innovations for the Pandemic-Precipitated Online Delivery of University Chinese Courses. In *Frontiers of L2 Chinese Language Education*, ed. Yanyin Zhang, and Xiaoping Gao, 51–67. Routledge.

Tao, Jian, and Xuesong (Andy) Gao. 2022. Teaching and Learning Languages Online: Challenges and Responses. *System* 107: 1–9. https://doi.org/10.1016/j.system.2022.102819.

*Too, Sharon. 2022. Online Mandarin Language Teaching and Learning during COVID-19 Pandemic at University of Mauritius in Africa. In *Teaching the Chinese Language Remotely: Global Cases and Perspectives*, ed. Shijuan Liu, 135–166. Cham: Springer. https://doi.org/10.1007/978-3-030-87055-3_6

*Wang, Danping, and Martin East. 2020. Constructing an Emergency Chinese Curriculum during the Pandemic: A New Zealand Experience. *International Journal of Chinese Language Teaching* 1 (1): 1–19. https://doi.org/10.46451/ijclt.2020.06.01

———. 2023. Integrating Translanguaging into Assessment: Students' Responses and Perceptions. *Applied Linguistics Review* (May): 1–27. https://doi.org/10.1515/applirev-2023-0087

*Wang, Qing, and Yuhong Jiang. 2022. A Positive Psychology Perspective on Positive Emotion and Foreign Language Enjoyment among Chinese as a Second Language Learners Attending Virtual Online Classes in the Emergency Remote Teaching Context amid the Covid-19 Pandemic. *Frontiers in Psychology* 12: 1–17. https://doi.org/10.3389/fpsyg.2021.798650

Wang, Yuntong, and Jie Xu. 2020. A Survey on the Use of Technology and Digital Resources in CFL Instruction before the COVID-19. *Journal of Technology and Chinese Language Teaching* 11 (2): 113–139.

Wang, Danping, and Yang Zhao. 2020. Introduction to the Special Issue. *International Journal of Chinese Language Teaching* 1 (1): I–V. https://doi.org/10.46451/ijclt.2020.06.06

*Wang, Yanjun, Pei-Ling Wei, and Van Thanh Nguyen. 2022. An Exploratory Intervention Program on Chinese Culture among CFL Students at a Vietnamese University. *Education Sciences* 12 (887): 1–18. https://doi.org/10.3390/educsci12120887

*Xu, Yi, Li Jin, Elizabeth Deifell, and Katie Angus. 2020. Facilitating Technology-Based Character Learning in Emergency Remote Teaching. *Foreign Language Annals* 55 (1): 72–97. https://doi.org/10.1111/flan.12541

———. 2021. Chinese Character Instruction Online: A Technology Acceptance Perspective in Emergency Remote Teaching. *System* 100: 1–12. https://doi.org/10.1016/j.system.2021.102542

*Zahradnikova, Michaela. 2022. Behind the Screen: Lessons Learnt from a Chinese Emergency Remote Teaching Experience in Czech Republic. In *Teaching the Chinese Language Remotely: Global Cases and Perspectives*, ed. Shijuan Liu, 23–55. Cham: Springer. https://doi.org/10.1007/978-3-030-87055-3_2

Zhang, Chun. 2020a. From Face-to-Face to Screen-to-Screen: CFL Teachers' Beliefs about Digital Teaching Competence during the Pandemic. *International Journal of Chinese Language Teaching* 1 (1): 35–52.

*Zhang, Qi. 2020b. Narrative Inquiry into Online Teaching of Chinese Characters during the Pandemic. *International Journal of Chinese Language Teaching* 1 (1): 20–34. https://doi.org/10.46451/ijclt.2020.06.02

Zhang, Phyllis Ni. 2021a. Typing to Replace Handwriting: Effectiveness of the Typing-Primary Approach for L2 Chinese Beginners. *Journal of Technology and Chinese Language Teaching* 12 (2): 1–28.

Zhang, Shenglan. 2021b. A Systematic Review of Pedagogical Research on Teaching Chinese as a Foreign Language in the United States—From 1960 to 2020. *Chinese as a Second Language Research* 10 (2): 207–238. https://doi.org/10.1515/caslar-2021-2003.

Zhang, Qi, and Ge Min. 2019. Chinese Writing Composition among CFL Learners: A Comparison between Handwriting and Typewriting. *Computers and Composition* 54 (December): 102522. https://doi.org/10.1016/j.compcom.2019.102522.

Zhang, Linlin, and Hongbing Xing. 2023. The Interaction of Orthography, Phonology and Semantics in the Process of Second Language Learners' Chinese Character Production. *Frontiers in Psychology* 14 (March). https://doi.org/10.3389/fpsyg.2023.1076810

Zhang, Qi, and Zhouxiang Lu. 2014. The Writing of Chinese Characters by CFL Learners: Can Writing on Facebook and Using Machine Translation Help? *Language Learning in Higher Education* 4 (2): 441–467. https://doi.org/10.1515/cercles-2014-0023.

Zhang, Qi, Xu Lin, and Caitríona Osborne. 2022. A Think-Aloud Method of Investigating Translanguaging Strategies in Learning Chinese Characters. *Applied Linguistics Review.* https://doi.org/10.1515/applirev-2022-0135.

*Zhao, Lucy Xia, Brittany Blankinship, Zhipeng Duan, Huihui Huang, Jiaxin Sun, and Thomas H Bak. 2020. Comparing Face-to-Face and Online Teaching of Written and Spoken Chinese to Adult Learners: An Edinburgh-Sheffield Case Study. *International Journal of Chinese Language Teaching* 1 (1): 83–98. https://doi.org/10.46451/ijclt.2020.06.05

Zhou, Xiaolin, and William Marslen-Wilson. 1999. Phonology, Orthography, and Semantic Activation in Reading Chinese. *Journal of Memory and Language* 41 (4): 579–606. https://doi.org/10.1006/jmla.1999.2663.

Zhou, Yanling, and Catherine McBride. 2018. The Same or Different: An Investigation of Cognitive and Metalinguistic Correlates of Chinese Word Reading for Native and Non-Native Chinese Speaking Children. *Bilingualism: Language and Cognition* 21 (4): 765–781. https://doi.org/10.1017/S1366728915000279.

3

Investigating the Student Perspective on the Present and Future of Teaching Chinese Characters Online

Caitríona Osborne

Introduction

The unique situation of COVID-19 emerging in early 2020 had a profound effect on the world. Social distancing measures and lockdowns put in place to protect the public against the spread of COVID-19 meant that many non-essential businesses were forced to close their doors, people were isolated from each other and indeed, universities and other educational institutions rapidly switched to distance learning to avoid large gatherings (see WHO 2020). While technologies such as learning platforms, specialised software and general computer programmes had been widely used in tandem with face-to-face classes in universities (e.g. Starkey 2020), this rapid and unprecedented switch challenged third-level educators and students alike. It is widely assumed that students in third-level

---

C. Osborne (✉)
Irish Institute for Chinese Studies, University College Dublin, Belfield, Dublin, Ireland
e-mail: caitriona.osborne@ucd.ie

© The Author(s), under exclusive license to Springer Nature Switzerland AG 2024
C. Osborne et al. (eds.), *Teaching Chinese Characters in the Digital Age*, Palgrave Studies on Chinese Education in a Global Perspective,
https://doi.org/10.1007/978-3-031-64784-0_3

education are competent in using computers and other technology in the classroom, however, this is not necessarily the case (Burns et al. 2020). In addition, other factors such as access to the internet, a reliable computer and even instructors' technological skills can negatively affect learners in this switch to online learning, while a student's wellbeing also suffers with a lack of face-to-face engagement (ibid.). Furthermore, students studying CFL (Chinese as a foreign language) are faced with additional and more specific challenges in the move to at-distance learning. Learning a language with a writing system different from one's own mother tongue means that even in a regular face-to-face setting, acquiring this new skill is challenging (see Osborne et al. 2018, 2022). Approximately 7000 characters are in use in modern China, and as these can be formed in one of six ways (be it pictures, symbols, sound-loans, sound-meaning compounds, meaning-meaning compounds or re-clarified compounds) (Yin 2016), students generally spend much time focusing on the written aspect of the language (e.g. Allen 2008). However, this handwriting practice is necessary for developing both reading and writing skills of Chinese (e.g. Chang et al. 2014; Guan et al. 2011).

In the move to at-distance learning around March 2020, the monitoring of handwritten tasks and written assignments became complicated. Apart from missing an instructor's real-time correction on handwriting practice in the classroom, the trend in moving assignments and exams online meant that assessing handwriting skills was sometimes replaced with typing (Wang and East 2020). While such interventions were made during an emergency period whereby all teaching had to be transferred online in a rapid timeframe, it is now worthwhile to examine the prolonged changes made to the curriculum from the student perspective and provide recommendations for current and future courses. The chapter therefore examines this under three headings: curriculum design, learning strategies and assessment. Specifically, the data highlight areas of student concern along with their primary needs in an online classroom, particularly when it comes to learning Chinese characters. From this, key characteristics are identified for new and/or existing online applications to support student learning. While invaluable research has been conducted during the emergency period to report on the situation from the teacher perspective (e.g. Jin et al. 2021; Wang and East 2020; Zhang 2020), it is now vital to document the experience of CFL learners in order to plan adequately for future curricula.

Literature Review

The migration to online teaching and learning had a major effect on instructors and students worldwide. Firstly, instructors were required to adapt their teaching methods to fit this new mode of delivery in a rapid timeframe. As a result, Wang and East (2020) note the problem of technology exhaustion experienced by faculty in New Zealand, and indeed worldwide, as they continuously explore digital platforms and other technologies to use in the CFL classroom. The lack of adequate training in these technologies and in adapting curricula to suit this new mode of delivery further adds to instructors' stress levels (ibid.) and has also been highlighted in-depth by Starkey (2020) in a systematic review of the literature between 2008 and 2018.

Instructors also had to adapt assessments to replace traditional in-person exams during this emergency period, with new methods introduced including at-home assignments, portfolios, multiple choice questions, open-book exams, practical examinations and viva voces to name but a few (Gamage et al. 2020). With these at-distance assessment strategies, however, comes a higher chance of academic dishonesty (Daniels et al. 2021), meaning that instructors must carefully design assessments to ensure that they can adequately assess student learning outcomes while also minimising opportunities for cheating.

While instructors grappled with this mammoth technological task in both teaching and assessment, it was generally assumed that students would adapt to this new mode of learning given the perceived—and blanket—reputation of students being able to manage computers and other devices with minimal issues (Burns et al. 2020; Link and Marz 2006). Even if students possessed high levels of technological competency, the availability of resources at home also would have impacted their ability to engage effectively. For example, access to technology, internet connection and even home responsibilities impact participation in online classes (Gao 2020; Jin et al. 2021; Zhang 2020).

Apart from these practical issues, the emotional toll taken on students must be considered when examining their experience of online learning. In particular, it has been reported that students' motivation and wellbeing are likely to decrease while learning at distance and therefore away from their peers (Burns et al. 2020; Gao 2020). Similarly, students' anxiety levels will rise as they navigate the uncertainty of online classes and assignments (ibid.).

Effects on the CFL Classroom

The move to online learning indeed has more specific effects on the CFL classroom as students navigate the unique writing system and mastery of the four tones in spoken Chinese. Firstly, the mode of a language class must include some synchronous delivery, ensuring that students can practise and receive immediate feedback on all four skills of reading, writing, speaking and listening (e.g. Padaguri and Pasha 2021; Riwayatiningsih and Sulistyani 2020). While asynchronous technology can be useful for at-distance assessment, the immediate feedback afforded by synchronous technology is generally found to be motivating to students in their language development (Helm 2015). Synchronous platforms also allow for monitored group work and for students to produce meaning-focused output, thus supporting their language acquisition (ibid.; Kohnke and Moorhouse 2022).

Learning Chinese as a Foreign Language

For native speakers of English who are learning CFL, there are very few similarities between their mother tongue and the Chinese language. Firstly, Chinese is a tonal language, meaning that incorrect tonal pronunciation can render spoken language difficult to understand, or simply incomprehensible, depending on the pronunciation (Abraham 2013).

Yet the most widely accepted challenge to CFL learners is undoubtedly learning the writing system, i.e., the characters (e.g. Hsiao et al. 2014; Osborne et al. 2018; Yang 2018; Zhang and Lu 2013). There are many debates surrounding the best approach(es) to teaching Chinese characters in the CFL classroom, however it is found that teachers and students alike tend to lean towards a method involving repetition in some way, presumably due to the popularity of such methods in the Chinese education system (e.g. Osborne et al. 2018; Wang and Lin 2018; Wang and Mcbride 2017; Winke and Abbuhl 2008). On the other hand, learning to handwrite the characters can be viewed as an inefficient use of a learner's time given the advances in and high use of technology (Allen 2008), which enables characters to be input through pinyin (the Romanisation of standard Chinese) or through a rough outline of the character (whereby an imperfect character can be recognised through fuzzy-matching software, see Zhang and Min (2019)). Nevertheless, characters are still deemed an important part of the CFL curriculum as handwriting practice can also positively impact a learner's reading skills as well as writing skills (e.g. Chang et al. 2014; Guan et al. 2011). In addition, the characters also reflect Chinese culture, which is inextricably linked to the language (see Jia and Jia 2005).

Research into Emergency Curricula Created for the CFL Classroom

A number of prominent themes have emerged from the continuous research during the pandemic period including the creation of emergency curricula for the CFL classroom, teaching Chinese characters online and inquiries into what future curricula may look like in the CFL classroom. The following sections therefore examine the emerging research under (1) perceptions on technology and (2) handling of Chinese characters in teaching and assessment.

Perceptions on Technology

In the very narrow window of time that instructors were required to adapt face-to-face courses into online courses, Jin et al. (2021) note that instructors were generally ill-equipped to cope with this task as pressures in increased workload and family matters rose. Even prior to this, instructors generally do not receive up-to-date instruction for online teaching in their training (ibid., Starkey 2020), meaning that creating online language courses under this time pressure becomes even more stressful. In a study of 133 CFL instructors in the United States, respondents firstly found it difficult to see the value of online tools when teaching characters as the action of pen to paper cannot be mimicked (Jin et al. 2021). In their study of 662 world language instructors in the United States, the lack of face-to-face interaction concerns the majority of respondents, demonstrating a vast preference for a blended approach or even fully face-to-face in some cases (ibid.).

In a study of 40 CFL learners in Australia (mainly beginner learners), Gao (2020) reports that respondents found their motivation for learning Chinese was negatively affected during this time through increased demands for self-discipline and time management. The lack of face-to-face interaction likely influenced their requirement to self-study after class, and they overwhelmingly adopted repetitive strategies in practising their handwriting of Chinese characters. In the context of New Zealand, the use of additional technology such as online games was actually minimised during the emergency remote period in order to alleviate technological concerns and/or pressures (Wang and East 2020). In an attempt to maintain the main pillars of their approach to teaching (student-centred, communicative and task-based), Wang and East (2020) prioritised opportunities for communication and collaboration among students and teachers alike.

Jin et al. (2021) present a number of interesting findings on the continuation of delivering online language courses in post pandemic times. Around 57% of respondents felt positive about adopting online teaching in the future, and the study notes that the experience of teaching in an online emergency course allowed some participants to gain more self-confidence in their online delivery as well as with other technologies. In analysing the delivery, pedagogy and assessment of an emergency CFL curriculum from the New Zealand perspective, Wang and East (2020) echo previous sentiments that synchronous learning is paramount in learning a language online, and so small groups were taught in a synchronous manner in order to allow for this vital practice and instruction. These classes were also recorded, which allowed for students to revisit the lesson at a later time and was reportedly well-received by students.

The vast majority of respondents in Jin et al. (2021) were confident in their ability to use tools associated with building character recognition skills, although less than half were confident in using tools for teaching and assessing the handwriting of characters. Animations of character stroke order and even online games were deemed helpful for engaging students. Respondents' intentions to continue to integrate such online tools for character instruction in the future seem to be determined by the perceived value, student readiness and instructors' usage of online tools in emergency remote character teaching.

Handling of Chinese Characters

Indeed, the lack of opportunity for writing characters by hand or receiving feedback on handwriting from an instructor in the online classroom also contributes to the difficulty of teaching Chinese characters online (Zhang 2020). Respondents from Jin et al. (2021) reported that teaching characters online was the biggest challenge for instructors, and a reduction of focus on characters was reported in many cases. With this came a negative impact not only on students' handwriting abilities but also their reading skills (ibid.). In Zhang's (2020) study, five CFL instructors' handling of Chinese characters in Ireland and the UK are captured. Main findings demonstrate that from a practical perspective, animations could be used to demonstrate the stroke order of a character, while clearly designed activities and tasks can also assist in the acquisition of Chinese characters. Participants also mentioned mimicking the handwritten experience through using a stylus and a tablet, however also realised that not all students would have access to such.

In a bid to avoid academic dishonesty in the assessment process, assignments in New Zealand were presented as images using anti-OCR (optical character recognition) whereby they could not be edited or copy-pasted into Google Translate, while students were also presented with an academic integrity statement (Wang and East 2020). The oral test became more heavily weighted (from 15% to 25%), while the final written exam was reduced from 40% to 20%. In this written exam, students had the option to write in characters (while being awarded an additional 5 marks), or to type their answers. More time was allocated for assessments, while it was also noted that the grading became more lenient. Gao (2020) also recognises that using typing in assessments, while incorporating formative assessments into the curriculum, seems to have eased the difficulties in learning Chinese characters. However, typing characters cannot replace handwriting in assessments if character composition is also being tested (e.g. Guan et al. 2011).

The literature review has demonstrated that a certain lack of technological affordances exists when it comes to teaching Chinese characters in the online CFL classroom. However, there is also a willingness to incorporate technology into the classroom in the future, albeit with a strong need to upskill instructors. Unsurprisingly, the emergency period reported here meant that in many cases, heavy emphasis was not placed on Chinese characters while oral assessments were sometimes more heavily weighted. However, this is not a long-term or sustainable solution, and character-teaching tools as well as assessment methods must be considered for future online CFL courses. Indeed, the student voice is primarily missing from these previous studies. Through questionnaires and follow-up interviews, information and feedback on online character-teaching practices and learning strategies are explored from the perspective of students in six English-speaking countries in order to gain an understanding of the current situation and to be better able to plan for present and future curricula. The research questions are:

1. What has been the student experience of learning Chinese online—particularly characters—in English-speaking countries after the outbreak of COVID-19?

2. What strategies were adopted by these students to learn Chinese characters during their online/at-distance courses?
3. What recommendations can be made for future online CFL curricula, particularly in relation to character teaching and assessment?

Methodology

In order to understand the student perspective on current online CFL curricula and decipher recommendations for those in the future, a mixed methods approach was adopted. In short, an online questionnaire was developed based on findings and gaps from the literature emerging primarily in 2020–2021 surrounding the mass migration to online CFL teaching and learning. A pilot questionnaire was first distributed locally for robustness in August 2021, and after this was finalised, the data collected from the questionnaire informed the semi-structured interview questions that were later refined and also pilot tested in April 2022. The online questionnaire was made live and disseminated by a link via email to colleagues in Ireland, the UK, the United States, Canada, Australia and New Zealand in October 2021, while the interviews were scheduled in the summers of 2022 and 2023. Figure 3.1 demonstrates an overview of this research process.

Research Instruments

Firstly, the anonymous questionnaire was hosted online in order to reach a wider network and consisted of questions under the specific themes of

Fig. 3.1 Overview of research process

(1) curriculum overview, (2) character learning strategies and (3) assessment. It consisted of 46 questions in total which were mainly tick-the-box questions with additional space for elaboration, while some Likert-scale and open-ended questions were also included in order to wholly capture the learner experience and recommendations for future curricula. The landing page of the link detailed a plain language statement and a box to tick for consent, while basic biographical details were also collected from the 35 participants. As the survey was voluntary, this number represents a sample of the participants, while the number of respondents for each question is specifically highlighted in Section "Data".

Secondly, towards the end of the questionnaire, participants were invited to provide their email address if they wished to take part in a follow-up interview. The purpose of the semi-structured interview was to interrogate the findings further and allow space to delve deeper into the main themes that were emerging from the questionnaire. Four participants took part in the online interviews conducted over Zoom. The interviews were recorded with full consent of the participants in order to gain access to the meeting transcription, which was also cross-checked by the author. The length of the four interviews ranged from 21:35 minutes to 34:56 minutes with an average of 26:11 minutes. In total, 104:46 minutes were recorded and transcribed.

Participants

The participants were learning Chinese as an additional/foreign language at varying levels in a university or tertiary institution. Most were learning it as a non-major (74%), with 17% learning it as part of a diploma course and 9% as a major. The majority of participants identified as women (60%) with 35% identifying as men. They were mostly aged 18–24 (75%) and based on the HSK (Hanyu Shuiping Kaoshi) 2.0, had varying levels from HSK 1-6.[1] Figure 3.2 demonstrates the participant profile information captured from the biographical questions of the online questionnaire.

---

[1] The HSK is an international, standardised Chinese proficiency test. The 2.0 version has six bands, whereby HSK 1 is the first/beginner level and HSK 6 is the final and most advanced level (see Zeng and Xiao 2021).

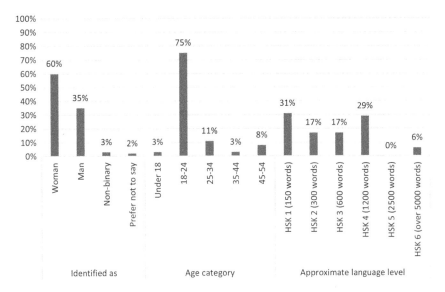

Fig. 3.2 Participant profile (n = 35)

Data Analysis

Data were collected in the form of online questionnaire responses and interview transcriptions. The questionnaire data and interview data were grouped and coded thematically and cross-checked by another researcher separately. The "Data" section will present the findings according to the themes of (1) curriculum overview, (2) character learning strategies and (3) assessment, while also describing the general learning experiences of participants as appropriate.

Data

The following data stem primarily from the questionnaire, while further information is clarified in information received from the follow-up interviews. As the questionnaire was set up to allow participants to skip some questions, the following sections indicate the number of responses per question.

Curriculum Overview

When asked whether they had ever enrolled in online Chinese language courses prior to the pandemic, 77.14% (of 35 respondents) stated that they had not. When asked about their overall experience of learning CFL online during the pandemic, the vast majority of 61 respondents had either a very positive (26.23%) or positive experience (45.90%), with almost half of these 61 respondents (47.54%) indicating their willingness to enrol in an online CFL course in the future (see Fig. 3.3).

Interestingly, when this latter finding was investigated in the student interviews, participants reported mixed feelings.

Student A:[2] I found that apps or online learning ... you can replay it—a character being written correctly, the right stroke order—and you can replicate it then. I find—especially if you have a tablet with a pen—I think it's very, em, very beneficial. That's just on my own experience, from writing

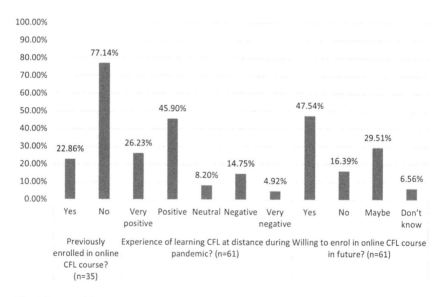

Fig. 3.3 Participants' general experience of learning CFL online

---

[2] The extracts here and throughout the chapter are verbatim.

with a paper and pen in a classroom trying to watch the board to see what the teachers do [which is] quite difficult.

Student B: I prefer the online classes where you don't see my face, and I just ask my question comfortably.

Student C: In the online classes it's also difficult for the teachers since they don't really get the reaction of the students. Maybe they thought: Oh, everyone got it … there are no questions. So, they just went on to the next topic.

Student D: I think attending classes online is much harder … It's just a different environment like that's something that I never really got used to. So, like my focus tends to wander even in class.

Next, participants answered questions on the effects of learning CFL online in relation to their character learning. Participants mostly had neutral feelings on their experience (39.02% of 41 respondents), followed by 34.15% gearing towards negative feelings and 26.83% towards positive feelings (see Fig. 3.4). A comment box followed this question

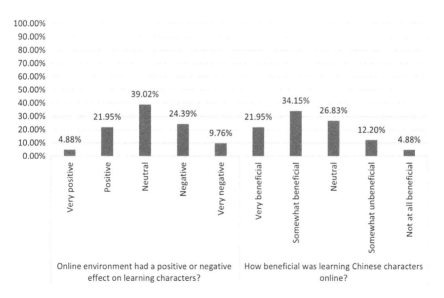

Fig. 3.4 Participants' experience of learning CFL online in relation to character learning (n = 41)

and asked participants to elaborate on their answers. Of the 28 responses received for this open-ended question, a mix of neutral, negative and positive reasons were given with the top answer (eight mentions) referring to the negative effect of the online environment on handwriting. However, when asked how beneficial learning Chinese characters was in the online environment, an overwhelming majority noted the experience as very beneficial or somewhat beneficial (21.95% and 34.15% of 41 respondents respectively). The specifics of this will be examined in a later section.

To gain a full picture of the student situation, participants were asked about their current learning experiences. Of the 35 participants who answered this question, 45.71% were learning Chinese online (16 respondents), with Zoom being the most popular online platform. When it came to independent learning, 35 participants estimated that approximately 56% of their learning time was spent using online resources. Some 34 respondents elaborated on the skill(s) that they practice with these resources. As participants were able to tick all answer options that applied, the total number of responses equalled 117. Figure 3.5 demonstrates that

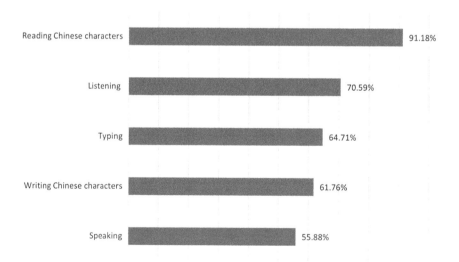

Fig. 3.5 Skills being supported during independent learning time through online resources (n = 34)

participants mostly practised their reading skills (91.18%) with the lowest number of answers stating that participants practised their speaking skills (55.88%).

This question was further investigated in the interviews. In general, participants were supportive of the use of online apps/websites, particularly for character recognition, with one mentioning the potential benefits for assisting handwriting with the right technology.

> Student A: You probably can't beat the rote learning. I think that's ... It's tried and tested. But you can make it more enjoyable ... I think gamification and apps would make a huge difference on just being more engaged with the handwriting.

Another student mentioned how online resources helped them in their independent learning.

> Student C: I listen to a lot of like Chinese music, and then sometimes I just um write down the lyrics and learn the words from the lyrics. Those might not be the words like in the workbook that we have to learn, but ... because it interests me, it's easier for me to remember ... And then, also, when I listen to the song, I get the pronunciation.

Character Learning Strategies

In order to explore the specifics of how participants learned characters in the online space, they were first asked to select any and all items that assist them when learning Chinese characters, firstly in terms of classroom setup/curriculum design, and secondly in terms of activities (see Fig. 3.6).

In terms of classroom setup/curriculum design, the top answer of 41 participants (82.93%) was "specific homework tasks to practice handwriting", with "dedicated time in class to practice handwriting" also scoring high at 70.73%. On the lower end of the scale, participants mentioned that typing characters (not via pinyin) was not so helpful (26.83%), while "communication with peers" was also not highly rated (29.27%). "Other" answers included flash cards, pinyin and using characters in sentences.

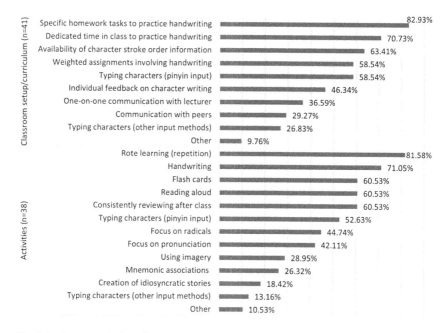

Fig. 3.6 Items assisting character learning

In terms of activities that assist learning characters, the answer options in Fig. 3.6 were adapted from a number of studies surrounding character learning strategies, namely: Everson (1998); McGinnis (1995); McGinnis (1999); Shen (2005); Shen (2010); Tseng (2000). In the current survey, 38 participants scored rote learning and handwriting highest (81.58% and 71.05% respectively). On the other hand, creating idiosyncratic stories and typing characters via an input method other than pinyin scored on the lower end (18.42% and 13.16% respectively). "Other" answers included using Quizlet, using/seeing characters in sentences or simply looking at the character. When further investigated in a later question, 23.68% and 52.63% of respondents (out of 31) mentioned that incorporating their character learning strategies in the online space was "very easy" and "easy" respectively.

To gain a sense of how at-distance learning affected students and their learning strategies, participants were asked to tick the main constraint faced from a list of options. Figure 3.7 demonstrates that out of 41 respondents, the top answer was "lack of hands-on approach from teacher for character practice corrections (i.e., guidance on correct stroke order, character shape etc.)" at 24.39%, followed closely by "lack of one-on-one communication with teacher" at 21.95%. After this, participants were asked how they tried to overcome this constraint. As this question supplied a text box for participants to answer, the responses were grouped thematically. In addition, some participants described more than one way that they overcame such constraints. Four categories were identified, of which independent methods (such as teaching themselves certain material, attempting to find answers to their own questions or working alone) was mentioned most (40%), followed by other technology (30%) and reaching out to friends or the teacher (15% respectively). Two participants mentioned that they could not find a solution to the constraint.

Giving participants the chance to reflect, a further question was posed asking whether participants had thought of another way to overcome these constraints (from Fig. 3.7). Of the 41 participants that answered, the vast majority could not think of any other solutions (32 participants, 78.01%). Of the 21.95% who could think of other solutions (9

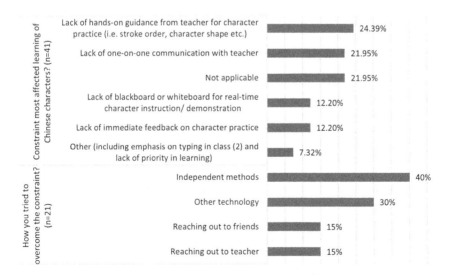

Fig. 3.7 Constraints in the online space when learning Chinese characters

participants), one-third mentioned independent learning (such as self-study and practice outside of class). Another third mentioned the importance of a "good"/dedicated teacher (1), systematic teaching of characters (1) and to have more emphasis on handwriting (1). The final third mentioned technology again, including Pleco and Google (1), an app that assists practice of handwriting characters (name not supplied—1) and finally, a proposed idea of an app that allows teachers to preside over students' character learning (1). Interviewed participants also had comments on this aspect.

> Student A: I can just think of my own experience in [university name] with the teachers walking in the class. They'd look into your notebook—if they saw it was incorrect they might put a circle on it show and you what it was. That kind of communication is more difficult online for learning characters.
>
> Student B: What we did as a classroom was we created a group chat, and everyone would just help everyone. … because we kind of see it was easier, because obviously we weren't having access to a teacher or professor all the time … So, what we tend to do then is … try to ah talk to each other and try to get it figured out.
>
> Student C: Some teachers don't really use the online classes to their fullest potential.

In asking specifically about software/technology that could meet participants' character learning needs, 16 participants (39.02% of 41 responses) commented with ideas. Some specific apps were mentioned in answers—the most popular being Duolingo—while in other answers specific features were mentioned, with the ability to write on screen as the most popular (see Fig. 3.8).

In the interview, a student also commented on the learning materials being used in their online classroom and issues with accessibility:

> Student D: I think they're good textbooks, actually, just the online version is really hard to use it like the PDF.

Finally, participants were asked to rate a series of statements on a Likert scale regarding their (1) experience of handwriting Chinese characters and (2) experience of typing Chinese characters. Participants rated each

3 Investigating the Student Perspective on the Present... 65

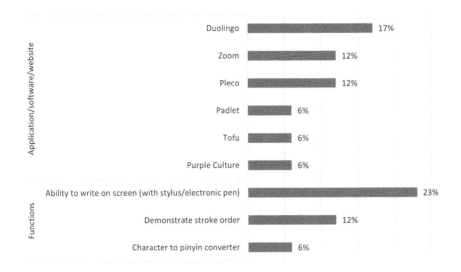

Fig. 3.8 Participant ideas on software/technology that could meet their character learning needs (n = 16)

sentence by choosing one of strongly agree (1), agree (2), neither agree nor disagree (3), disagree (4) and strongly disagree (5). A total of 37 participants answered this section. Chapter 5 addresses this data in greater detail; however, the following is worth noting in relation to learning strategies.

Regarding the first 15 statements on handwriting Chinese characters (Fig. 3.9), the statement scoring strongest in terms of agreement was "practicing handwriting is the most time-consuming part for me in Chinese" at 1.7. Also scoring closely were the statements relating to handwriting helping participants memorise the characters better than typing (1.86) and the helpfulness of handwriting as levels of Chinese advance (1.97). On the other hand, the statements scoring highest on disagreement were "I'd feel more confident in learning Chinese if my handwriting skills were no longer assessed" (2.84), "I feel handwriting is the least useful skill we need for real-life communication" (2.73) and "handwriting is the most fascinating part of Chinese that has attracted me to study the language" (2.59). At an aerial view, it seems that

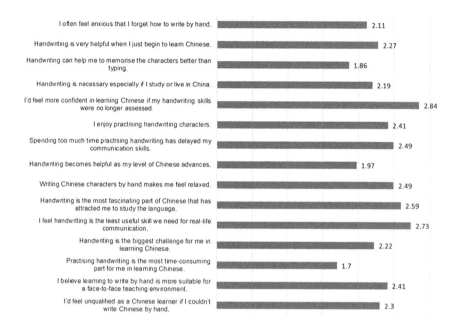

Fig. 3.9 Likert-scale questions relating to handwriting Chinese characters (n = 37)

participants believe handwriting to be an important practice for advancing their learning (albeit time-consuming).

For the typing-related questions, Fig. 3.10 shows the weighted average for each of the 13 statements (n = 37). In terms of the statements showing most agreement among participants, top statements include the helpfulness of typing as levels of Chinese advance (1.92), a preference for typing over handwriting in assessments (2.11) and the helpfulness of pinyin typing in character recognition (2.19). On the other hand, participants disagreed most with the following statements: "typing can be more complicated than handwriting" (3.81), "the technical issues can be challenging when I type Chinese" (3.35) and "I feel frustrated when I have to use pinyin typing but I lack pinyin knowledge of Chinese characters" (3.3). From these responses, it appears that participants believe typing to be a useful task that is straightforward to incorporate to their learning.

Students in the interviews also weighed in on the aspect of handwriting versus typing in more detail. The following excerpts echo the

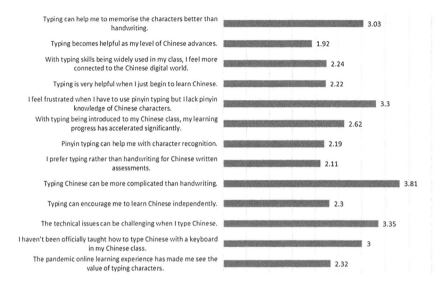

Fig. 3.10 Likert-scale questions relating to typing Chinese characters (n = 37)

Likert-scale results in that participants acknowledge the time-consuming yet beneficial aspects of handwriting, while also appreciating the usefulness of typing.

> Student A: Maybe teachers should dedicate more time to handwriting, because students might be—I don't want to say lazy, but reluctant to spend more time … You spend a lot of time learning how to write characters … I'm disappointed I can't write them better. But in terms of work—it's not going to be a huge barrier for me in a professional sense.
>
> Student B: Ninety percent of my studying was more focused on the characters and memorising what each character meant and how to write each character.
>
> Student C: I would prefer handwriting because like typing is always the easy answer, and I feel like nowadays I can type a lot of characters, but I can only like write sixty percent of them.
>
> Student D: There's no need to write, I guess, in society … everyone's just forgetting about the handwriting … I think it's a bit sad to be honest, because … what if you couldn't write English like that'd be so weird.

Assessment

Firstly, when asked about the mode of their most recent online/at-distance assessment, Fig. 3.11 demonstrates that participants' answers were quite split. Of the 35 who answered, 31.43% of participants had live assessments that took place during online synchronous sessions, while 34.29% of participants had at-home/at-distance assessments that took place outside the online synchronous sessions. Next, 25.71% of participants had open-book assessments only and closed-book assessments only respectively, while 48.57% of participants had a mix of open- and closed-book assessments. When it came to using characters in assessments, 37.14% of 35 participants were asked to handwrite answers only, while 22.86% were asked to type assessments only and 40% were asked to do both. A text box attached to this question revealed that this "mix" of both typing and handwriting could be present on the exam paper itself (i.e. type a paragraph but handwrite key characters), or split across assessments (i.e. typing for presentations and handwriting for formative assessments) or even presented as a choice (i.e. participants could answer using either mode).

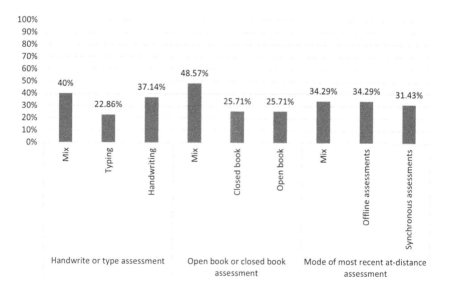

Fig. 3.11 Assessment mode completed online/at-distance (n = 35)

3 Investigating the Student Perspective on the Present... 69

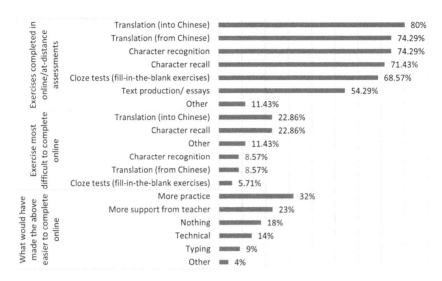

Fig. 3.12 Assessment exercises completed online/at-distance (n = 35)

Next, participants were asked about the specific exercises that they completed in the online/at-distance space (see Fig. 3.12). In a question that allowed participants to choose multiple answers, the most prominent one among 35 participants was translation into Chinese at 80% of all answers, with text production scoring lowest (54.29%). Others (11.43%) included sentence creation, reading comprehensions and true-or-false questions. After this, participants could only choose one answer to describe the most difficult exercise to complete online. This time, 35 participants noted that both translation into Chinese and character recall were most difficult (22.86% respectively), with cloze tests being reported as least difficult (5.71%). "Other" answers (11.43%) included no difference in difficulty, pronunciation and translating into pinyin. When asked what could have made these exercises easier to complete online through a comment box, 21 participants described various—and sometimes multiple—scenarios that came under the main headings of (1) more practice, (2) more support from teacher, (3) nothing, (4) technical (including larger font and better Wi-Fi connection), (5) typing and (6) other (including being in China to be fully immersed in the language). Of these, the top scoring answer related to practising more (32%) and having more support from their teacher (23%).

These answers were further explored in the student interviews. Here, participants described how the various modes and exercises listed in Fig. 3.12 were put into practice and how they affected their learning experience.

> Student A: I think listening exercises are much better online because you have headphones.
>
> Student B: [The teacher] did make [the assessments] easy ... We had some mix and matching ... filling the blanks ... a true or false ... a [reading] passage. We did have to write some sentences like she'll give us some characters or some words, and we had to put them into a sentence. She had the papers, and then she just gave to us to complete online ... But we had to write it down ... so we could either print out the paper and write on that paper and send her a copy of it, or we could just take it in our notes and just write question one etc.
>
> Student C: She sent us like a document with questions or like just a few words. And then we had to mute ourselves. So, the Zoom was just for her to monitor us, and we had to like record an audio file on our phones, answering those questions.
>
> Student D: The first question is, you like, fill in the blank with the character—like I just copy paste the character, and I don't have to write a character, and even like for the long sections it's just a bunch of typing ... And also, actually, I think that is an advantage ... you don't have to know the characters, for some parts you'll type the pinyin because you know the word.

Discussion and Concluding Remarks

This chapter has demonstrated the student perspective of learning Chinese online with particular reference to learning characters. In order to address the research questions (1) encompassing the student experience of learning Chinese characters online, (2) their learning strategies adopted and (3) recommendations for future curricula, questionnaire and interview data have been presented. From this, a number of important findings and recommendations are found and summarised below.

Firstly, in terms of their overall experience, students noted benefits to learning CFL both online and in-person. While there is a consistent theme emerging of the negative effects on handwriting in the online space from the data, students seem to be able to forecast some benefits, however these are yet to be developed and/or experienced by them. Students therefore note that online learning may be better suited to skills of reading, listening and typing as it stands. Still, the existing learning materials need major updates so that they can be accessed online, mirroring the current hybrid learning environment.

Secondly, in terms of learning strategies adopted, students note that their independent learning strategies were not majorly affected in the online space. However, more structured work in- and outside the virtual classroom is necessary for handwriting development. This structured work should include handwriting and rote learning, while typing is not necessarily useful for character learning despite its usefulness in communicating, according to the data. Interestingly, Chap. 5 describes that teachers are also of the opinion that individual feedback and structured exercises are vital for advancing character learning. A more prominent teacher presence and clear communication channels are crucial when learning characters, while students tried to overcome the lack thereof with technology. It could be that students feel that teachers are unapproachable in the online space, thus highlighting an even greater need for clear communication channels.

From these findings, it appears that a heavy burden is placed on students when trying to cope with learning characters online while interestingly, the inclusion of more technology is resorted to. This demonstrates not only an ever increasing mental load and burden on the student, but it could also lead to technology exhaustion as previously described (e.g. Wang and East 2020). Still, students' suggestions on the applications or technology that could meet character learning needs online describe the physical action of pen to paper, which has also been documented in previous research (e.g. Zhang 2020). Although time-consuming, students note that handwriting characters is helpful as their learning of Chinese advances.

In terms of assessment, students report that their experiences are quite mixed with regard to online/offline, open-book/closed-book and typing/

handwriting. Of course, in the initial stages of COVID-19 when learning was transferred to the online environment, many adaptations were made worldwide. However, there could be serious implications to prolonged varied assessment methods in different regions. That is, for a student who takes an online (monitored) assessment that is closed-book and involves handwriting, the mental load and knowledge requirement will be much greater than an offline (not monitored), open-book exam that involves typing.

The issue of cheating in online assessments is also reported by students in the current research, and so more stringent methods or technology are necessary for online assessments. For students, more targeted practice and support from teachers could have made their assessments more manageable. Indeed, teachers should endeavour to align teaching to the learning outcomes of their course, while also preparing students sufficiently for assessments and the exercises therein (e.g. Guan et al. 2011).

Indeed, the view on typing presents two distinct themes in the data (e.g. Figs. 3.9 and 3.10). While handwriting is viewed as more time-consuming yet beneficial for learning Chinese characters, the idea of typing being useful for daily communication and as an assessment mode is prevalent. This finding echoes Gao (2020) in that typing eases difficulties for students when completing assessments and allows them to focus on other unique features of Chinese that may also cause difficulties, such as grammar. In determining what mode of writing to use in the CFL classroom and assessments, instructors should draw inspiration from Coss (2024) who advises that "writing proficiency" should be systematically and clearly defined in individual courses. In this way, handwriting and typing can complement each other in meeting the learning outcomes and specific needs of learners.

To sum up, analysis of the data enables recommendations to be made for future CFL curricula. In terms of character learning, the data demonstrates the crucial and pressing matter that this aspect should be systematically supported through the development of a new or existing online application. Useful features of such applications could include elements of rote learning and handwriting mimicry that allow students to practise handwriting in the classroom and in their own time. Better still would be an enhanced communication feature whereby teachers could provide real-time feedback in the classroom, while the ability to playback students' writing through a screen-record feature could provide the opportunity to log feedback on student homework and independent learning in viewing their writing practice stroke-by-stroke. At the same time, the learning materials used should be easily accessible in both the online and offline environment for a smoother learning process for students, thereby relieving them of an increased mental load and learning burden that could lead to technology exhaustion. In terms of recommendations for assessment, a feature to monitor students' handwriting could diminish cheating in closed-book exams. For example, an "assessment mode" could notify the teacher whenever the student leaves the application during a timed exam to presumably use a translator or online dictionary.

The next step for this research would be to firstly examine how existing applications and software can support the recommendations made in this section. In this way, a more structured curriculum and effective assessment mode could be explored while utilising current resources. Further steps could be to collaborate with a software developer to develop an application or platform to holistically host the features mentioned. Indeed, specific research into defining these potential features should first be completed with empirical data before a prototype is developed.

The study is not without limitations. First, it involves a relatively small sample size. Second, the questionnaire and interview required participants to self-report on past experiences, which may have led to some exaggerations or certain biases. Still, the results echo some previous findings from the literature while also providing the vital student voice for the future of teaching and learning CFL online.

Ethical Approval
Ethical approval was granted by University College Dublin Ethics Committee in 2021 (HS-E-21-183-Osbourne).

Competing Interests This study was funded by University College Dublin's Global Engagement Seed Fund 2021 and the Chinese Embassy in Ireland.

References

Abraham, Wendy. 2013. *Chinese for Dummies*. 2nd ed. Hoboken, N.J.: John Wiley & Sons, Inc.

Allen, Joseph R. 2008. Why Learning to Write Chinese is a Waste of Time: A Modest Proposal. *Foreign Language Annals* 41 (2): 237–251. https://doi.org/10.1111/j.1944-9720.2008.tb03291.x.

Burns, Danielle, Neil Dagnall, and Maxine Holt. 2020. Assessing the Impact of the COVID-19 Pandemic on Student Wellbeing at Universities in the United Kingdom: A Conceptual Analysis. *Frontiers in Education* 5 (582882): 1–10. https://doi.org/10.3389/feduc.2020.582882.

Chang, Li-Yun, Yi Xu, Charles A. Perfetti, Juan Zhang, and Hsueh-Chih Chen. 2014. Supporting Orthographic Learning at the Beginning Stage of Learning to Read Chinese as a Second Language. *International Journal of Disability, Development and Education* 61 (3): 288–305. https://doi.org/10.1080/1034912X.2014.934016.

Coss, Matthew D. 2024. Towards a Curricularized Approach to L2 Hanzi Teaching and Learning. In *Transforming Hanzi Instruction in the Digital Age: Theory, Research, and Pedagogy*, ed. Chengzhi Chu, Matthew D. Coss, and Phyllis N. Zhang. Routledge.

Daniels, Lia M., Lauren D. Goegan, and Patti C. Parker. 2021. The Impact of COVID-19 Triggered Changes to Instruction and Assessment on University Students' Self- Reported Motivation, Engagement and Perceptions. *Social Psychology of Education* 24: 299–318. https://doi.org/10.1007/s11218-021-09612-3.

Everson, Michael E. 1998. Word Recognition among Learners of Chinese as a Foreign Language: Investigating the Relationship between Naming and Knowing. *Modern Language Journal* 82 (2): 194–204. https://doi.org/10.1111/j.1540-4781.1998.tb01192.x.

Gamage, Kelum A.A., Dilani I. Wijesuriya, Sakunthala Y. Ekanayake, Allan E.W. Rennie, Chris G. Lambert, and Nanda Gunawardhana. 2020. Online Delivery of Teaching and Laboratory Practices: Continuity of University Programmes during COVID-19 Pandemic. *Education Sciences* 10 (10): 291. https://doi.org/10.3390/educsci10100291.

Gao, Xiaoping. 2020. Australian Students' Perceptions of the Challenges and Strategies for Learning Chinese Characters in Emergency Online Teaching. *International Journal of Chinese Language Teaching* 1 (1): 83–98. https://doi.org/10.46451/ijclt.2020.06.04.

Guan, Connie Qun, Ying Liu, Derek Ho Leung Chan, Feifei Ye, and Charles A. Perfetti. 2011. Writing Strengthens Orthography and Alphabetic-Coding Strengthens Phonology in Learning to Read Chinese. *Journal of Educational Psychology* 103 (3): 509–522. https://doi.org/10.1037/a0023730.

Helm, Francesca. 2015. The Practices and Challenges of Telecollaboration in Higher Education in Europe. *Language Learning & Technology* 19 (2): 197–217.

Hsiao, Ya Ping (Amy), and Peter Broeder. 2014. Let's Tweet in Chinese! Exploring How Learners of Chinese as a Foreign Language Self-Direct in Their Use of Microblogging to Learn Chinese. *Journal of the European Confederation of Language Centres in Higher Education (CERCLES)* 4 (2): 469–488. https://doi.org/10.1515/cercles-2014-0024.

Jia, Yuxin, and Xuerui Jia. 2005. Chinese Characters, Chinese Culture and Chinese Mind. *Intercultural Communication Studies* XIV (1): 151–157. https://www-s3-live.kent.edu/s3fs-root/s3fs-public/file/12-Yuxin-Jia-Xuerui-Jia.pdf.

Jin, Li, Yi Xu, Elizabeth Deifell, and Katie Angus. 2021. Emergency Remote Language Teaching and U.S.-Based College-Level World Language Educators' Intention to Adopt Online Teaching in Postpandemic Times. *The Modern Language Journal* 105 (2): 412–434. https://doi.org/10.1111/modl.12712.

Kohnke, Lucas, and Benjamin Luke Moorhouse. 2022. Facilitating Synchronous Online Language Learning through Zoom. *RELC Journal* 53 (1): 296–301. https://doi.org/10.1177/0033688220937235.

Link, Thomas Michael, and Richard Marz. 2006. Computer Literacy and Attitudes Towards E-Learning among First Year Medical Students. *BMC Medical Education* 6 (34). https://doi.org/10.1186/1472-6920-6-34.

McGinnis, Scott. 1995. *Student Attitudes and Approaches in the Learning of Written Chinese.* Paper presented at the Annual Conference of the Chinese Language Teachers Association, Long Beach, California.

———. 1999. Student's Goals and Approaches. In *Mapping the Course of the Chinese Language Field: Chinese Language Teachers Association Monograph Series, Vol. III,* ed. Madeline Chu, 151–168. Kalamazoo, MI: Chinese Language Teachers Association, Inc.

Osborne, Caitríona, Qi Zhang, and Bob Adamson. 2022. The Next Steps for Teaching Characters in CFL: Investigating the Effects of Four Character-Teaching Methods on Beginner Learners. *International Journal of Chinese Language Education* 11: 45–82. https://doras.dcu.ie/27617/1/IJCLE_No.11_Jun22_03.pdf.

Osborne, Caitríona, Qi Zhang, and George Xinsheng Zhang. 2018. Which is More Effective in Introducing Chinese Characters? An Investigative Study of Four Methods Used to Teach CFL Beginners. *The Language Learning Journal* 48 (4): 385–401. https://doi.org/10.1080/09571736.2017.1393838.

Padaguri, Vijay G., and Syed Akram Pasha. 2021. Synchronous Online Learning versus Asynchronous Online Learning: A Comparative Analysis of Learning Effectiveness. *Proceedings of the AUBH E-Learning Conference 2021: Innovative Learning & Teaching—Lessons from COVID-19.* https://doi.org/10.2139/ssrn.3878806.

Riwayatiningsih, Rika, and Sulistyani Sulistyani. 2020. The Implementation of Synchronous and Asynchronous E-Language Learning in EFL Setting: A Case Study. *Journal Basis* 7 (2): 309–318. https://doi.org/10.33884/basisupb.v7i2.2484.

Shen, Helen H. 2005. An Investigation of Chinese-Character Learning Strategies among Non-Native Speakers of Chinese. *Department of Asian Languages and Literature* 33 (1): 49–68. https://doi.org/10.1016/j.system.2004.11.001.

———. 2010. Analysis of Radical Knowledge Development Among Beginning CFL Learners. In *Research Among Learners of Chinese as a Foreign Language*, ed. Michael E. Everson and Helen H. Shen, 45–66. University of Hawaii: National Foreign Language Resource Center.

Starkey, Louise. 2020. A Review of Research Exploring Teacher Preparation for the Digital Age. *Cambridge Journal of Education* 50 (1): 37–56. https://doi.org/10.1080/0305764X.2019.1625867.

Tseng, Chin-Chin. 2000. Deguo xuesheng xuexi Hanzi de qingkuang ji qi xuexi celue [Character Learning Strategies among German Students]. *Language Research June*: 85–93.

Wang, Danping, and Martin East. 2020. Constructing an Emergency Chinese Curriculum during the Pandemic: A New Zealand Experience. *International Journal of Chinese Language Teaching* 1(1): 1–19. https://doi.org/10.46451/ijclt.2020.06.01.

Wang, Junju, and Jia Lin. 2018. Traditional Chinese Views on Education as Perceived by International Students in China: International Student Attitudes and Understandings. *Journal of Studies in International Education* 23 (2): 195–216. https://doi.org/10.1177/1028315318797356.

Wang, Ying, and Catherine McBride. 2017. Beyond Copying: A Comparison of Multi-Component Interventions on Chinese Early Literacy Skills. *International Journal of Behavioral Development* 41 (3): 380–389. https://doi.org/10.1177/0165025416637212.

WHO. 2020. Considerations for Implementing and Adjusting Public Health and Social Measures in the Context of COVID-19. Accessed July 18, 2023. https://apps.who.int/iris/bitstream/handle/10665/336374/WHO-2019-nCoV-Adjusting_PH_measures-2020.2-eng.pdf.

Winke, Paula M., and Rebekha Abbuhl. 2008. Taking a Closer Look at Vocabulary Learning Strategies: A Case Study of a Chinese Foreign Language Class. *Foreign Language Annals* 40 (4): 697–712. https://doi.org/10.1111/j.1944-9720.2007.tb02888.x.

Yang, Juan. 2018. What Makes Learning Chinese Characters Difficult? The Voice of Students from English Secondary Schools. *Journal of Chinese Writing Systems* 2 (1): 35–41. https://doi.org/10.1177/2513850217748501.

Yin, John Jing-Hua. 2016. Chinese Characters. In *The Routledge Encyclopedia of the Chinese Language*, ed. Sin-Wai Chan, Florence Li Wing Yee, and James W. Minett, 51–63. Oxon, UK: Routledge.

Zeng, Yun, and Jingfan Xiao. 2021. Review on Chinese Proficiency Grading Standards for International Chinese Language Education. *Frontiers in Educational Research* 4 (6): 116–121. https://doi.org/10.25236/FER.2021.040619.

Zhang, Jie, and Xiaofei Lu. 2013. Variability in Chinese as a Foreign Language Learners' Development of the Chinese Numeral Classifier System. *The Modern Language Journal* 97 (S1): 46–60. https://doi.org/10.1111/j.1540-4781.2012.01423.x.

Zhang, Qi. 2020. Narrative Inquiry into Online Teaching of Chinese Characters during the Pandemic. *International Journal of Chinese Language Teaching* 1 (1): 20–34. https://doi.org/10.46451/ijclt.2020.06.02.

Zhang, Qi, and Ge Min. 2019. Chinese Writing Composition among CFL Learners: A Comparison between Handwriting and Typewriting. *Computers and Composition* 54 (December): 102522. https://doi.org/10.1016/j.compcom.2019.102522.

Theme II

Critical Perspectives Regarding Typing Chinese Characters in the CFL Classroom

4

The E-writing Approach to L2 Chinese Pedagogy: Educational Imperative and Empirical Evidence

Matthew D. Coss

Introduction

A primary goal of Chinese as an additional language (L2 Chinese) instruction should be to equip learners with the functional proficiency and intercultural competence to meet their personal and professional goals vis-à-vis Chinese language use in a variety of contexts and situations. Mandarin and other Chinese varieties are described as being "Category IV languages" by the US State Department, meaning that due to linguistic distance from alphabetic Indo-European languages, Chinese (purportedly) requires an excessive amount of time to achieve desirable levels of functional and professional proficiency (U.S. State Department Foreign Language Training n.d.). However, Chinese language learners and programmes are constrained by a number of limited resources as they

---

M. D. Coss (✉)
Michigan State University, East Lansing, MI, USA
e-mail: mattcoss@msu.edu

© The Author(s), under exclusive license to Springer Nature Switzerland AG 2024
C. Osborne et al. (eds.), *Teaching Chinese Characters in the Digital Age*, Palgrave Studies on Chinese Education in a Global Perspective,
https://doi.org/10.1007/978-3-031-64784-0_4

strive collectively towards this goal. Whether students are enrolled in a single course or an intensive language programme, *time* is perhaps the scarcest resource for L2 (Chinese) learning. The often extremely limited amount of time, therefore, necessitates high degrees of careful planning for resource allocation in order to maximize proficiency attainment.

One of the most contentious debates in L2 Chinese pedagogy is the best way ('best' meaning 'most efficient path through the necessary challenges and hurdles') for developing *literacy* in Chinese. It is generally recognized that although Chinese is a tonal language and pronunciation accuracy may also be a challenge for L2 learners (e.g. Pelzl et al. 2022), it is also widely accepted as a truism that the primary barrier to high levels of competence, and, for example, professional prospects in Chinese as an additional language, is the writing system (for an early discussion, see Moser 1991), and contentious debate runs rampant in the field about the best ways to develop proficiency in reading and writing. This debate has multiple perspectives and many sides and is a complex, often convoluted argument in which scholars have pointed out that we (the field) are often talking past one another (Coss 2024a). The present chapter will focus on a relatively recent proposal which is gaining ground both in conceptual as well as empirical and importantly practical applications for the efficient achievement of literacy in L2 Chinese: the 电写为主 or 'e-writing' approach. I first define this approach and provide an overview of its many affordances, explaining why it has been argued to be preferable to handwriting as the primary means of literacy development in L2 Chinese programmes, in other words, why it is, in my view, an *educational imperative*. Following this, I provide an overview of relevant lines of research examining various aspects of the e-writing approach for L2 Chinese. At the end of the chapter, I offer a framework for language instructors and programmes to integrate e-writing in a principled fashion and document the impact(s) of this curricular shift.

E-writing for L2 Chinese

E-writing is the shorthand of the 'e-writing as primary, handwriting as secondary' (电写为主, 手写为辅) approach to L2 Chinese literacy development (Chu et al. 2024).[1] The core idea of this approach is that the primary method of written production in L2 Chinese from the very beginning of learning should be typing rather than handwriting. In other words, in the e-writing approach, the vast majority of the written communication in which learners engage in the L2 Chinese classroom is technology-based (typed), primarily using (Hanyu) pinyin or other sound-based input systems, rather than (on-screen or paper-based) handwriting. Coss (2024a) explains e-writing as follows:

> The simple fundamental principle underpinning the e-writing approach is that L2 Chinese reading and writing proficiency (literacy) should be developed and measured primarily using digitally produced texts. In other words, the four skills of '听说读写' (listening, speaking, reading, writing) should be reconceptualised as five skills: 听说读打 + (手)写: listening, speaking, reading, typing and handwriting. Within this approach, Hanzi are generally first encountered and learned as whole unanalysed (not decomposed) units in the words, phrases and chunks in which they appear in meaningful textual contexts through a combination of intentional and incidental learning. By engaging in receptive, productive and interactional practice and communicative tasks, learners develop reading and writing skills using Hanzi and are able to engage in meaningful communication in and outside of class in both oral-aural and written modalities. Handwriting, in turn, occupies a secondary supporting role for a limited and purposefully selected subset of Hanzi. E-writing is compatible with a variety of models of L2 instruction, including various instantiations of Communicative Language Teaching (or proficiency-oriented language teaching), Task-Based Language Teaching and approaches based on Skill Acquisition Theory.

---

[1] Although scholars have proposed various iterations of this approach under a variety of names (e.g. 'penless Chinese' Xu and Jen 2005; 'computer Chinese' He 2009, He and Jiao 2010; '电脑输入汉字 [pinyin Hanzi input]' Feng and Yang 2013; 'typing-primary' Zhang 2021), the core principles of the approach are consistent with those described in this chapter.

The e-writing approach advocates for holistic chunk-based initial processing of characters that is often referred to as the 字不离词 (characters appearing in words) and/or 词本位 (word-based, as opposed to 字本位/character-based) approach at the beginner level, engendering in even novice Chinese users a word-level (as opposed to character-level) reading approach (see Jiang et al. 2020). How this manifests within the e-writing approach, as detailed by Feng and Yang (2013) and Zhang (2021, 2024), is that for written communication, starting at the novice (Common European Framework of Reference/CEFR) level, learners are explicitly taught and required to produce chunks of language, rather than individual characters. Zhang (2021, p. 4) argues that "Pinyin-typing transforms the Hanzi processing from a sub lexical-based visual-motor procedure into a lexical-based phonological–visual chunking procedure", noting that instead of producing single characters stroke-by-stroke (sub-lexical written production), typing enables learners to produce words (lexical written production). This, Zhang argues, alleviates excessive cognitive load and facilitates dual-encoding and retrieval of new language in and from long-term memory. Importantly, scholars have argued that along with this primarily holistic, chunk-based, non-analytic learning approach, it is possible, and in fact, by some accounts advisable, to engage learners in some amount of analytical character learning (e.g. Coss 2024b). In other words, while primary emphasis in acquiring and using new language is placed on ('unanalysed') chunks—words, phrases and structures, rather than individual characters or their sub-character components—students can be selectively but systematically taught to analyse individual characters and thereby make meta-character connections between the functional components of characters they repeatedly encounter. The notion of 'functional components' comes from work by Henson and colleagues (e.g., Henson 2022). Somewhat different from the notion of 'radicals' (which Renfroe (2018) argues does not systematically capture the functions of Hanzi components), functional components (or 功能部件) can be defined as components which serve one of a limited number of functions in the compound characters in which they appear (Coss 2024b). These functions can be and, as I have argued (see Coss 2024b), should be learned and systematically analysed with a subset of Hanzi as learners' vocabulary repertoires develop. However, this analytical single-character, sub-character component and meta-character system learning should be secondary to the holistic, chunk-based learning and communication prioritized in the e-writing approach.

Importantly, to head off a common misconception, the e-writing approach does *not* typically advocate for a complete abandonment of handwriting. In the recent edited volume that serves as the first comprehensive introduction to the e-writing approach in the field (Chu et al. 2024), options for the secondary supporting roles of handwriting were proposed (see Coss 2024a). Specifically, students can be assigned a limited amount of handwriting (not all necessarily from memory) for (a) communicative purposes; (b) character-learning purposes; and/or (c) cultural/experiential purposes. Respectively, this could involve (a) filling out a paper-based form; (b) tracing recurring functional components of key vocabulary words and connecting these to a growing systematic understanding of Hanzi; and (c) experiencing brush calligraphy or other traditional methods of Hanzi writing, each as a principled part of a curriculum primarily focused on digital communication and Hanzi (system) literacy development.

E-writing has been argued to have a number of advantages over handwriting-focused approaches to L2 Chinese. First, e-writing is the primary writing medium that L2 Chinese users use for twenty-first-century communication (see Allen 2008). Alignment between curricular goals and L2 user needs affords learners clear learning targets, which can increase and sustain motivation. Unlike handwriting, which is burdensome and demotivating (see Ke and Shen 2003), e-writing offers learners the immediate satisfaction of being able to communicate in both oral and written Chinese from day one (Feng and Wu 2024). From a psycholinguistic perspective, e-writing is also advantageous over handwriting in that pinyin and other sound-based input systems induce multimodal (i.e. sound, meaning, form) encoding and storage of new words, whereas handwriting does not necessarily require or induce this level of multimodal encoding (primarily encoding stroke-by-stroke written form, see Zhang (2021, p. 4) for a detailed overview). Pinyin-based typing for communicative purposes also engages communicative intent (meaning; learners know what they are trying to convey) with phonetic retrieval (sound information in order to type in pinyin) and character form identification, forming a natural feedback loop every time a learner types anything.

It has been argued that (massive amounts of memorized) handwriting is ideal or even necessary for successful L2 Chinese learning. However, much of the research that is cited as justification for this point of view is limited for a number of reasons (for a more in-depth discussion, see Coss 2024a). Some of this research is conducted in first language Chinese learning contexts, and while some cognitive mechanisms may be similar, it is crucial to point out the key differences between L1 learners, L2 learners and even heritage learners, in terms of available time for L2 learning, needs and goals for L2 Chinese use, etc. Furthermore, many of these studies are lab based and use participants who are not actually language learners of Chinese and are provided with very short-term treatments while potentially even only tested for learning gains in the short term. Unfortunately, some of these lab-based studies do not use pedagogical approaches that are common in the Chinese classroom, in other words, they lack ecological validity, and are therefore not ready to be generalized to classroom-based teaching contexts. The citation of some of this research is also an oversimplification of actually nuanced positions (e.g. citing Guan et al. 2011) as evidence against typing, or citing Allen (2008) as a position eschewing all handwriting. Careful reading and interpretation of research are critical in order to move the field forward in terms of both research and pedagogy.

While there can be no doubt that developing L2 Chinese literacy is a complex endeavour, and it is certainly true that we are not yet ready to draw firm conclusions from the available body of research evidence, it is also true that L2 language—including Chinese—programmes are faced with ever-increasing challenges related to enrolment and student retention (Lusin et al. 2023). Though perhaps not a fix-all solution, the many affordances of e-writing as a highly relevant, self-efficacy-engendering, learning-affordance-rich pedagogical alternative to the status quo of handwriting-based L2 Chinese instruction should, therefore, not be underestimated, and merit open-minded scholarly attention as well as programmatic and pedagogical consideration.

E-writing: Empirical Evidence

Now that we have established a clear definition of e-writing and an overview of its potential affordances, we turn to the small but growing body of empirical research and overviews of implementations of the e-writing approach to summarize the evidence available to date. A recent edited volume (Chu et al. 2024) has made a sizable contribution to this body of evidence. Though this edited volume features prominently in the summary provided in this chapter, efforts have been made to include a variety of studies in different contexts from various sources in the literature. Rather than offering a direct comparison between the research on e-writing and handwriting (available in Zhang et al. 2024) or a theoretical argument to make the case for e-writing (available in Coss 2024a), this chapter focuses on summarizing areas of scholarship related to the affordances of e-writing for L2 Chinese learning. In what follows, I provide overviews focusing on five interrelated areas: (1) character and vocabulary learning and retention; (2) learner interaction and feedback; (3) emerging new technologies; (4) writing assessment and (5) stakeholder perceptions. I conclude this section with a brief summary of the limitations of the current research literature and potential future directions, which are continued in the subsequent section.

Character and Vocabulary Learning

Hanzi learning (retention, recall, etc.) has been the primary focus of the vast majority of L2 Chinese reading and writing research to date (Fedewa et al. 2022). As such, it is natural to begin evaluations of e-writing as a pedagogical alternative by judging the extent to which learners using e-writing are able to learn and retain Hanzi, both in isolation (single characters and words) and in productive use. Complementing lab-based studies which compare handwriting and typing, a recent study by Zhang (2021) offers insight into e-writing's potential from multi-year student cohort data situated in a language learning programme. Zhang examined the learning outcomes of 108 *ab initio* ("true beginner") L2 Chinese students. By comparing multiple cohorts of data, Zhang concluded that students whose out-of-class practice prioritized e-writing significantly outperformed peers who prioritized handwriting on a number of representative measures. Namely, e-writing students performed better in end-of-term typed essay-length writing, in-context (in-sentence) word recognition and isolated Hanzi recall. Additionally, e-writing students performed just as well as handwriting students in measures of reading comprehension and Hanzi production accuracy in typed essays. Zhang concluded that handwriting and typing Chinese involve distinct types of processing (handwriting being sub-lexical, stroke by stroke; typing being lexical and involving multimodal encoding of sound and form simultaneously) which has consequences for learning/retention as well as communicative ability.

In a more recent study, Zhang (2024) further corroborated these findings. Here, she compared the end-of-term performance of students who prioritized e-writing ('typing only'), students who regularly practised both e-writing and handwriting ('balanced'), and a new cohort of students who received what she called 'audio-enhanced chunk-based typing' training. While all groups achieved comparable results in terms of linguistic (Hanzi) accuracy in writing and word-level recognition, the e-writing groups both outperformed the balanced group in sentence-level typing (reading + retrieval to type out sentences), with an advantage for the audio-enhanced group.

In terms of vocabulary learning specifically, the most robust study available at present was a multi-site multi-replication of Lu et al. (2019) conducted by Lu et al. (2024) with novice and intermediate Chinese as a foreign language (CFL) learners. Students assigned to learning conditions involving any amount of handwriting systematically performed poorer on vocabulary recognition than students who did not handwrite. Lu et al. (2019) operationalized handwriting practice based on an ecologically valid range, basing groups on student-reported typical amounts of out-of-class handwriting practice when required and not required to do so. Whether students handwrote a lot or a little, they did not perform better than students who did not handwrite at all. Though doubt has been cast repeatedly on whether students who do not handwrite will be able to learn, retain and use Hanzi, the evidence presented in these studies suggests that e-writing is more than sufficient across a wide variety of measures.

Learner Interaction and Feedback

By now, the value of interaction for additional language development is a well-established component of the literature on L2 learning (see Loewen and Sato (2018) for a detailed overview). Like face-to-face interactions between learners of similar and different language backgrounds and proficiency levels, both synchronous and asynchronous technology-mediated interaction have been repeatedly demonstrated to benefit various aspects of language development (Ziegler 2016). Research findings for L2 Chinese have specifically shown that synchronous text interaction, for example, via mobile apps like WeChat, is highly beneficial both for linguistic and for intercultural development (Jin 2018; Jin and Erben 2007). Handwritten communication cannot compete with the affordances of digital communication, both in terms of the potential to be physically distant (i.e., in different locations) or the real-time speed (of turn-taking) and multimodality which digital communication provides. Especially when it comes to feedback, which is one of the primary drivers of language development from inter-individual interaction (Loewen and Sato 2018), e-writing is advantageous over handwriting. Recent research findings (e.g., Fu and Li 2022) suggest that synchronous and immediate feedback leads to uptake and sustained changes (i.e. learning) for L2 learners when communicating via writing. As such, the capacity for a teacher or even a peer to work collaboratively in a live document and provide feedback in real-time is an affordance of e-writing, but not one of handwriting. Handwriting, therefore, is much more limited in terms of real-time interaction and feedback potential than e-writing, which limits the former's prospects for necessary elements for interaction-driven L2 development.

For L2 Chinese specifically, though research on both technology-mediated digital interaction and synchronous feedback is still somewhat scarce, recent studies have identified multiple benefits of digital collaborative writing, both for language development and for positive affect gains. Specifically, Zhai (2021) triangulated multiple data sources in a longitudinal classroom-based study of intermediate Chinese learners and found that though in the short-term group dynamics sometimes caused fluctuations in motivation, overall motivation was higher at the end of the treatment period than at the beginning due to perceived gains in language ability from live e-writing collaborations. Extending this line of research, Zhang and Liu (2023) compared synchronous and asynchronous collaborative e-writing for novice (second semester) L2 Chinese students. Both synchronous and asynchronous writing led to learning gains, but synchronous writing afforded many more opportunities for language learning (e.g. negotiation of form and meaning). Similarly, Yang and Polin (2023) found a clear advantage in terms of end-of-semester individual writing ability for groups of students assigned to their collaborative writing condition as opposed to the independent writing condition. Research on L2 Chinese interaction and collaborative writing has only recently begun in earnest, but it is clear from the existing literature that e-writing is beneficial for language learning for the reasons outlined here and further will afford researchers unprecedented opportunities to study these affordances and their underlying L2 development mechanisms for a variety of contexts and learners.

Emerging Technologies

Technology is changing at an unprecedented rate, and educational programmes face the recurring challenge of incorporating (or suppressing) new technologies into the teaching, learning and assessment cycle. Importantly, the argument to prioritize e-writing over handwriting for L2 Chinese should not be misunderstood as limiting learners only to keyboard-based typing to communicate via digital media. Instead, e-writing (as Chu et al. 2024 conceptualize it) is an open category which includes any technology-based language production tool (see discussion in Coss et al. 2024). For example, a recent study by Da et al. (2024) explored the pedagogical viability of a freely available speech-to-text tool. They argued that while not without issues, this technology allows learners to produce text for digitally-mediated communication with the added benefit of pronunciation practice and immediate feedback—if the speech-to-text software is unable to correctly convert speech to desired text to convey the intended meaning, learners are (1) immediately aware of the site(s) of the issue(s) and (2) able to reattempt their utterance and receive feedback again. Though Da et al. (2024) only examined one tool, their study opens an exciting potential direction for L2 Chinese language teaching and research within the e-writing paradigm—the integration of speech and text (i.e. multimodal communication) with automatic feedback loops.

Though sometimes perceived to be antithetical to language learning, machine translation tools have been used with increasing enthusiasm by language teachers and learners for various communicative tasks. Among other benefits, these tools offer opportunities for repeated engagement with multiple sources of input to cross-reference translation accuracy (e.g. Chang 2022), as well as the possibility to train students to independently use these tools to improve their writing and language proficiency (Xu 2020). At present, artificial intelligence (e.g. large language model, or LLM, tools like ChatGPT) are being developed and are (mostly) freely available. Various scholars have argued that these tools can be used for a range of language learning and teaching purposes including decreasing teacher workload (e.g. Poole 2022) and engaging learners in digital communication for language development as well as development of digital literacies (e.g. Poole and Polio 2024). To date, no study has been published on the efficacy of ChatGPT-like tools for L2 Chinese learning, but I am sure we will see these studies published any day now.

Speech-to-text, machine translation and (generative/LLM) AI tools are only a few of the many emerging technologies which can potentially be leveraged for language learning in the digital age. By embracing e-writing, L2 Chinese programmes will be able to exploit these technologies for in- and out-of-class communication and learning while also fostering learners' abilities to use these technologies for a variety of academic, social, and professional purposes.

Writing Assessment

The debate about the need for handwriting in L2 Chinese has largely focused on *pedagogy* (see Allen 2008; Everson 2011). However, in addition to refining pedagogical approaches to best meet the needs of our learners, it is also critical that we *assess* learners in a way that we are able to obtain reliable information and draw supportable and valid inferences upon which we base decisions. While many language programmes are grappling with how much handwriting to require for students at various proficiency levels, the majority of L2 Chinese assessments which are used for mid- and high-stakes purposes (e.g. placement into programmes, awarding of credentials including college credit, job eligibility, and study abroad readiness) either *require* handwriting or allow learners to *choose* to type or handwrite (Coss In press; Zhao et al. 2023). The fundamental premise of any test which offers parallel versions—including many standardized proficiency tests available today—is that these tests would elicit equivalent scores from the same learners. That is, no matter whether a test taker handwrites or types a response, their score will be equivalent (i.e. the test versions would show evidence of *convergent validity*).

Several studies have compared handwritten and typed writing by L2 Chinese learners by having the same group of learners take both a handwritten and typed assessment. These studies have found that typed writing consistently receives higher scores. Zhu et al. (2016) found higher scores for typed writing by 32 Chinese learners from various L1s in China. Similarly, Zhang and Min (2019) found higher typed scores for 12 learners in the UK/Ireland. However, these studies had limitations including no control for prompt or modality order, simple statistics and writing being measured in untimed non-test conditions. That said, more methodologically robust studies by Bourgerie et al. (2023), Liao (2023) and Coss (In press) also found higher scores for typing than handwriting in within-subjects study designs. Overall, these studies have shown that typed writing consistently outperforms handwriting for L2 Chinese learners across proficiency levels on timed writing tests. The consistent score discrepancies for the same learners (i.e. learners who are tested in both typing and handwriting) undermine validity arguments for handwritten tests as measures of overall writing proficiency. Namely, if the construct of interest is L2 learners' ability to *use written Chinese to meet communicative needs*, empirical evidence consistently shows typing and handwriting capturing this ability differently, that is, they do not present evidence of convergent validity. Given this lack of score equivalence, the validity of handwritten tests is questionable as the sole or primary form of assessment of Chinese writing ability. As such, language programmes should reconsider the modality they prioritize for a variety of testing purposes, including formative, summative and diagnostic test uses.

This does not necessarily mean that handwriting tests should be completely eliminated or that they are entirely without value. Instead, in order to maximize positive test impact and ensure that tests guide instructional—and therefore student—priorities in the desired direction, L2 Chinese programmes should test the skill(s) which they value at the level of competence that each skill is needed for. Concretely, for example, a programme might choose to prioritize most writing test tasks using e-writing for a variety of communicative purposes, including sending emails, writing academic papers and interpersonal text chatting, among others. Simultaneously, the programme may choose to selectively require handwriting for some assessment tasks, including, for example, filling out a paper-based form with personal information or writing a greeting card. Which tasks learners need in which writing modality could be determined via a needs analysis (see Long (2005) for a detailed treatment and Lambert (2010) for practical guidance) to optimize instruction and assessment to best meet the needs and expectations of local stakeholders.

Stakeholder Perceptions

When comparing pedagogical approaches, especially when attempting to shift from one approach to another, one critical component of responsible educational practice is to understand stakeholder perceptions. This line of research, however, is deceptively complicated, as perceptions are not fixed. Instead, they can be shaped by a number of factors, including individual past experiences, direct and indirect teacher (or other expert) influence and experiences of success or challenge, among others. Lyu et al. (2021) summarize findings from a number of studies which reported (mostly 'CSL' as opposed to 'CFL') learners' perceptions of the affordances of typing and handwriting. Generally speaking, learners tended to prefer typing over handwriting, though they often noted that handwriting was beneficial for some aspects of character learning. Other studies (e.g. Morgan 2012) have reported extensive data from both learners and teachers, illustrating the complex relationship between learner and teacher perceptions and a variety of relevant individual background and learning experience factors. The onset of the COVID-19 pandemic brought about another wave of studies investigating teachers' approaches and students' responses to these approaches as classroom teaching abruptly went online (Gao 2020; Wang and East 2020; Xu et al. 2022). Again, these studies show a complex array of findings and factors which shape perceptions and preferences related to typed and handwritten Chinese production abilities.

While we should not discount these studies or their findings outright, it is important to contextualize their findings and not over-extrapolate or overgeneralize. First, as with any study, there is a question of the extent to which findings generalize to larger populations (and this generalizability, in turn, is predicated on the reliability and validity and/or trustworthiness of the instruments or procedures being used to elicit learner perceptions). Given the contextual differences across the current body of available research, we are not yet ready to make generalizations or draw firm conclusions. Furthermore, without *time zero* data, that is, data about learners' perceptions at the onset of L2 Chinese learning, it is very difficult to disentangle students' *perceptions* from their *experiences* or, more specifically, to deduce the *directionality* of the influence (i.e. a cause-and-effect relationship) between learners' experiences and their beliefs. For example, is it that learners were predisposed to like or prefer handwriting before even starting L2 Chinese learning which explains their preferences, or were learners exposed to teachers who implicitly or explicitly emphasized that handwriting was necessary to successfully learn characters? Conversely, if learners found success with typing as compared to handwriting (e.g. on assessments, as discussed previously), might their experiences change their perceptions? When conducting questionnaire/survey-based research, especially longitudinally, researchers must be able to prove what is called measurement invariance—that the construct being measured (in this case 'preference') has not shifted as learners themselves have changed (e.g. become more proficient). As many of the studies referenced in the previous paragraph have shown, past experience is often a predictor of preferences and perceptions, as is teacher influence. Therefore, while this line of research is fundamental and should be continued, it must be conducted and reported carefully, taking careful consideration of the initial state of learners' preferences and concurrently documenting the many experiences with handwriting and e-writing, as well as overt and implicit teacher influence on students, which might influence those preferences to draw useful conclusions for the field to benefit from.

Limitations in Current Research

While interest in e-writing for both language programmes and researchers has steadily increased in recent years (Fedewa et al. 2022), it is important to acknowledge the limitations of the current body of available research, in terms of both research methods and research scope. Research on languages, especially "less commonly taught languages" like Chinese, often suffers from small sample sizes, especially in classroom-based research (Loewen and Hui 2021). For quantitative research, these small sample sizes (i.e. of less than 30 participants per group) limit the range of inferential statistical tests that can be reliably applied to analyse data, and therefore conclusions extrapolating research findings beyond the sample of a given study must be drawn cautiously. Similarly, statistical reporting and interpretation in L2 Chinese reading and writing research have not yet risen to meet the standards expected in educational or L2 research across the board (e.g. reporting statistics like confidence intervals, effect sizes, etc.; see Norris et al. (2015)), which will be important for understanding the magnitude of the effects of e-writing compared to, say, handwriting beyond mere statistical significance. For qualitative studies, lack of data triangulation and lack of interrogation of the relationship between the researcher(s) and the participants (who are often students of the researchers) can undermine or limit the trustworthiness of the research design, and conclusions must again be drawn with caution. Of course, all research designs inherently come with relative advantages and disadvantages. All well-conducted studies, whether intended to generalize beyond a particular sample or context or whether conducted specifically to document practices and catalyse local change, as in action research, have the potential to enhance our understanding of the complex and multifaceted nature of L2 Chinese literacy development. Triangulation of diverse research approaches in diverse contexts by both independent research teams and programme-internal teacher-researchers will no doubt continue to provide us with a complex but ever-clearer understanding of how we might best approach the task of facilitating L2 Hanzi literacy development for the diverse learners of Chinese across the world.

Most importantly, perhaps, is the issue of scope which plagues L2 research in general and from which the current body of e-writing research also suffers. Namely, the majority of this research has been conducted on college learners, some of whom are already in contexts which prioritize e-writing. Language learners in college programmes tend to be voluntary (i.e. self-enrolled), and their motivational profiles may well differ from those of less voluntary learners (e.g. grade school students). The latter are highly underrepresented in the current e-writing literature, and the extent to which e-writing can truly meet the needs of all (or even most) L2 Chinese learners must be examined within the context and constraints of a variety of educational programmes if the model is to be considered viable enough to be widely accepted. Similarly, the majority of the research on e-writing so far has focused on non-heritage 'L2' learners. Heritage learners, for example, or non-school-based learners (e.g. adults learning independently) have not yet been sufficiently studied. While continuing to refine research designs and maintaining a priority on curricular-situated classroom- and programme-based research, it will be important to expand the scope of the samples included in e-writing research to identify both opportunities and challenges for the field.

E-writing: An Educational Imperative

As I have previously argued, "language programmes should be focused on making the Chinese learning process as engaging, as efficient, as effective and as enjoyable and relevant as possible, allowing learners to achieve more in the same amount of time in a more enjoyable way than would be possible if they were learning on their own" (Coss 2024a). Therefore, especially in the present 'digital age' or 'age of technology', I firmly believe it is our obligation as educators to adjust our practice to meet the needs of our students and that the e-writing approach is one option with clear benefits to accomplishing this. However, shifting educational practice is a challenging endeavour. As Everson (2011) notes, particularly when it comes to handwriting, Chinese programmes may encounter great inertia when attempting to change. This inertia often manifests itself as colleague disagreements, inflexible programme policies or challenges for students when moving between one educational level and another (e.g. high school to college, from study abroad back to home institutions, etc.)—each of these in turn resulting in challenges for language learners as they are forced to deal with inconsistent requirements and success criteria.

To aid in attempts at (usually difficult) educational change, scholars of 'change management' have developed a framework for gradually "de-implementing" one practice in favour of other more effective or efficient practices (Hamilton et al. 2023). Namely, they propose four 'Rs' which can be employed to gradually shift individual and programme-level practices to, as they say, 'make room for impact'. These 'Rs' are:

- Remove (eliminate a practice)
- Reduce (lessen the frequency or intensity of the practice)
- Re-engineer (change the practice in some substantive way other than quantity)
- Replace (do something instead of the current practice)

These four 'Rs' offer a concrete set of possibilities for Chinese programmes to gradually adopt e-writing to supplant handwriting as the primary means of communication and assessment. While some instructors or teachers may be ready to jump straight to 'replace' or 'remove', others may prefer, as (Coss 2024a) describes, a significant reduction and re-engineering of handwriting to play a supporting role. In some contexts (e.g. heritage learners, young children in bilingual education), handwriting and e-writing may need to coexist in a model that is acceptable to stakeholders and takes into account the developmental needs and capacities of children in a way that college programmes need not be concerned with. For some programmes, it may be sufficient to 're-engineer' the curriculum as has been suggested by scholars like Allen (2008) or Feng and Yang (2013) so that e-writing is the initial sole modality for communication and assessment, but that after foundational communicative abilities and motivation are securely in place, handwriting can be gradually added for some or all learners. This can be done, perhaps, as Everson (2011) argues, by giving learners the option to choose. A balance of e-writing with handwriting will be particularly necessary for contexts in which high-stakes assessments (e.g. the International Baccalaureate exam, the General Certificate of Secondary Education, etc.) require some amount of handwriting. Importantly, though, before a programme 'removes' or 'reduces' handwriting, it should be ready to 'replace' it with viable alternatives in a systematic fashion, rather than leaving learners or instructors to their own devices and assuming that desirable learning outcomes will be reached. To this end, Coss (2024b), Hu and He (2024), Wang and Wang (2024) and Zhang (2024) each offer viable possibilities for curricula at varying levels of granularity, from programme and course design (Hu and He; Wang and Wang) to specific pedagogical approaches (Coss; Zhang).

As teachers and language programmes use one or more of these 'Rs' to systematically adjust their practice, it will be critical to document the results of these educational shifts. As Byrnes (2019) argued, a language programme's curriculum offers a robust site for a sustained programme of high quality and highly informative research. That is, pedagogical experiments attempting a replacement, reduction or re-engineering of handwriting situated in the context of a language programme afford teacher-researchers the potential to measure various outcomes (e.g. learning, motivation and self-efficacy) longitudinally. Furthermore, one of the most important parts of documenting the efficacy of pedagogical or curricular change is a gradual and principled approach to rollout and data collection. For example, programmes might pilot novel instruction with a subset of classes and measuring outcomes and will ideally triangulate data with other converging data sources (interviews, observations, document analysis, etc.). This of course requires careful planning and design such that variable confounds do not undermine the trustworthiness of results (e.g. confound with teacher and treatment, lack of comparison groups). However, when done well, this type of curriculum-situated research can afford a single classroom or programme the evidence necessary to confidently continue expanding the shift or innovation and can offer important evidence to the field beyond the local context that the new pedagogical approach (i.e. e-writing) might be effective in other contexts.

With this in mind, I would like to offer two additional 'Rs' to build on Hamilton et al.'s (2023) framework as we explore the viability of e-writing: *researching* and *reporting*. As our field explores e-writing in our own contexts, which I truly believe is an educational imperative for learners in the twenty-first century, we must do so in a justifiable way, where we document the successes, the challenges, the impact(s) on students and the questions that continue to emerge, of which, for now, there are likely to be many. By documenting our processes and reporting them in settings like conferences, social media groups and practitioner and scholarly publication venues, we can contribute to collective confidence that our efforts are resulting in meaningful educational change while avoiding attempting to innovate without understanding other similar contexts' experiences. As educators, we owe it to our learners to give them the optimal educational experience to prepare them to meet their goals and to do so in a way that fully supports their language and intercultural development. As colleagues interested in evidence-informed pedagogy, we owe it to ourselves to carefully and honestly document our attempts to improve our educational programmes. Together, we can offer the optimal learning experience for L2 Chinese students at every level of education. E-writing is the next important step in this direction.

Competing Interests The author has no conflicts of interest to declare that are relevant to the content of this chapter.

References

Allen, Joseph R. 2008. Why Learning to Write Chinese is a Waste of Time: A Modest Proposal. *Foreign Language Annals* 41 (2): 237–251. https://doi.org/10.1111/j.1944-9720.2008.tb03291.x.

Bourgerie, Dana Scott, Troy L. Cox, and Steven L. Riep. 2023. Does Text Entry Method Make a Difference on Chinese Writing Test Scores? *Chinese as a Second Language* 57 (3): 270–273. https://doi.org/10.1075/csl.22012.bou.

Byrnes, Heidi. 2019. Affirming the Context of Instructed SLA: The Potential of Curricular Thinking. *Language Teaching Research* 23 (4): 514–532. https://doi.org/10.1177/1362168818776666.

Chang, Li-Ching. 2022. Chinese Language Learners Evaluating Machine Translation Accuracy. *JALT CALL Journal* 18 (1): 110–136. https://doi.org/10.29140/jaltcall.v18n1.592.

Chu, Chengzhi, Matthew D. Coss, and Phyllis Ni Zhang, eds. 2024. *Transforming Hanzi Pedagogy in the Digital Age: Theory, Research, and Practice [电写时代的汉字教学——理论与实践]*. Routledge.

Coss, Matthew D. 2024a. The E-Writing Approach to L2 Chinese instruction: Clarifying Fundamental Principles and Core Concepts. In *Transforming Hanzi Pedagogy in the Digital Age: Theory, Research, and Practice*, ed. Chengzhi Chu, Matthew D. Coss, and Phyllis Ni Zhang, 34–54. Routledge.

———. 2024b. Towards a Curricularized Approach to L2 Hanzi Teaching and Learning. In *Transforming Hanzi Pedagogy in the Digital Age: Theory, Research, and Practice*, ed. Chengzhi Chu, Matthew D. Coss, and Phyllis Ni Zhang, 211–238. Routledge.

———. In press. Are We Testing What We Think We Are? A Multi-Site Investigation of Typed and Handwritten L2 Chinese Writing Assessments. *Language Learning & Technology*.

Coss, Matthew D., Chengzhi Chu, and Phyllis Ni Zhang. 2024. Introduction. In *Transforming Hanzi Pedagogy in the Digital Age: Theory, Research, and Practice*, edited by Chengzhi Chu, Matthew D. Coss, and Phyllis Ni Zhang, 1–12. Routledge.

Da, Jun, Yanlin Wang, and Chengxu Yin. 2024. Voice-Writing Chinese Characters Using Speech-To-Text Technology for CSL Learning and Instruction: An Exploratory Study. In *Transforming Hanzi Pedagogy in the Digital Age: Theory, Research, and Practice*, edited by Chengzhi Chu, Matthew D. Coss, and Phyllis Ni Zhang, 127–147. Routledge.

Everson, Michael E. 2011. Best Practices in Teaching Logographic and Non-Roman Writing Systems to L2 Learners. *Annual Review of Applied Linguistics* 31: 249–274. https://doi.org/10.1017/S0267190511000171.

Fedewa, Kevin, Charlene Polio, and Matthew D. Coss. 2022. *Researching Chinese Reading and Writing: Past, Present, and Future.* Paper presented online at the ACTFL Convention, Boston, MA, USA.

Feng, Yu, and Hao Wu. 2024, May 18. 震撼课：第一课就确立电写教学的方向. Conference presentation at 电写时代汉字教学模式国际学术研讨会 International Symposium on L2 Chinese Teaching. Online.

Feng, Yu, and Qingyu Yang. 2013. The Implementation Principles of Computer Input of Chinese Characters in Chinese Language Teaching in North American Universities. *Chinese Language Globalization Studies* 1: 33–40.

Fu, Mengxia, and Shaofeng Li. 2022. The Effects of Immediate and Delayed Corrective Feedback on L2 Development. *Studies in Second Language Acquisition* 44 (1): 2–34. https://doi.org/10.1017/S0272263120000388.

Gao, Xiaoping. 2020. Australian Students' Perceptions of the Challenges and Strategies for Learning Chinese Characters in Emergency Online Teaching. *International Journal of Chinese Language Teaching* 1 (1): 83–98. https://doi.org/10.46451/ijclt.2020.06.04.

Hamilton, Arran, John Hattie, and Dylan Wiliam. 2023. *Making Room for Impact: A De-Implementation Guide for Educators*. SAGE Publications.

He, Wenchao Wayne. 2009. *Listening, Speaking, Reading, Typing, and Writing: Development Directions in Teaching Chinese as a Foreign Language*, 45–60. Nanjing University Press.

He, Wenchao Wayne, and Xiaoxiao Jiao. 2010. Curriculum Design and Special Features of 'Computer Chinese' and Chinese for Tomorrow. In *Teaching and Learning Chinese: Issues and Perspectives*, ed. Jianguo Chen, Chuang Wang, and Jinfa Cai, 217–235. North Carolina: Information Age Publishing.

Henson, Ash. 2022. Semantic Components: Meaning and Form Components. Accessed April 25, 2022. https://www.outlier-linguistics.com/blogs/chinese/semantic-components-meaning-and-form-components.

Hu, Xiaoyan, and Wenchao Wayne He. 2024. Computerized Chinese to Promote the Three Modes of Communication in an Intermediate-Level Chinese Class. In *Transforming Hanzi Pedagogy in the Digital Age: Theory, Research, and Practice*, ed. Chengzhi Chu, Matthew D. Coss, and Phyllis Ni Zhang, 196–210. Routledge.

Jiang, Nan, Fengyun Hou, and Xin Jiang. 2020. Analytic Versus Holistic Recognition of Chinese Words among L2 Learners. *The Modern Language Journal* 104 (3): 567–580. https://doi.org/10.1111/modl.12662.

Jin, Li. 2018. Digital Affordances on WeChat: Learning Chinese as a Second Language. *Computer Assisted Language Learning* 31 (1-2): 27–52. https://doi.org/10.1080/09588221.2017.1376687.

Jin, Li, and Tony Erben. 2007. Intercultural Learning via Instant Messenger Interaction. *CALICO Journal*: 291–311. https://www.jstor.org/stable/24147913.

Ke, Chuanren, and Helen Shen. 2003. Looking Backward and Forward: A Review of Chinese Character Instruction Research in the United States. *Yuyan Jiaoxue yu Yanjiu [Language Teaching & Research]* 3: 1–17.

Lambert, Craig. 2010. A Task-Based Needs Analysis: Putting Principles into Practice. *Language Teaching Research* 14 (1): 99–112. https://doi.org/10.1177/1362168809346520.

Liao, Jianling. 2023. What Skills are being Assessed? Evaluating L2 Chinese Essays Written by Hand and on a Computer Keyboard. *Assessing Writing* 57: 100765. https://doi.org/10.1016/j.asw.2023.100765.

Loewen, Shawn, and Bronson Hui. 2021. Small Samples in Instructed Second Language Acquisition Research. *The Modern Language Journal* 105 (1): 187–193. https://doi.org/10.1111/modl.12700.

Loewen, Shawn, and Masatoshi Sato. 2018. Interaction and Instructed Second Language Acquisition. *Language Teaching* 51 (3): 285–329. https://doi.org/10.1017/S0261444818000125.

Long, Michael H., ed. 2005. *Second Language Needs Analysis*. Cambridge University Press.

Lu, Xiwen, Korinn S. Ostrow, and Neil T. Heffernan. 2019. Save Your Strokes: Chinese Handwriting Practice Makes For Ineffective Use of Instructional Time in Second Language Classrooms. *AERA Open* 5 (4): 1–15. https://doi.org/10.1177/2332858419890326.

Lu, Xiwen, Korinn S. Ostrow, Qingyu Yang, and Neil T. Hefferman. 2024. Save Your Strokes: Further Studies on the Efficiency of Learning Chinese Words without Hand-writing. In *Transforming Hanzi Pedagogy in the Digital Age: Theory, Research, and Practice*, ed. Chengzhi Chu, Matthew D. Coss, and Phyllis Ni Zhang, 103–126. Routledge.

Lusin, Natalia, Terri Peterson, Christine Sulewski, and Rizwana Zafer. 2023. Enrollments in Languages other than English in US Institutions of Higher Education, Fall 2021. *Modern Language Association.* https://www.mla.org/content/download/191324/file/Enrollments-in-Languages-Other-Than-English-in-US-Institutions-of-Higher-Education-Fall-2021.pdf.

Lyu, Boning, Chun Lai, Chin-Hsi Lin, and Yang Gong. 2021. Comparison Studies of Typing and Handwriting in Chinese Language Learning: A Synthetic Review. *International Journal of Educational Research* 106: 1–15. https://doi.org/10.1016/j.ijer.2021.101740.

Morgan, Yuan-Yu Karen. 2012. *Attitudes toward Hanzi Production Ability Among Chinese Teachers and Learners*. PhD diss., Purdue University.

Moser, David. 1991. Why Chinese is so Damn Hard. *Sino-Platonic Papers* 27: 59–70.

Norris, John M., Luke Plonsky, Steven J. Ross, and Rob Schoonen. 2015. Guidelines for Reporting Quantitative Methods and Results in Primary Research. *Language Learning* 65 (2): 470–476. https://doi.org/10.1111/lang.12104.

Pelzl, Eric, Jiang Liu, and Chunhong Qi. 2022. Native Language Experience with Tones Influences Both Phonetic and Lexical Processes when Acquiring a Second Tonal Language. *Journal of Phonetics* 95. https://doi.org/10.1016/j.wocn.2022.101197.

Poole, Frederick J. 2022. Using ChatGPT to Design Language Material and Exercises. FLTMAG.com. Accessed February 24, 2024. https://fltmag.com/chatgpt-design-material-exercises/.

Poole, Frederick J., and Charlene Polio. 2024. From Sci-Fi to the Classroom: Implications of AI in Task-Based Writing. *TASK: Journal on Task-Based Language Teaching* 3 (2): 243–272.

Renfroe, John. 2018. Getting Radical About Radicals: Why You Should Think of Characters in Terms of Functional Components. Accessed November 6, 2018. https://www.outlier-linguistics.com/blogs/chinese/getting-radical-about-radicals.

U.S. State Department Foreign Language Training. n.d. Accessed February 24, 2024. https://www.state.gov/foreign-language-training/.

Wang, Danping, and Martin East. 2020. Constructing an Emergency Chinese Curriculum during the Pandemic: A New Zealand Experience. *International Journal of Chinese Language Teaching* 1 (1): 1–19. https://doi.org/10.46451/ijclt.2020.06.01.

Wang, Qian, and Hsiang-Ning Wang. 2024. E-writing Based Pedagogy to Advance Chinese Language Learning: Practices from Heritage and Non-Heritage Teaching at a Major Canadian University. In *Transforming Hanzi Pedagogy in the Digital Age: Theory, Research, and Practice*, ed. Chengzhi Chu, Matthew D. Coss, and Phyllis Ni Zhang, 167–195. Routledge.

Xu, Jun. 2020. Machine Translation for Editing Compositions in a Chinese Language Class: Task Design and Student Beliefs. *Journal of Technology & Chinese. Language Teaching* 11 (1) http://www.tclt.us/journal/2020v11n1/xu.pdf.

Xu, Ping, and Theresa Jen. 2005. Penless Chinese Language Learning: A Computer-Assisted Approach. *Journal of the Chinese Language Teachers Association* 40 (2): 25–42.

Xu, Yi, Li Jin, Elizabeth Deifell, and Katie Angus. 2022. Facilitating Technology-Based Character Learning in Emergency Remote Teaching. *Foreign Language Annals* 55 (1): 72–97. https://doi.org/10.1111/flan.12541.

Yang, Li, and Lini G. Polin. 2023. Exploring the learning Benefits of Collaborative Writing in L2 Chinese: A Product-Oriented Perspective. *International Review of Applied Linguistics in Language Teaching*. https://doi.org/10.1515/iral-2023-0034.

Zhai, Mengying. 2021. Collaborative Writing in a Chinese as a Foreign Language Classroom: Learners' Perceptions and Motivations. *Journal of Second Language Writing* 53. https://doi.org/10.1016/j.jslw.2021.100836.

Zhang, Phyllis Ni. 2021. Typing to Replace Handwriting: Effectiveness of the Typing-Primary Approach for L2 Chinese Beginners. *Journal of Technology and Chinese Language Teaching* 12 (2): 1–28.

———. 2024. The Typing-Based Approach to CFL Beginner Instruction: Hanzi Instructional Design and Learning Outcomes. In *Transforming Hanzi Pedagogy in the Digital Age: Theory, Research, and Practice*, ed. Chengzhi Chu, Matthew D. Coss, and Phyllis Ni Zhang, 77–102. Routledge.

Zhang, Meixiu, and Qi Liu. 2023. Synchronous and Asynchronous Online Collaborative Writing: A Study on Chinese Language Learners. *Foreign Language Annals*. https://doi.org/10.1111/flan.12704.

Zhang, Qi, and Ge Min. 2019. Chinese Writing Composition among CFL Learners: A Comparison between Handwriting and Typewriting. *Computers and Composition* 54 (December): 102522. https://doi.org/10.1016/j.compcom.2019.102522.

Zhang, Luyao, Yang Gong, and Boning Lyu. 2024. E-Writing in Chinese as a Second/Foreign Language (CSL/CFL) Learning: A Systematic Review. In *Transforming Hanzi Pedagogy in the Digital Age: Theory, Research, and Practice*, ed. Chengzhi Chu, Matthew D. Coss, and Phyllis Ni Zhang, 148–164. Routledge.

Zhao, Ran, Matthew D. Coss, Henry Ruan, Bailu Li, and Jing Ma. 2023. Examining Secondary-Postsecondary Articulation of Chinese Language Programs: A Survey of US College Placement Procedures. *Foreign Language Annals* 56 (3): 690–719. https://doi.org/10.1111/flan.12709.

Zhu, Yu, Shiu-Kee Mark Shum, Shek-Kam Brian Tse, and Jinghui Jack Liu. 2016. Word-Processor or Pencil-and-Paper? A Comparison of Students' Writing in Chinese as a Foreign Language. *Computer Assisted Language Learning* 29 (3): 596-617. https://doi.org/10.1080/09588221.2014.1000932.

Ziegler, Nicole. 2016. Synchronous Computer-Mediated Communication and Interaction: A Meta-Analysis. *Studies in Second Language Acquisition* 38 (3): 553-586. https://doi.org/10.1017/S027226311500025X.

5

Embodied Learning of Chinese Characters Through Typing and Handwriting in the Multimodal Virtual Space: Implications for a Digital Future

Qi Zhang

Introduction

With the increasing use of digital input systems in our daily lives, there has been a call for the early introduction and employment of typing in learning Chinese characters. In emergency remote teaching (ERT; Hodges et al. 2020), the forced shift of almost every aspect of learning online due to COVID-19 further encouraged typing and marginalised handwriting in virtual learning environments. However, the study of the complex system of Chinese script conventionally requires labour-intensive handwriting because of its orthographic nature, especially among Chinese as a

Q. Zhang (✉)
School of Applied Language and Intercultural Studies, Dublin City University, Dublin, Ireland
e-mail: qi.zhang@dcu.ie

foreign language (CFL) beginners (Zhang and Min 2019). This chapter presents results collected from an online survey on the co-deployment of handwriting and typing among CFL learners and teachers, as well as their perceptions of the two writing modalities during ERT.

This chapter first introduces the challenges that the Chinese writing system poses for learning, with a focus on the advantages and limitations of handwriting and typing for learning Chinese characters. It then provides an overview of embodiment and explains how embodied cognition is engaged in handwriting and typing Chinese. Data from an online survey from six English-speaking countries are analysed specifically in terms of the use and perceptions of the two writing modalities. Further details regarding the design of the survey for both learners and teachers can be found in Chap. 3 of this book.

This chapter then discusses the awareness and employment of embodied cognition through an investigation of handwriting and typing practice. The possible reasons for the exploitation or neglect of the embodied cognition potential are also considered, especially in terms of the multimodal encoding of typing and the dual-modal nature of the Chinese literacy route. While this study focuses on teaching and learning practice during the pandemic, it is at the frontier of the study of the embodied learning of Chinese characters in an online environment. It exemplifies the application of embodiment as a theoretical framework to examine Chinese language learning in the multimodal virtual space.

Challenges of Learning Chinese Characters

Chinese characters have a three-tier orthographic structure. Strokes—the smallest units in a character—are used as building blocks to form a radical, and one or more radicals can construct a character (Shen and Ke 2007; Zhang and Reilly 2015). Unlike the linear arrangement of alphabetic-based letters, Chinese characters "are packed into a square configuration, possessing a high, nonlinear visual complexity" (Tan et al. 2005, p. 5). In addition, characters can generally be categorised as integral or compound according to the physical structure (Shen 2013). An integral character is composed of inseparable crossed strokes, whereas a compound one is composed of at least two radicals (Lyu et al. 2021).

Approximately 80% of modern Chinese characters are phonetic-semantic compound characters (Kuo et al. 2014; Shu et al. 2003). While the semantic radical usually provides information on meaning and the phonetic radical tends to offer cues for pronunciation, the correspondences are not always systematic or even reliable (Zhang and Reilly 2020). In fact, phonetic radicals function as morphemes rather than phonemes (Shen 2013). This means that a graphic unit—such as a Chinese character—is mapped to a whole morpheme syllable rather than to a phoneme (Chan et al. 2021; Perfetti et al. 2013). In addition, Chinese has a large number of characters. Approximately 3000 of its 56,000 characters are commonly used and should consequently be acquired by a literate person (Shen 2013).

The visual complexity and the large quantity of characters within the Chinese writing system therefore lead to uneven development in reading and writing versus listening and speaking. Because of the memory-demanding script, it takes longer to learn to write Chinese characters, compared to learning to speak (Kubler 2020). While reading and writing skills can usually catch up with listening and speaking at the intermediate level, it is suggested that the curriculum be designed to have separate tracks accommodating oral and written skills development (Kubler 2020; Zhang and Leahy 2022).

These features of Chinese characters pose significant challenges to CFL learners accustomed to an alphabetic system. The US government rates Chinese as a Category IV language since it "requires learners to spend up to three times more time to reach an equivalent proficiency in languages such as Spanish" (Everson and Xiao 2009).

Typing—a writing mode which younger generations are accustomed to in the digital era—further complicates the study of Chinese writing script. Handwriting and typing can contribute to and at the same time restrict certain aspects of Chinese character learning. Handwriting supports establishing the spatial configuration of strokes and radicals, along with a temporal sequence of motor movements associated with stroke composition (Zhang and Reilly 2015). Consequently, handwriting shows positive effects on character recognition and boosts CFL learners' grapheme-morpheme mapping capacity, which ultimately contributes to reading development (Cao et al. 2013; Guan et al. 2011, 2015). Typing, on the other hand, not only requires less physical workload than handwriting but also contributes to reducing the cognitive load at lower levels of character processing and allowing higher-order thinking (Allen 2008; Zhang and Min 2019). Typing Chinese characters on a Latin alphabet keyboard requires the use of a pinyin input system, as well as an extra step of transcribing Chinese characters into pinyin—a Romanised form representing the pronunciation of each character (Wong et al. 2011). Typing therefore exhibits a significant positive effect on phonology recognition and phoneme-morpheme mapping (Lyu et al. 2021).

However, typing does not encourage the learning of visual representation of characters, which is the main concern when applying typing to CFL learning. This is because after typing pinyin on a keyboard, the input system generates a list of possible characters with the same pronunciation based on the pinyin input. The user then simply chooses the intended character from the list, which means he/she is required to be able to correctly recognise the intended character (Zhang and Min 2019). This means character recognition rather than character composition is put in the foreground in typing; however, one of the best ways to reinforce character recognition is through handwriting rather than typing, as stated earlier.

As outlined in Table 5.1, the strengths of one writing modality may compensate for the limitations of the other. Therefore, the study examined the co-deployment of handwriting and typing by CFL learners and teachers to assist Chinese character acquisition in an online learning environment.

Table 5.1 Strengths and limitations of two writing modalities

	Strengths	Limitations
Handwriting	Establishes graphic-motor planning and allograph-shape conversion; benefits character recognition; contributes to reading development	Heavy cognitive and physical workload; marginalised writing modality in the digital era
Typing	Indispensable writing modality in modern life; benefits phonology recognition and phoneme-morpheme mapping; contributes to higher-order thinking and quality of writing compositions	Does not encourage learning whole-character representation; relies on character recognition

Embodied Cognition for Learning Chinese Characters

Embodied cognition, or embodiment, is a concept that challenges the body-mind dichotomy. Conventionally, cognition has been considered an internal operation of processing abstract information in the mind, separate from other bodily experiences in the environment (Atkinson 2010; Michaels and Palatinus 2014). However, embodiment perceives cognition as embodied, highlighting the body as a crucial part of linking the brain with the environment, known as "organism-environment mutuality" (Craighero 2014, p. 51). It recognises the ecological flow between cognition and bodily experiences and interactions with the environment, as well as the fact that "the mind and body interact 'on the fly' as a single entity" (Ellis 2019, p. 41).

In language learning, embodiment does not narrowly conceptualise language as an internalised product in the mind. Instead, it views language learning as more than just a cognitive process by taking into account physical, sensory experiences and actions in the eco-social world (Atkinson 2019; Ellis 2019). Although the online environment looks like it entails minimal corporeal contact, Blackledge and Creese (2017) maintain that a person's established biographies are brought along in any social encounters. Thus, learners certainly need to activate their prior corporeal and sensory experiences to interact with the multimodal semiotics in the virtual space. Under these circumstances, embodied cognition while engaged in online learning is as salient as for offline learning.

Specific to learning Chinese characters using computer technologies, Lu (2011; see also Lu et al. 2013) outlines five types of instructional embodiment. One is haptic embodiment (HE): the sense registry through a haptic channel such that learners use their hands to write, touch or click a mouse. For handwriting, a learner uses his/her hand to write a Chinese character on paper. For typing, a learner's fingers first press various keys on a keyboard to spell the pinyin of a Chinese character before the intended character is chosen from a list of characters with the same pronunciation generated by the input system.

The bodily movements involved via either writing modality can consolidate the learner's sensorimotor experience with the character he/she writes, which ultimately contributes to the memorisation of the character. In other words, the HE engaged in the sensorimotor experiences—established from either handwriting or typing—can assist with the acquisition of Chinese characters.

While previous literature points out the engagement of embodied cognition in the study of Chinese characters (Lu et al. 2013; Zhang et al. 2022), there has been no research examining whether and to what extent CFL learners and teachers are aware of and exploit its potential for character acquisition. For this reason, this study investigates the practice and perceptions of handwriting and typing in the online environment.

Learning Chinese Characters Online

Since almost every aspect of learning had to move online due to COVID-19, typing was inevitably pervasively used, regardless of the preferences of teachers and learners. However, the merits of handwriting meant it was not abandoned, despite all the difficulties. In this case, the practice of two writing modalities in ERT can to a large extent represent the co-deployment of handwriting and typing for the digital future of Chinese language learning and was therefore chosen for the study.

This chapter analyses survey data collected from 38 CFL learners and 20 instructors from six English-speaking countries: Australia, Canada, Ireland, New Zealand, the UK and the US.[1] The survey aimed to examine the overall experience of learning Chinese characters online from three perspectives: learning, teaching and assessment strategies. This chapter will solely focus on learning strategies and teaching methods involving handwriting and typing. In other words, the results presented below consist only of items/questions from the questionnaire that are related to these two writing modalities.

---

[1] While 69 CFL learners and 34 CFL teachers completed the survey, not everyone answered every question, since the survey was taken on a completely voluntary basis. Approximately 38 learners and 20 teachers were valid respondents.

Of the 38 student respondents, about 34% were male and 60% female, with 3% non-binary and 3% preferring not to say. More than 70% were aged 18–24. Approximately 74% were studying Chinese as a non-major in a university. Around 43% had been studying CFL for less than a year, 37% for 1–3 years and 15% for 4–7 years. About 3% had been studying for either 8–10 years or 10+ years.

Of the 20 teacher respondents, 11% were male and 84% female, with 5% preferring not to say. More than 74% were aged 25–44 and about 21% were aged 45–64. More than 42% had been teaching CFL for 4–7 years and another 42% for more than 10 years. Around 11% had been teaching CFL for 8–10 years.

In short, most student respondents were young CFL learners in the early stages of learning Chinese when the survey was carried out. The majority of teacher respondents were middle-aged. None of them were new to teaching, and most of them had a reasonable amount of teaching experience. More details of the student and teacher participants in the survey can be found in Chap. 3 of this book.

Survey of CFL Learners

There are four questions related to handwriting and typing in the questionnaire for CFL learners. Questions 19 and 20 are in relation to learners' strategies while Questions 23 and 24 are about their perceptions of the two writing modalities.

Options provided in Questions 19 and 20 are informed by previous literature (Everson 1998; Shen 2005, 2010). Similar options are also used in Questions 21 and 22 for the teachers' survey, which will be discussed later. In addition to previous literature (Morgan 2012; Xu et al. 2021; Zhang and Min 2019), the statements for Questions 23 and 24 were drawn from interviews with 20 students enrolled in a Chinese language programme in New Zealand. The interviews were carried out in March 2020 when the pandemic started to have a global impact and consequently academic study took place in an exclusively online environment. They were conducted by the authors of Chap. 2 of this book.

While Question 20 has the same options as Question 19, it asks respondents to choose only the one item they believe is most helpful for their acquisition of Chinese characters.

Question 19:	Please tick all items that assist your learning of Chinese characters.
•	Rote learning (repetition)
•	Focus on radicals
•	Using imagery
•	Mnemonic associations
•	Flash cards
•	Creation of idiosyncratic stories
•	Consistently reviewing characters after class
•	Reading aloud
•	Focus on pronunciation
•	Handwriting
•	Typing characters (pinyin input)
•	Typing characters (other input methods)
•	Other (please specify)

Question 20:	Which one of these do you believe is most helpful for development of character acquisition?
•	Rote learning (repetition)
•	Focus on radicals
•	Using imagery
•	Mnemonic associations
•	Flash cards
•	Creation of idiosyncratic stories
•	Consistently reviewing characters after class
•	Reading aloud
•	Focus on pronunciation
•	Handwriting
•	Typing characters (pinyin input)
•	Typing characters (other input methods)
•	Other (please specify)

Figure 5.1 shows the results of Questions 19 and 20. Of 69 respondents, 38 answered these questions and 31 skipped them. While the majority of CFL learners (71.1%) reported that handwriting assisted with their study of Chinese characters, a substantial number of them also

5 Embodied Learning of Chinese Characters Through Typing... 113

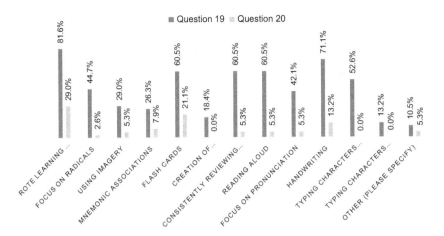

Fig. 5.1 Strategies for learning Chinese characters online

used typing, either with pinyin (52.6%) or with other input methods (13.2%). Interestingly, the top strategy that the vast majority of learners employed was rote learning (81.6%). In other words, regardless of which writing modality a learner adopted, he/she was likely to repeatedly handwrite or type characters.

However, when it came to the single most helpful strategy for learning Chinese characters, 13.2% of them chose handwriting. Handwriting was also the third most selected option among all strategies, after rote learning (29%) and flash cards (21.1%). Although many CFL learners also used typing in their learning, as shown in the results of Question 19, none of the respondents thought it to be the most helpful method of character acquisition.

Question 23 asks respondents to rate 15 statements on a scale ranging from 'strongly agree' to 'strongly disagree'. Of 69 respondents, 37 answered this question and 32 skipped it. The statements are on their positive or negative perceptions of handwriting. The positive ones consist of the values and benefits of handwriting, such as its pragmatic or emotional value. The negative ones consist of the disadvantages of handwriting, such as its being time-consuming.

Interestingly, Statement 2 relates to the situation in which handwriting can assist learning, namely face-to-face in the classroom. While the statement itself can be a neutral perception of handwriting, given the fact that the survey is about learning Chinese characters in an era of online learning, this statement suggests that handwriting is not suitable for the online environment. It is therefore grouped into the negative category. Statement 1 perceives handwriting to be an indispensable skill for the study of the Chinese language. It is consequently grouped into the positive category.

Question 23:	Please rate the following statements based on your experience of handwriting Chinese characters.			
1)	I'd feel unqualified as a Chinese learner if I couldn't write Chinese by hand.			
Strongly agree	Agree	Neither agree nor disagree	Disagree	Strongly disagree
2)	I believe learning to write by hand is more suitable for a face-to-face teaching environment.			
Strongly agree	Agree	Neither agree nor disagree	Disagree	Strongly disagree
3)	Practising handwriting is the most time-consuming part for me in learning Chinese.			
Strongly agree	Agree	Neither agree nor disagree	Disagree	Strongly disagree
4)	Handwriting is the biggest challenge for me in learning Chinese.			
Strongly agree	Agree	Neither agree nor disagree	Disagree	Strongly disagree
5)	I feel handwriting is the least useful skill we need for real-life communication.			
Strongly agree	Agree	Neither agree nor disagree	Disagree	Strongly disagree
6)	Handwriting is the most fascinating part of Chinese that has attracted me to study the language.			
Strongly agree	Agree	Neither agree nor disagree	Disagree	Strongly disagree
7)	Writing Chinese characters by hand makes me feel relaxed.			
Strongly agree	Agree	Neither agree nor disagree	Disagree	Strongly disagree
8)	Handwriting becomes helpful as my level of Chinese advances.			
Strongly agree	Agree	Neither agree nor disagree	Disagree	Strongly disagree

(continued)

(continued)

Question 23:	Please rate the following statements based on your experience of handwriting Chinese characters.
9)	Spending too much time practising handwriting has delayed my communication skills.
Strongly agree	Agree Neither agree nor disagree Disagree Strongly disagree
10)	I enjoy practising handwriting characters.
Strongly agree	Agree Neither agree nor disagree Disagree Strongly disagree
11)	I'd feel more confident in learning Chinese if my handwriting skills were no longer assessed.
Strongly agree	Agree Neither agree nor disagree Disagree Strongly disagree
12)	Handwriting is necessary especially if I study or live in China.
Strongly agree	Agree Neither agree nor disagree Disagree Strongly disagree
13)	Handwriting can help me to memorise the characters better than typing.
Strongly agree	Agree Neither agree nor disagree Disagree Strongly disagree
14)	Handwriting is very helpful when I just begin to learn Chinese.
Strongly agree	Agree Neither agree nor disagree Disagree Strongly disagree
15)	I often feel anxious that I forget how to write by hand.
Strongly agree	Agree Neither agree nor disagree Disagree Strongly disagree

In short, seven of them (Statements 2, 3, 4, 5, 9, 11 and 15) are oriented towards negative perception and the other eight (Statements 1, 6, 7, 8, 10, 12, 13 and 14) are oriented towards positive perception. The results are aggregated in the categories of positive and negative and presented in Table 5.2. Figure 5.2 shows the response rate of every statement.

For the purpose of concision, the respondents who chose 'agree' and 'strongly agree' are added together, as are those who chose 'disagree' and 'strongly disagree'.

Table 5.2 Overall learner perceptions of handwriting

	Agree	Neutral	Disagree
Positive statements	62.9%	20.5%	16.6%
Negative statements	58.3%	22.4%	19.3%

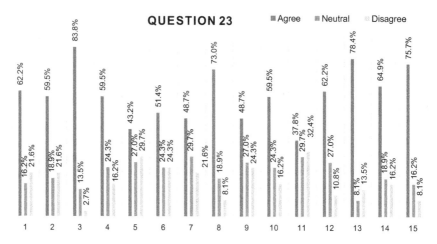

Fig. 5.2 Learner perceptions of handwriting

The fact that most respondents agree with the statements—both negative and positive—indicates that they are indeed a good representation of the general perceptions of handwriting. However, slightly more respondents (62.9%) agreed with the positive perceptions of handwriting than agreed with the negative ones (58.3%). In addition, a substantial number of respondents were either neutral on (22.4%) or disagreed with (19.3%) all the negative statements. These results suggest that there are likely mixed feelings about handwriting among CFL learners: despite recognising its disadvantages, they also acknowledge its benefits for their study of Chinese.

Details from Fig. 5.2 confirm this finding. Statement 3 ("Practising handwriting is the most time-consuming part for me in learning Chinese") was most agreed with (83.7%). However, the second most agreed statement was Statement 13 ("Handwriting can help me to memorise the characters better than typing"), with 78.3%. That is to say, while CFL learners identify the challenges of handwriting, they are also aware that this writing modality can help with their study of Chinese script.

In contrast, Question 24 consists of statements specific to typing. Similarly, these statements are also developed from interviews with CFL learners in New Zealand, as well as previous research. Of the 13 statements, nine (Statements 1, 4, 6, 7, 8, 10, 11, 12 and 13) are oriented towards positive perceptions, and four (Statements 2, 3, 5 and 9) are negative.

5 Embodied Learning of Chinese Characters Through Typing...

Question 24:	Please rate the following statements based on your experience of typing Chinese characters.
1)	The pandemic online learning experience has made me see the value of typing characters.
Strongly agree	Agree Neither agree nor disagree Disagree Strongly disagree
2)	I haven't been officially taught how to type Chinese with a keyboard in my Chinese class.
Strongly agree	Agree Neither agree nor disagree Disagree Strongly disagree
3)	The technical issues can be challenging when I type Chinese.
Strongly agree	Agree Neither agree nor disagree Disagree Strongly disagree
4)	Typing can encourage me to learn Chinese independently.
Strongly agree	Agree Neither agree nor disagree Disagree Strongly disagree
5)	Typing Chinese can be more complicated than handwriting.
Strongly agree	Agree Neither agree nor disagree Disagree Strongly disagree
6)	I prefer typing rather than handwriting for Chinese written assessments.
Strongly agree	Agree Neither agree nor disagree Disagree Strongly disagree
7)	Pinyin typing can help me with character recognition.
Strongly agree	Agree Neither agree nor disagree Disagree Strongly disagree
8)	With typing being introduced to my Chinese class, my learning progress has accelerated significantly.
Strongly agree	Agree Neither agree nor disagree Disagree Strongly disagree
9)	I feel frustrated when I have to use pinyin typing but I lack pinyin knowledge of Chinese characters.
Strongly agree	Agree Neither agree nor disagree Disagree Strongly disagree
10)	Typing is very helpful when I just begin to learn Chinese.
Strongly agree	Agree Neither agree nor disagree Disagree Strongly disagree
11)	With typing skills being widely used in my class, I feel more connected to the Chinese digital world.
Strongly agree	Agree Neither agree nor disagree Disagree Strongly disagree
12)	Typing becomes helpful as my level of Chinese advances.
Strongly agree	Agree Neither agree nor disagree Disagree Strongly disagree
13)	Typing can help me to memorise the characters better than handwriting.
Strongly agree	Agree Neither agree nor disagree Disagree Strongly disagree

For the purpose of concision, the respondents who chose 'agree' and 'strongly agree' are added together, as are those who chose 'disagree' and 'strongly disagree'. Table 5.3 shows that the majority of respondents agreed with the positive statements, and more than half of them disagreed with the negative statements. In comparison with the results for handwriting, the CFL learners seem to demonstrate a clear positive attitude towards typing.

It is worth noting that there are seven negative statements (Statements 2, 3, 4, 5, 9, 11 and 15) for handwriting, but only four (Statements 2, 3, 5 and 9) for typing. As mentioned earlier, these statements were derived from interviews with 20 CFL learners in New Zealand. The positive perceptions of typing were already evident in the comparatively small number of negative statements for this writing modality in the interview data.

Figure 5.3 presents the response rate for statements 1–13. Based on the evaluations of 37 respondents, the most agreed statements were Statement 7 ("Pinyin typing can help me with character recognition") and Statement

Table 5.3 Overall learner perceptions of typing

	Agree	Neutral	Disagree
Positive perception	61.6%	23.1%	15.3%
Negative perception	27.7%	20.3%	52.0%

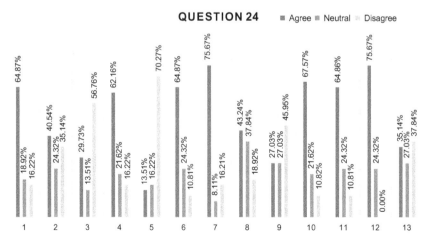

Fig. 5.3 Learner perceptions of typing

12 ("Typing becomes helpful as my level of Chinese advances"). Both were agreed with by 75.6% of respondents. Interestingly, no respondents disagreed with Statement 12.

Also interestingly, the most disagreed statement was Statement 5 ("Typing Chinese can be more complicated than handwriting"), with 70.2% disagreeing, followed by Statement 3 ("The technical issues can be challenging when I type Chinese"), with 56.7% disagreeing.

These results indicate that CFL learners not only recognise the support provided by typing but also show confidence about the technical complexity that may be involved in this writing modality.

Survey of CFL Teachers

Five questions in the survey are related to handwriting and typing: Questions 11, 12 and 15 explore the student needs identified by teachers in relation to the writing modalities, while Questions 21 and 22 are related to methods for teaching Chinese characters used in the online environment. There were 20 respondents for each question.

Question 11:	What have you identified as major needs for student character acquisition? Tick all that apply.
•	Dedicated time in class to practise handwriting
•	Specific homework tasks to practise handwriting
•	Weighted assignments involving elements of handwriting
•	Availability of character stroke order information
•	Individual feedback on character writing
•	One-on-one communication with their lecturer
•	Communication with their peers
•	Typing characters (pinyin input)
•	Typing characters (other input methods)
•	Other (please specify)

Question 11 asked the CFL teachers to identify students' needs for character acquisition. Question 12 had the same choices as Question 11, this time asking teachers to indicate any needs that could not be met in the online environment.

Question 12:	Were there any of these student needs that could not be met in an online, at-distance environment? Tick all that apply.
• • • • • • • • • •	Dedicated time in class to practise handwriting Specific homework tasks to practise handwriting Weighted assignments involving elements of handwriting Availability of character stroke order information Individual feedback on character writing One-on-one communication with their lecturer Communication with their peers Typing characters (pinyin input) Typing characters (other input methods) Other (please specify)

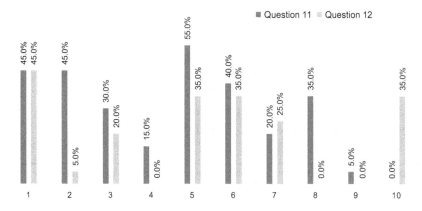

Fig. 5.4 Teachers' identification of student needs for character acquisition

Figure 5.4 shows the results of Questions 11 and 12 together. A total of 55% of teacher respondents felt that individual feedback on character writing is most needed when teaching online. The second need that 45% of teachers identified relates to practising handwriting, either with dedicated time or with specific homework. When it came to any needs that were not met during the online learning period, "dedicated time in class to practise handwriting" was ranked first (45%), followed by the lack of opportunities to offer one-on-one attention to individual learners (35%).

In contrast, teachers perceived typing to be less needed in the online environment, with only 35% choosing "typing characters (pinyin input)" and 5% choosing "typing characters (other input methods)". Interestingly, none of the respondents (0%) felt that the needs of typing were not being

5 Embodied Learning of Chinese Characters Through Typing… 121

met, which suggests that CFL teachers are quite confident about students' digital literacy. Their main concern was still "dedicated time in class to practise handwriting", an option selected by 45% of respondents.

The purpose of Question 15 was to investigate which writing modality dominates in teaching, or if both modalities are generally employed equally.

Question 15:	In relation to teaching characters in the online environment, tick the statement that is more representative of your teaching style.
•	More time is spent handwriting rather than typing characters in class.
•	More time is spent typing rather than handwriting characters in class.
•	Roughly the same amount of time is spent on handwriting and typing in class.

Of the 20 respondents who answered the question, the vast majority (75%) indicated that typing was employed more than handwriting, followed by 15% who used both modalities roughly the same amount of time (see Fig. 5.5). Interestingly, there were still a small number of

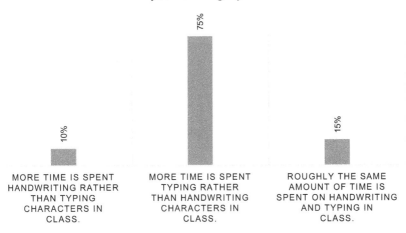

Fig. 5.5 Teaching style in relation to writing modalities

teachers (10%) who spent more time on handwriting than on typing in the online environment.

Question 21 examined the teaching methods commonly used. Question 22 followed up on this, in order to further examine which method the CFL teachers thought most helpful.

Question 21:	Please tick all character teaching methods that you usually employ in the classroom
•	Rote learning
•	Focus on radicals
•	Using imagery
•	Mnemonic associations
•	Creation of own idiosyncratic stories
•	Systematic preview and review of characters
•	Using the character in context (i.e. a sentence) to demonstrate use and meaning
•	Reading aloud
•	Focus on pronunciation
•	Handwriting
•	Typing characters (pinyin input)
•	Typing characters (other input methods)
•	Other (please specify)
Question 22:	Which one of these do you believe is most helpful for student development of character acquisition?
•	Rote learning
•	Focus on radicals
•	Using imagery
•	Mnemonic associations
•	Creation of own idiosyncratic stories
•	Systematic preview and review of characters
•	Using the character in context (i.e. a sentence) to demonstrate use and meaning
•	Reading aloud
•	Focus on pronunciation
•	Handwriting
•	Typing characters (pinyin input)
•	Typing characters (other input methods)
•	Other (please specify)

Figure 5.6 shows the results of both Questions 21 and 22. In terms of which methods were used, imagery was the most popular (75%), followed by "using the character in context" (70%). "Typing characters (pinyin input)", together with "systematic preview and review of

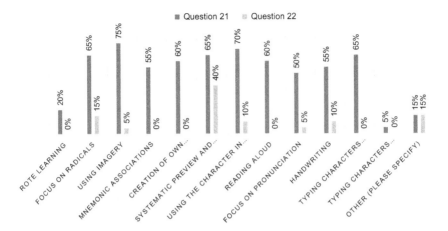

Fig. 5.6 Teaching methods in relation to writing modalities

characters" and "focus on radicals", was the third most employed (65%). However, none of these were considered very helpful for student development of characters. "Systematic preview and review of characters" was thought to be most helpful for students (40%).

Discussion

This section discusses the combined findings of the student and teacher surveys. In terms of handwriting, both learners and teachers show awareness of the potential of embodied cognition for the study of Chinese characters. Learners perceive handwriting to be the most helpful strategy for learning Chinese characters, while teachers identify practising handwriting during class time in an online environment as a major need for student character acquisition.

In terms of typing, a positive attitude of students towards typing and teacher confidence in the use of typing among learners were found in the results. While both groups acknowledge the pervasive use of typing in learning and teaching, the overall perception of this writing modality seems to be that it is unhelpful for learning Chinese characters. That is to say, neither learners nor teachers are fully aware of the embodied cognition engaged in typing and consequently do not think typing enhances the study of the Chinese writing system.

Taking a closer look at the results of the student survey (see Statements 7 and 12 in Fig. 5.3), CFL learners identified the benefits of typing in terms of character recognition, especially in the long term. As stated earlier, embodied cognition is activated in the sensorimotor experience of typing, which contributes to the learning of Chinese characters. However, the contributing effect is not as straightforward as in the case of handwriting (see Fig. 5.7), which might be why respondents perceive handwriting to be more helpful and typing to only help in the long term.

Typing Chinese requires a person to know the pronunciation of Chinese characters—'auditory encoding'—and be able to convert this to pinyin, the 'pinyin encoding' in Fig. 5.7. He/she first types the pinyin of a Chinese character. From a list of characters sharing the same pronunciation generated by the pinyin input system, he/she needs to be able to recognise and choose the intended character from the list. The pinyin typing and choosing—both done by pressing keys on a keyboard—are both examples of 'motor encoding'.

In comparison, handwriting Chinese involves looking at the visual representation of a character, the 'visual encoding' in Fig. 5.7, and then using a pen to copy the character, which is 'motor encoding'. As Zhang

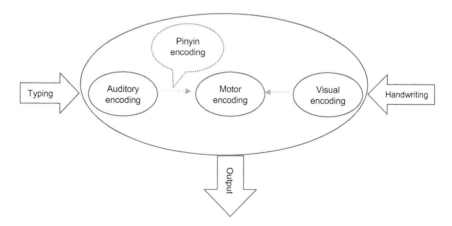

Fig. 5.7 Schematic representation of the multimodal encoding process underlying typing and handwriting. (Adapted from Zhang and Reilly 2015)

and Reilly (2015) point out, learners can go straight from the visual representation of a character to motor encoding, which potentially enhances the reciprocal connections between visual and motor representations.

Rather than being a straightforward link between visual and motor encoding, typing first auditorily encodes the visual representation of a character. An intermediate step is then needed to transform the sound of the character into its corresponding pinyin code. In this way, a reciprocal connection between the sound and its motor encoding is established.

As a result, the embodied cognition engaged in typing mainly supports the learning of the pronunciation of Chinese characters. Thus, typing is likely to contribute to phonology recognition. In contrast, the embodied cognition involved in handwriting strongly supports the acquisition of a character's visual-orthographic representation. Consequently, CFL teachers prefer handwriting for the purpose of linking the sensory-motor experience with the visual representation of a character.

Unlike the literacy route of grapheme-sound-meaning for European alphabetic languages, the pictographic origin and logographic nature of Chinese script lead to a lack of fixed and transparent grapheme-phoneme mapping (Zhang and Min 2019). For this reason, literacy in Chinese can take the route of grapheme-visualisation-meaning, with sound barely involved (Lu 2020). Indeed, the literacy route of Chinese seems to suggest that learning the pronunciation of characters could be neglected, which also explains the prominence of handwriting and lack of attention to typing in teaching and learning.

In these circumstances, Lu (2020) proposes that Chinese is a dual-modal language. Learners need to go through dual-modal processing of a new character—grapheme-phoneme and grapheme-morpheme mappings in parallel—to acquire its sound, shape and meaning. As mentioned above, embodied cognition of typing includes conversion of the grapheme > pronunciation (auditory encoding) > phoneme (pinyin encoding). It is therefore possible for typing to (indirectly) assist with the establishment and consolidation of grapheme-phoneme mapping (see Fig. 5.8).

While the value of typing in learning Chinese characters seems to be underestimated, learners and teachers also demonstrate awareness of the unsustainability of handwriting in the online environment (see the results

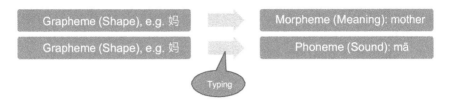

Fig. 5.8 Dual-modal processing in learning Chinese characters

of Statements 2 and 3 in Fig. 5.2 and Fig. 5.4). Indeed, online learning provides learners with multimodal repertoires which consist of traditional linguistic features (lexical, morphological, syntactical, etc.) and other meaning-making signs embodied in semiotic modes such as gestures, posture and broader semiotic practices of using technologies (Vogel et al. 2018).

For example, "focusing on radicals" and "using imagery" are predominant methods used by teachers (see Fig. 5.6) and also employed by a small number of students (see Fig. 5.1). Some teacher respondents specified that pictures and animations of radicals can be generated and shared with students. Learners also stated that image-processing software allows users to circle different radicals of a character, which can assist their study of the character. Moreover, both students and teachers consider reviewing characters to be very helpful (see Figs. 5.2 and 5.6). Software, such as PowerPoint and Quizlet, was also mentioned by both teachers and students as assisting with systematic preview and review of characters.[2]

While CFL learners and teachers both recognise the multimodal semiotics afforded by technologies in the virtual world, they seem to overlook the fact that most of them rely on typing. Importantly, typing Chinese is in itself a multimodal process requiring conversions between visual and auditory modes. However, as shown earlier, it is exactly this multimodal process that leads learners and teachers to undervalue this writing modality for character acquisition.

Although the pervasive use of typing and the marginalisation of handwriting have become significant in ERT, the practice of these two writing

---

[2] These findings were also obtained from the open-ended questions in the survey, such as "Based on your answer to Question 22, how can this be incorporated online?". However, the results are not presented in detail in this chapter due to space limitations.

modalities in the future online environment does not need to be a choice between one and the other. Electronic devices already penetrate almost every aspect of our daily life, making typing an integral part of day-to-day communication; however, members of Generation Z, who never experienced life before the Internet (Turner 2015), still see the advantages of handwriting, whether in assisting their character acquisition or for personal enjoyment (see results for Statements 10 and 13 in Fig. 5.2). The intriguing thing is that these digital natives accustomed to typing are unaware of the potential embodied cognition engaged in the multimodal process of typing and therefore do not see its immediate benefits for the study of characters.

Since the survey shows that most CFL teachers tend to either mainly employ typing or balance the two writing modalities (see Fig. 5.5), it may contribute to increasing acknowledgement of the contributing effect of the embodied cognition engaged in typing. In addition, when learners are already members of a generation with unprecedented exposure to multimodal semiotics in their social milieu, embodiment offers a theoretical framework to capture the bodily activities and sensory experiences—including typing—engaged in the virtual, multimodal space. A scrutiny of embodied cognition involved in distributed and extended teaching and learning may provide insights into the digital future of language learning.

Conclusion

This chapter examines the CFL teaching and learning practice during ERT, with a specific focus on handwriting and typing. The findings indicate that handwriting is perceived as more helpful for character acquisition than typing. An overall positive attitude can be observed towards typing, especially for learning character pronunciation and long-term study. However, the potential of the embodied cognition engaged in typing to assist the study of Chinese characters is not recognised by learners or teachers, probably due to the multimodal process of conversion between auditory and visual encoding involved in typing. Even though they are aware of the multimodal repertoires offered in the virtual space, they seem to overlook the fact that typing is the essential tool to access these resources.

Because of the unsustainability of handwriting in an online learning environment, CFL teachers mainly employ typing or at least endeavour to have a balanced use of handwriting and typing to teach Chinese characters. With the inevitably increasing use of typing in the virtual learning space, it is essential to raise awareness of the potential of the embodied cognition engaged in typing, in order to assist and guide teachers and learners to move between the two writing modalities to help with the learning of Chinese characters. This study employs embodiment as the theoretical framework to depict the practice and perceptions of handwriting and typing, which exemplifies the application of embodiment in future research to investigate teaching and learning in the virtual space.

One of the main limitations of this study that ought to be considered for generalising the results is the relatively small number of participants. There were only 58 valid questionnaires—38 from students and 20 from teachers—returned from a survey across six English-speaking countries. The small sample size restricts further statistical analysis, including any potential effects of variables such as the language proficiency of learners and the teaching experience of language instructors. For the same reason, factor analysis cannot be performed for the perception statements of handwriting and typing. As noted earlier, there were seven negative statements for handwriting and only four negative ones for typing. Without sophisticated statistical modelling, the findings do not necessarily lead to definite conclusions. Future research is recommended to address this limitation by enlarging the number of participants and using statistical inquiry to enhance the generalisability of findings.

Ethical Approval Ethical approval was granted by the University College Dublin Ethics Committee in 2021 (HS-E-21-183-Osbourne).

Competing Interests This study was funded by University College Dublin's Global Engagement Seed Fund 2021 and the Chinese Embassy in Ireland.

References

Allen, Joseph R. 2008. Why Learning to Write Chinese is a Waste of Time: A Modest Proposal. *Foreign Language Annals* 41 (2): 237–251. https://doi.org/10.1111/j.1944-9720.2008.tb03291.x.

Atkinson, Dwight. 2010. Extended, Embodied Cognition and Second Language Acquisition. *Applied Linguistics* 31 (5): 599–622. https://doi.org/10.1093/applin/amq009.

———. 2019. Beyond the Brain: Intercorporeality and Co-Operative Action for SLA Studies. *The Modern Language Journal* 103 (4): 724–738. https://doi.org/10.1111/modl.12595.

Blackledge, Adrian, and Angela Creese. 2017. Translanguaging and the Body. *International Journal of Multilingualism* 14 (3): 250–268. https://doi.org/10.1080/14790718.2017.1315809.

Cao, Fan, Ben Rickles, Vu Marianne, Ziheng Zhu, Derek Ho Lung Chan, Lindsay N. Harris, Joseph Stafura, Yi Xu, and Charles A. Perfetti. 2013. Early Stage Visual-Orthographic Processes Predict Long-Term Retention of Word Form and Meaning: A Visual Encoding Training Study. *Journal of Neurolinguistics* 26 (4): 440–461. https://doi.org/10.1016/j.jneuroling.2013.01.003.

Chan, Tikky S. P., Elizabeth K. Y. Loh, and Cathy O. Y. Hung. 2021. A Longitudinal Study of Chinese as a Second Language Kindergarteners' Orthographic Awareness and Its Association with Their Lexical Learning Performance. *Current Psychology*, May. https://doi.org/10.1007/s12144-021-01797-2

Craighero, Laila. 2014. The Role of the Motor System in Cognitive Functions. In *The Routledge Handbook of Embodied Cognition*, ed. Lawrence Shapiro, 51–58. London and New York: Routledge, Taylor & Francis Group.

Ellis, Nick C. 2019. Essentials of a Theory of Language Cognition. *The Modern Language Journal* 103 (January): 39–60. https://doi.org/10.1111/modl.12532.

Everson, Michael E. 1998. Word Recognition among Learners of Chinese as a Foreign Language: Investigating the Relationship between Naming and Knowing. *The Modern Language Journal* 82 (2): 194–204. https://doi.org/10.2307/329208.

Everson, Michael E., and Yun Xiao. 2009. *Literacy Development in Chinese as a Foreign Language*. Boston: Cheng & Tsui Company.

Guan, Connie Qun, Ying Liu, Derek Ho Leung Chan, Feifei Ye, and Charles A. Perfetti. 2011. Writing Strengthens Orthography and Alphabetic-Coding Strengthens Phonology in Learning to Read Chinese. *Journal of Educational Psychology* 103 (3): 509–522. https://doi.org/10.1037/a0023730.

Guan, Connie Qun, Charles A. Perfetti, and Wanjin Meng. 2015. Writing Quality Predicts Chinese Learning. *Reading and Writing* 28 (6): 763–795. https://doi.org/10.1007/s11145-015-9549-0.

Hodges, Charles, Stephanie Moore, Barb Lockee, Torrey Trust, and Aaron Bond. 2020. The Difference Between Emergency Remote Teaching and Online Learning. *EDUCAUSE Review*, March 27, 2020. https://er.educause.edu/articles/2020/3/the-difference-between-emergency-remote-teaching-and-online-learning.

Kubler, Cornelius. 2020. Considerations in Preparing Pedagogical Materials for Adult Native English-Speaking Learners of Chinese as a Second/Foreign Language. In *The Routledge Handbook of Chinese Language Teaching*, ed. Chris Shei, Monica McLellan Zikpi, and Der-Lin Chao, 321–335. London and New York: Routledge.

Kuo, Li-Jen, Ying Li, Mark Sadoski, and Tae-Jin Kim. 2014. Acquisition of Chinese Characters: The Effects of Character Properties and Individual Differences among Learners. *Contemporary Educational Psychology* 39 (4): 287–300. https://doi.org/10.1016/j.cedpsych.2014.07.001.

Lu, Ming-Tsan Pierre. 2011. *The Effect of Instructional Embodiment Designs on Chinese Language Learning: The Use of Embodied Animation for Beginning Learners of Chinese Characters*. Ph.D. diss., Columbia University. http://academiccommons.columbia.edu/catalog/ac:132065.

Lu, Rugang. 2020. Multimodal Pedagogy and Chinese Visual Arts in TCFL Classrooms. In *The Routledge Handbook of Chinese Language Teaching*, ed. Chris Shei, Monica E. McLellan Zikpi, and Der-Lin Chao. Oxon: Routledge.

Lu, Ming-Tsan Pierre, Gregory L. Hallman Jr., and John B. Black. 2013. Chinese Character Learning: Using Embodied Animations in Initial Stages. *Journal of Technology and Chinese Language Teaching* 4 (2): 1–24.

Lyu, Boning, Chun Lai, Chin-Hsi Lin, and Yang Gong. 2021. Comparison Studies of Typing and Handwriting in Chinese Language Learning: A Synthetic Review. *International Journal of Educational Research* 106 (101740). https://doi.org/10.1016/j.ijer.2021.101740.

Michaels, Claire F., and Zsolt Palatinus. 2014. A Ten Commandments for Ecological Psychology. In *The Routledge Handbook of Embodied Cognition*, ed. Lawrence Shapiro, 19–28. London and New York: Routledge, Taylor & Francis Group.

Morgan, Yuan-Yu Karen. 2012. *Attitudes toward Hanzi Production Ability among Chinese Teachers and Learners*. PhD diss., Purdue University. https://docs.lib.purdue.edu/dissertations/AAI3545325.

Perfetti, Charles, Fan Cao, and James Booth. 2013. Specialization and Universals in the Development of Reading Skill: How Chinese Research Informs a Universal Science of Reading. *Scientific Studies of Reading* 17 (1): 5–21. https://doi.org/10.1080/10888438.2012.689786.

Shen, Helen H. 2005. An Investigation of Chinese-Character Learning Strategies among Non-Native Speakers of Chinese. *System* 33 (1): 49–68. https://doi.org/10.1016/j.system.2004.11.001.

———. 2010. Analysis of Radical Knowledge Development among Beginning CFL Learners. In *Research among Learners of Chinese as a Foreign Language*, ed. Michael Everson and Helen H. Shen. Hawaii: National Foreign Language Resource Center.

———. 2013. Chinese L2 Literacy Development: Cognitive Characteristics, Learning Strategies, and Pedagogical Interventions. *Language and Linguistics Compass* 7 (7): 371–387. https://doi.org/10.1111/lnc3.12034.

Shen, Helen H., and Chuanren Ke. 2007. Radical Awareness and Word Acquisition among Nonnative Learners of Chinese. *The Modern Language Journal* 91 (1): 97–111. https://doi.org/10.1111/j.1540-4781.2007.00511.x.

Shu, Hua, Xi Chen, Richard C. Anderson, Wu Ningning, and Yue Xuan. 2003. Properties of School Chinese: Implications for Learning to Read. *Child Development* 74 (1): 27–47. https://doi.org/10.1111/1467-8624.00519.

Tan, Li Hai, John A. Spinks, Guinevere F. Eden, Charles A. Perfetti, and Wai Ting Siok. 2005. Reading Depends on Writing, in Chinese. *Proceedings of the National Academy of Sciences* 102 (24): 8781–8785. https://doi.org/10.1073/pnas.0503523102.

Turner, Anthony. 2015. Generation Z: Technology and Social Interest. *The Journal of Individual Psychology* 71 (2): 103–113. https://doi.org/10.1353/jip.2015.0021.

Vogel., S, L. Ascenzi-Moreno, and Ofelia García. 2018. 'An Expanded View of Translanguaging: Leveraging the Dynamic Interactions between a Young Multilingual Writer and Machine Translation Software'. In Plurilingualism in Teaching and Learning: Complexities Across Contexts, edited by J. Choi and S. Ollerhead. London and New York: Routledge, Taylor & Francis Group.

Wong, Lung-Hsiang, Ching-Sing Chai, and Ping Gao. 2011. The Chinese Input Challenges for Chinese as Second Language Learners in Computer-Mediated Writing: An Exploratory Study. *The Turkish Online Journal of Educational Technology* 10 (3): 17.

Xu, Yi, Li Jin, Elizabeth Deifell, and Katie Angus. 2021. Facilitating Technology-based Character Learning in Emergency Remote Teaching. *Foreign Language Annals*, June, 1–26. https://doi.org/10.1111/flan.12541.

Zhang, Qi, and Angela Leahy. 2022. A Multimodal Approach to the Technological Representations in CFL Textbooks: *Chinese as a Second Language [漢語教學研究—美國中文教師學會學報]* 56 (3): 229–254. https://doi.org/10.1075/csl.21002.zha.

Zhang, Qi, and Ge Min. 2019. Chinese Writing Composition among CFL Learners: A Comparison between Handwriting and Typewriting. *Computers and Composition* 54 (December): 102522. https://doi.org/10.1016/j.compcom.2019.102522.

Zhang, Qi, and Ronan G Reilly. 2015. Writing to Read: The Case of Chinese. *29th Pacific Asia Conference on Language, Information and Computation*: 345–54.

Zhang, Qi, and Ronan G. Reilly. 2020. What Regions of Chinese Characters Are Crucial for Recognition? A Web-Based Study. *Journal of Chinese Writing Systems* 4 (4): 297–311. https://doi.org/10.1177/2513850220950020.

Zhang, Qi, Xu Lin, and Caitríona Osborne. 2022. A Think-Aloud Method of Investigating Translanguaging Strategies in Learning Chinese Characters. *Applied Linguistics Review*, October. https://doi.org/10.1515/applirev-2022-0135.

Theme III

Development of Methodologies and Theories for Character Teaching

6

Enhancing Understanding and Engagement with the Chinese Writing System in Second Language Classrooms

Andrew Scrimgeour

Introduction

The challenges the Chinese writing system presents to young Chinese as a second language (CSL) learners are well understood (Orton 2016b; Loh et al. 2018; Orton and Scrimgeour 2019). The Chinese character system is a complex and distant orthography from an English alphabetic perspective. The number of characters, and range and arrangement of stroke patterns within them appears endless, and the functional properties of semantic and phonetic radicals in compound characters are both unreliable and take time to emerge (Everson 2007, 2011; Švarcová 2023). Yet the time on task to come to terms with these challenges in school-based contexts is notoriously limited (Orton 2016b). For the majority of CSL students, the time spent learning Chinese in school is typically short, perhaps six years (around 40 hours per year) at primary school, and/or

---

A. Scrimgeour (✉)
University of South Australia, Adelaide, SA, Australia
e-mail: andrew.scrimgeour@unisa.edu.au

© The Author(s), under exclusive license to Springer Nature Switzerland AG 2024
C. Osborne et al. (eds.), *Teaching Chinese Characters in the Digital Age*, Palgrave Studies on Chinese Education in a Global Perspective,
https://doi.org/10.1007/978-3-031-64784-0_6

two or three years (around 80 hours per year) in junior secondary school (Orton 2016a; Scrimgeour 2023). Data on student retention in languages in Australian schools (Scrimgeour 2023) indicate that across languages it is common for the majority of students to 'drop out' of language study by the middle secondary years, with less than 15% of students remaining in Chinese language courses after three years of secondary study (Years 7–9). Perceptions of difficulty, the workload required and competition for grades with learners who use Chinese at home or attend community school are often put forward as reasons for leaving the Chinese classroom 'early' (Scrimgeour 2014b; Orton 2016c). Thus, while rationale for learning Chinese in schools typically refer to future-focused vocational and educational opportunities, the reality is that for most young learners the actual outcomes are limited, and often negative, as their limited learning experience and exposure to the system reinforces perceptions of the difficulties in achieving any meaningful communicative outcomes in the CSL classroom (Orton 2016b, 2016c; Scrimgeour 2014a).

Orton and Scrimgeour (2019), for example, report on a study of learners completing six years of Chinese study at primary school in Australia. When asked to describe a Chinese character, some students were able to refer to radicals, pictographs and rules for stroke order, but overall, their appreciation of Chinese writing was best reflected in the comment 'A Chinese character is … "a whole lot of lines going everywhere to make a word"' (Orton and Scrimgeour 2019, p. 54). Finding ways to overcome learner misconceptions and train the hand, eye and mind of novice learners to understand and appreciate at least the visual properties of Chinese characters, if not their functional roles, may contribute to an improved overall perception of recurrent components in the Chinese writing system and enhance the experiences of those engaging with it, no matter how limited the exposure.

The Nature of the Chinese Writing System

The orthographic structure of the Chinese writing system is usually described at three levels, with the Chinese character (hanzi 汉字) considered the basic unit of the system, composed of radicals (both semantic and phonetic) which are in turn composed of strokes (Shen 2005). In general terms, the character system contains two types of characters, basic and compound. Basic characters (独体字) are composed of a single stroke pattern or component, which is not decomposable into smaller discernible parts. According to Xu Shen's six-character classifications (六书) as outlined in Yin and Rohsenow (1994), basic characters are typically derived from pictographs (象形字) and ideographs (指事字). Compound characters (合体字) contain (at least) two discernible stroke patterns or components, organised into two sides.

These two sides are commonly referred to as radicals: the semantic radical, which conveys information related to the meaning of the character, and the other, the phonetic radical, likely to indicate the sound (in 形声字) or further semantic information (会意字) in a limited number of cases. The way the system functions to convey sound and meaning information in the majority of compound characters is typically described as inconsistent and unreliable. Shu (2003) estimates the 200 or so semantic radicals provide meaningful semantic information in only 58% of cases, while the 1100 or so phonetic radicals indicate precise sounds of compound characters in which they appear in only 39% of cases. A few basic and compound characters are now used as grammatical morphemes and are no longer easily explained (专注字 and 假借字) by their etymological origins (e.g., 也, 都, 不). Basic characters make up around 5% of the character corpus, semantic-phonetic compounds 80%, semantic compounds 10% and reused characters 5% (Shu 2003).

Learner's Exposure to Form and Function in the Chinese Writing System

The list of 8105 characters in the Table of General Standard Chinese Characters (通用规范汉字表) (Ministry of Education 2013) includes 3500 commonly used (high frequency) characters. A shorter list of 3000 characters is included in the Chinese Proficiency Grading Standards for International Chinese Language Education (Ministry of Education 2021). Semantic and phonetic information conveyed in radicals tends to be more reliable in lower frequency characters (Shu et al. 2003) (i.e., characters not commonly used), suggesting that access to reliable sound and meaning information in radicals encountered is lower for both young Chinese learners and for second language learners.

In a study of the 2570 characters taught in primary school in China, Shu et al. (2003) found that while average stroke number (i.e., visual complexity) per character was lower, the phonetic regularity and semantic transparency in compound characters on this list was significantly lower than in larger studies of the entire character system. Of the 436 characters taught at the start of formal literacy education in the first year of primary school, basic characters (which convey no semantic or phonetic information) comprise 26% of the total, (significantly higher than the 5% in larger studies), while semantic compounds comprise 22% (10% in larger studies) and semantic-phonetic compound characters constitute only 45% of the total, compared to around 80% in larger studies. In the semantic-phonetic compounds encountered in primary school, there are 563 phonetic radical families (characters sharing a common phonetic side), but the transfer of phonetic information is very low, with 90% of these phonetic radicals recurring in only one to three characters, providing little opportunity for young learners to gain any deeper appreciation of how such phonetic information applies. The 124 semantic radical families included in the primary school character list have relatively higher frequencies of use and may be more beneficial as learners progress in their character learning and use. Overall, however, while patterns in how clues to sound and meaning are conveyed and the reliabilities of this information in compound characters do emerge, these patterns are unlikely to emerge early, and may only become a source of useful information as learners' literacy skills develop over time.

The implications for CSL learners are also significant. Given the limited exposure to characters in such contexts, developing awareness of how sound and meaning information is represented in compound characters is particularly slow and uncertain (Loh et al. 2018; Orton and Scrimgeour 2019). A comparative study of two character lists designed for CSL learners (The HSK Graded list (900 characters) and the EBCL A2 list (630 characters)), Zhang et al. (2019) found similar trends to Shu et al.'s (2003) study. The visual-orthographic information in many characters encountered at the early stages of Chinese second language learning appears less complex (contains fewer strokes) and includes more basic characters (around 20% of the total); however, compound characters on both lists are less transparent semantically and phonetically than found in larger character corpus. The challenges in learning to understand the nature of the Chinese writing system for new CSL learners in school-based contexts are even greater as they will encounter a much smaller number of characters across their years of school-based Chinese language learning. The Victorian Certificate of Education Character list (VCAA 2018), for example, includes a list of 440 characters that students are expected to know after a minimum of 200 hours of study (by the end of Year 10), prior to their senior secondary years (Year 11 and 12). The emerging awareness of the functional reliability of semantic and phonetic information emerging in compound characters encountered in that limited set of characters is likely to be even more limited.

While some explicit teaching of higher frequency semantic radical function in individual character samples is common in such school-based CSL contexts, evidence of the reliability or variability in phonetic radical function is incidental at best for novice CSL learners. Consequently, the primary focus of learners' attention is typically directed more to the visual-orthographic properties of each character, typically presented as stroke sequences for writing practice (Everson 2007, 2011; Osborne et al. 2018; Orton and Scrimgeour 2019; Švarcová 2023). Coming to terms with unfamiliar visual-orthographic features of each new character—in terms of both the range of strokes used and the diversity of stroke patterns and their configurations in each character—is in itself a significant learning task. Chinese language textbooks encourage learners to rely on routine stroke-by-stroke character practice to hopefully internalise the whole-of-character form, and perhaps its sound and meaning. Unable to rely on prior knowledge of the semantic and phonetic function of radical sides, learning to map a new character form onto its specific sound and meaning depends largely on basic memorisation skills, typically supported by routine writing practice and regular exposure to such characters in reading and writing activity. Developing an enhanced level of understanding of the Chinese writing system, limited by both low input (in terms of the number of characters) and low exposure (in terms of time on task) needs significant pedagogical intervention if outcomes in terms of learning to read and write in Chinese are to be improved. The role for teachers and for resources in appreciating these challenges from the learner's perspective is even more crucial to improving initial literacy skills in Chinese in such contexts.

Research into Teaching and Learning of the Chinese Writing System

Issues with Terminology

Research on character teaching and learning is typically founded on the premise that the Chinese writing system is composed of three-tiers of orthographic structure: characters, radicals and strokes (Shen 2005), which prioritises learning to understand the functional properties of semantic and phonetic radicals when learning compound characters in particular. However, descriptions of the nature of the orthographic features of the Chinese writing system often display some inconsistencies or complexities in how some key features of the system are described.

There remains a lack of consensus about terminology for defining key structural and functional properties of the Chinese writing system (Isselé et al. 2022). The use of the terms 'radical' and 'component' to describe features of the internal structure of compound characters appears occasionally interchangeable and consequently confusing. Myers (2019), for example, refers to a 'phonetic component' when referring to a phonetic radical or side, which may be composed of more than one 'stroke pattern', as in the phonetic side 各 (in the characters 阁 or 格) which is, in effect, composed of two components: 夂 and 口. A significant number of phonetic radicals are multi-component units (Isselé et al. 2022), many of which occur as compound characters themselves (i.e., 各). A smaller number of semantic radicals are also multi-component units (e.g., 香食音麻鼻). Consequently, in this discussion, the term 'radical' is preferred when referring to the *functional* classification of a particular side in a compound character, irrespective of the number of constituent components, be it the semantic radical side (部首 bùshǒu) or the phonetic radical side (声旁 shēngpáng). The term 'component' (部件 bùjiàn) is hereafter used to refer to the smallest visual-orthographic units in a character, each distinguishable stroke pattern that cannot be readily decomposed into simpler, identifiable parts. The Ministry of Education *Specification of Common Modern Chinese Character Components and Component Names* (M.O.E. 2009) describes a component as "a character formation unit consisting of strokes that has the function of forming Chinese characters" (由笔画组成的具有组配汉子功能的构字单位). Each individual stroke pattern/component may form a basic character (独体字) on its own or be used in combination with other components to form a compound character (合体字) (Loh et al. 2018). The terms 'radical' and 'component' may refer to the same orthographic unit when both sides of a compound character are single components, as in the characters 汉, 名, 岁 and 床. However, multi-component characters such as 敏 contain two *functional* radical sides, 每+攵, but three *structural* components, 人+母+攵.

Orthographic Levels of the Chinese Writing System for CSL Learners

This distinction between the functional radical-sides and structural components is important when discussing the character system from the L2 learner's perspective. Loh et al. (2018) argue that given the notoriously unreliable and largely inaccessible functional information provided by semantic and phonetic radicals, components may be a more important focus for character learning for CSL students. Loh et al. (2018) therefore argue that, from the learner's perspective, describing the orthographic tiers of the Chinese writing system at the levels of strokes, components (rather than radicals) and characters may be more appropriate in CSL contexts. However given the important, albeit unreliable function of phonetic radicals in particular, it may be more appropriate to describe the orthographic structure at four levels; strokes, which are used to create components (which may also be basic characters), which compose radicals, which in turn create compound characters (which in turn create words).

The Component System

The logic of taking a component-oriented approach to character learning is reinforced by the fact that these 300 characters on the HSK1 300 list are composed of a smaller number of 226 components.

Identifying the number of components in any list of characters is problematic. Myers (2019) argues that proponents of a component inventory are attempting the impossible, given the challenges in determining the degree of deconstruction and in identifying and naming of each component included on such a list. Nevertheless, it has become increasingly common for component lists to be included in character inventories for educational purposes. Fei (1996) identified 384 components, and the more recent M.O.E. (2009) list, 514 components. The list of components compiled in Hong Kong for full form characters contains 644 components (Loh et al. 2018). An analysis undertaken by the author of the 300 characters included in the new HSK Level 1 character list (M.O.E. 2021) (HSK1 300 hereafter) identifies components new CSL learners are likely to encounter within an initial period of learning. A total of 68 basic (single component) characters and 232 compound (multi (two to four) component) characters are included on the list. Using a process of character decomposition (i.e., identifying the minimal character formation units comprised of a stroke pattern of more than one stroke) to identify components, a total of 226 individual components were identified, 119 (52%) of which occur more than once and 107 (48%) appearing only once in the list. Of these 107 single-use components, 30 are basic characters (characters such as 东, 个, 中, 么, 九, 书, 了), the rest (77) occur only once as character components, such as 宀, 凵, 匚, 卩, 垂, 幺, 彡 (some of which may be low-frequency whole characters, not included on the HSK list). Of the 119, recurrent components, 38 occur as basic characters as well as character components, including such high-frequency components such as 口 (48 times), 日 (21), 人 (14), 儿 (13) and 月 (11). The remainder are 'dependent' components (or 'bound forms' – 非成字) and include high frequency (semantic radical) forms such as 亻 (15 times), 讠 (13), 又 (8), 宀 (8), 辶 (8) and 匕 (7), most of which have a (pinyin) sound and (English) meaning and are readily named. There are, however, a large number of additional components which are seldom referenced (or named) in Chinese as they are sub-component forms which typically only occur in combination in a radical side (typically the phonetic). These component types also typically do not have a 'digital identity' (a Unicode number) and cannot be created digitally via pinyin input or other means. Examples of such components include the top-left component in 有 and 在, the upper component in 老, the lower component in 官 and the enclosing sides of 商 and 南. These remain, however, orthographic units that learners will encounter and must learn, and somehow relate to in order to instil them in the memory, while differentiating between them and other similar forms.

Research on CSL Learner Perceptions of Learning to Read and Write in Chinese

The important role that components do play as a key unit of character perception or identification in character learning is well recognised (Anderson et al. 2013). Young first language learners who do acquire insight into character structure by identifying (or discriminating between) components are likely to make more progress in learning to read (Shu et al. 2003). For novice second language learners keen to grasp the basics of a new orthography, a component-oriented approach—a focus on the individual stroke patterns or components as the smallest integral stroke patterns within a character, like letters in a word—may be more pedagogically valuable than current practices.

While a deeper appreciation of distinctive features of the Chinese writing system—the structural arrangement of components (including positional regularities) in compound characters and the functional properties of radicals—may develop through input and experience over time, there is significant likelihood that for most school-based CSL learners few insights into how to deal with the visual complexity of characters beyond mundane writing practice would be achieved. For learners who abandon their Chinese language studies after a few years of study, their experience is likely to reinforce the general perception of the difficulties inherent in learning to read and write in Chinese. The Chinese writing system itself may not be the only problem, however. Yang's (2022) study of teenage perceptions of character learning indicates that students do value learning Chinese characters and see writing practice as a useful means to memorise characters, but highlights the challenges they face with memorising stroke order in particular. Yang's (2022) study highlights the fact that despite learner interest and keenness for character learning, students appear to lack a well-developed metalanguage or set of terms for talking about their knowledge and experience. While learners in Yang's (2022) study show awareness in their explanations of the function of (semantic) radicals and the potential value in knowing this information, they appear less aware of emerging patterns in, and structural regularities of, recurring components. This suggests that broader appreciation of all levels of the orthographic system is neither emerging nor widely applied in their learning. Students did, however, recognise the need to pay attention to finer details in stroke patterns when they encounter characters or components that display similarity in form (such as in 王 and 玉, for example).

A recent study by Deng and Hu (2022) on character writing errors indicates a basic awareness of a component-level structure in characters, with constituent parts generally positioned correctly even if the stroke patterns of those parts were not yet well internalised. The study identified the types of errors found in a large corpus of L2 student character writing. Errors in the size and configuration (intersection etc.) of strokes, omissions of individual strokes or overreliance on similar, probably more familiar stroke patterns, suggest that visual ambiguity, or uncertainty with specific stroke patterns, remains a key impediment to accurate reproduction of the entire character, and consequently to the quality of their writing overall. Focusing on assisting students to overcome the visual ambiguity between recurrent stroke patterns with variable stroke configurations or additional strokes (i.e., 土-上, 主-王, 刀-力, 办 -为, 头-太) may be crucial to promoting rapid development of orthographic awareness and successful writing development (Deng and Hu 2022).

Švarcová's (2023) study of dropout rates in school-based elective Chinese classes in Czechia also indicates a high degree of learner interest in Chinese character study, despite the challenges and obstacles they face. Švarcová notes there is a fine line between enjoyment and boredom in character learning, especially where excessive handwriting practice is seen as the only way to internalise characters effectively. While students show enthusiasm for the handwriting challenge, the memory load and necessity for ongoing repetitive practice are seen as an impediment to their sense of satisfaction and success. This is particularly so, Švarcová suggests, where memorisation testing in dictation activities—requiring accurate recall of character stroke sequences—is used as a measure of progress, for example. The studies by Yang (2022) and Švarcová (2023) both indicate that while students find interest in characters and are initially keen to learn more, the demands of routine practice without systematic development of learners' understanding of recurring visual-orthographic features—the components—may in the long run be detrimental to both motivation and a sense of achievement in the CSL classroom.

A study of character learning strategies by Osborne et al. (2018) also highlights learners' reliance on routine character practice to memorise characters. Their study showed character practice to be more effective than other strategies such as an integrated macroskill approach, or a delayed start to character learning. There was, however, no evidence of teachers applying alternative strategies which might provide deeper conceptual, orthographic insights into the structural features of characters encountered as a means of facilitating character learning in a more conceptual, systematic manner.

What has always been a significant element of the CSL experience is the seemingly inordinate amount of time and attention given to routine character practice. There are some good reasons for this. Handwriting training has been found to play a critical role in reading development across languages and orthographies, with skilled reading in Chinese first language learners highly correlated to the ability to copy characters (from memory) (Tan et al. 2005) and is particularly useful in learning discrete variations between characters (Xu et al. 2020). Handwriting practice helps promote awareness of visual features of characters. It strengthens the connection between form and meaning (Hsiung et al. 2017), providing a mental model of the orthographic form which becomes stabilised and long lasting in the memory (Guan et al. 2011). However, students often describe their writing practice experience as mindless and repetitive, suggesting that during their practice routines, students are not encouraged to attend to the finer orthographic details within and across characters they encounter (Allen 2008; Lu et al. 2019; Švarcová 2023).

The issues with over-reliance on routine character practice as a means of literacy development in Chinese have been debated for some time (Allen 2008; Lu et al. 2019). In a review of recent literature on research into character teaching and learning, Li (2020) noted a number of debates over the manner in which characters are taught in second language contexts. One debate (Ye 2013) focuses on the timing of the introduction of character teaching and learning; whether characters be introduced from the outset or character learning be delayed until a degree of oral language proficiency has been achieved. Ye (2013) suggests that reading development in Chinese is likely to be slow, which may hinder the growth in oral language development and consequently reduce efficiency and effectiveness of overall instruction. Proposals for a separation of curriculum into oral and written strands are countered by the argument that there is no such precedent in second language curriculum, nor any consensus on what the optimal timing for the reintegration of oral-based and character-based learning may be (Zhao 2011).

A more recent debate has emerged over whether pinyin typing is now so pervasive in online text communication that it should in fact fully replace routine character practice, and character handwriting more generally. A range of studies undertaken over recent years indicate that creating digital texts using pinyin input, typically done at the bi-syllabic word-centred level, enhances word recognition and reading efficiency, strengthens sound to form relationships and leads to significant improvements in length and accuracy of digitally generated texts (Zhang, 2021). Proponents of pinyin typing naturally find issue with the traditional handwriting practice method, especially at the outset where the demands of time and mental energy required when coming to terms with graphic features of so many characters are so great, hindering oral language development. Zhang (2021) describes the 'meaningless stroke-based pedagogy' of routine character writing as counterproductive, distracting, inefficient and likely to have a negative impact on form-focused production. Zhang and Min (2019), however, argue that some initial, introductory handwriting training may assist learners in character identification or recognition during later typing-based activities. CSL learners still view handwriting experience as an essential means to remember characters (Jiang 2023), noting that while university students overwhelmingly preferred pinyin keyboarding for communication, a significant proportion were unwilling to give up character practice as the best means of instilling a specific stroke sequence in the motor-memory. Handwriting training is clearly as much about perceptual learning as it is about motor-memory. Handwriting training seems to boost recognition of visual graphs and has a consequential effect on learning to read. Therefore, it is still relevant to literacy instruction in the digital age (Araújo et al. 2022).

Criticisms of the routine writing practice as a method of character learning tend to focus on the lack of meaningfulness or systematicity in having to learn individual characters in isolation, attempting to memorise each new character as a unitary whole, seemingly unaware of regularities in structure and recurrence of constituent components (Everson 2007). Everson argues that the need for processing and routine memorisation of characters as merely an assemblage of strokes would be reduced if learners were taught to identify and internalise the individual components in characters they encounter. Everson (2011) proposes that information about the character system must be woven into the fabric of classroom pedagogy in order to facilitate learning and productive use of characters in reading. Fan (2010) also recommends a teaching focus on orthographic knowledge of components (and radicals) as components represent a form of chunking, which facilitates memory. There are fewer 'chunks' per character to recall compared with strokes alone and, importantly, that the ability to name these chunks (components), or to know their meaning, also facilitates memorisation.

Overall, there does appear to be a special role for component-level processing by CSL learners (Loh et al. 2018). Evidence indicates that learners do deconstruct characters analytically into component parts for copying and processing, and this component awareness may play an important role in their character learning (Nguyen et al. 2023), suggesting that explicit teaching of components may enhance character literacy development. However, while analytical, sub-lexical processing of new characters is characteristic of less-skilled CSL learners; this process of character and word recognition is ultimately slow and inefficient when compared with holistic reading processes evident in first language and more proficient CSL learners (Jiang and Feng 2022). Using a component-centred analytic approach to teaching characters to novice learners appears to be well supported, but there are concerns that overreliance on such a method in the longer term may hinder the development of more efficient holistic (words and character-level) processing in reading tasks (Jiang et al. 2020).

The Role of Textbooks in Developing Literacy Skills in CSL Classrooms

Two key sources of pedagogical input available to assist learners in developing the skills needed to learn to read and write in Chinese are their teacher and their textbook. Native speaker teachers bring with them their own first language experiences of learning to read and write Chinese, their own appreciation of how that system functions and how it should be taught (Orton 2016c). Textbooks typically influence the way the system is introduced to students and the types of activities learners engage in to internalise characters as they progress. How the Chinese writing system is introduced and explained at the outset and the types of engagement with characters provided to learners are likely to have significant implications for their learning and success in reading and writing in Chinese. Three contemporary textbooks, *Jinbu* (Zhu and Bin 2011), *Amazing Chinese (Zhenbang)* (Yeh et al. 2019) and *Step Up with Chinese* (Lee and Chen 2021), all of which have some Australian connection in their authorship, are reviewed in terms of the how features of the orthographic system are introduced, and the activities learners are to engage with to learn their character-vocabulary.

The Introduction to Character Structures and Features

Across all three textbooks there is limited explanation of structural features of characters, stroke types and sequences, component forms and relationships, character structure types and the configuration of sides and sub-components, let alone of the potential functional applications and

6 Enhancing Understanding and Engagement with the Chinese... 149

reliabilities of semantic and phonetic radicals. Characters are learned as isolated, logographic wholes. Terminology is kept simple, and opportunities to build an appropriate metalanguage for talking about characters is limited, and often confusing. In all three textbooks, each whole character to be practiced and learned is presented with the sequence of strokes required to complete the whole character with no sound (pinyin) or meaning (English) information provided on the practice pages. Explanations of the stroke system (the number and nature of strokes) are relatively consistent across the three textbooks, with reference typically to the six basic strokes and three extra movements (or 'dependent' strokes). However, none of this stroke data introduced at the outset is referenced in relation to characters to be practiced, with little reference to the range of lower frequency but more complex stroke types that emerge, as in the characters 马, 了, 辶 and 亻 (etc.). All three texts provide a set of general 'rules for stroke order' (i.e., left to right, top to bottom etc.), but little reference is made to the application of these rules or the complexities of stroke types and the rules of stroke order, in particular, stroke patterns or character structures (e.g., 这, 包, 我, 弟 and 家) or in complex compound forms (e.g., 酸 and 瘦).

Analysis of Structural Features in Individual Characters

None of the texts attempt to reduce the visual, graphic complexity of each character through analysis of character structure by, for example, identifying structure types and component configurations (number and arrangement of components). There is no decomposition into sides and sub-components and no identification (naming) of recurrent components, unless they are mentioned in the introduction to semantic radicals. Radical function and positional regularity are not regularly highlighted, despite some references to these features in the character introduction sections. The number of semantic radicals introduced varies considerably, from 24 to a small sample set of 6. The two larger sets of radicals (*Zhenbang* = 24, *Jinbu* = 22) share 16 radicals in common, the smaller set of 6 in *Step Up* shares 5 radicals in common. Where semantic radicals are introduced, reference to these radicals in the characters to be practised is absent. In terms of phonetic radical awareness, only one textbook makes one reference to what appears to be a reliable phonetic side (青-清请情晴), but no analysis of the variable phonetic function in, for example, 猜 or 静 is provided. In general, the phonetic function is left unaddressed, as no characters are deconstructed into sides or unit-by-unit, so no sound or meaning data is provided.

Character Coverage in Individual Textbooks

Whatever understanding of the Chinese writing system that emerges from textbook input and classroom interaction will also depend largely on exposure to that system—on the number and range of characters that learners encounter. The overall character coverage, that is, the total number of characters introduced for character practice, varies considerably across the three textbooks, from 70 characters in *Jinbu* to 253 characters in *Zhenbang*. Using the HSK1 300 list (M.O.E. 2021) as a benchmark for recommended character coverage within an initial period of learning, some interesting variations emerge. The HSK1 300 list is designed for all new learners of Chinese irrespective of age or context. School-based programmes are likely to include more student-centred topical vocabulary, resulting in variations to character coverage.

As shown in Table 6.1, of the 70 characters introduced for practice in *Jinbu*, the vast majority (96%) are included in the HSK1 300 list. In *Step Up*, 100 of the 143 characters are included in the HSK1 300 list, but 43 characters (30%) are not. In *Zhenbang*, 157 of the 253 characters introduced are also found in the HSK1 300 list, but 96 (38%) of the characters are not. There is also wide variability in the characters each textbook has in common with the HSK1 300 list. This is consistent with a larger analysis of college and pre-college textbooks which found that there was

Table 6.1 Comparison of HSK1 300 characters included in each textbook

Textbook	Jinbu	Step Up	Zhenbang
Characters included in the HSK1 300 list	67	100	157
Characters not included in HSK1 300 list	3	43	96
Total characters	70	143	253

only a 25% commonality in characters introduced across the five most commonly used textbooks at that time (Jiang 2006). Consequently, the—albeit—incidental learning of features of the system emerging is likely to be both varied and inconsistent across courses using each of these three textbook series.

The characters that are introduced in each textbook are typically those of greatest communicative value in the context of the topic in each unit or chapter. In the context of the communicative curriculum where purposeful use of language is deemed a priority, the topic-based selection and sequencing of characters is necessarily vocabulary-oriented; however, learners' access to systematic information and exploration of the system may well be restricted as a result.

The typical lack of analysis of stroke types and configurations, component forms and relationships and character structure and component arrangements reinforces the idea to learners that there is little systematic or productive data to be gleaned from within each character they encounter. The apparently routine learning moment of character writing practice, where learner attention is ideally focused on the finer detail of each character (limited to whole-of-character stroke sequence at present, however), presents a valuable lost opportunity to explore the Chinese writing system and enhances learners' understandings of that system in a more consistent, systematic way.

The Implications for Character Teaching and Learning in School-Based CSL Contexts

The implications of these representations of the Chinese writing system and how to learn it for developing learners' knowledge of that system and promoting useful orthographic awareness for future character learning and use are significant. The conceptualisation of the system, while understandably kept simple for young novice learners, is varied and inconsistent between the three texts. In the introduction to Chinese writing section in each of the textbooks, pictographs, strokes and stroke sequences and, to a lesser extent, semantic radicals are introduced. After this 'nice to know' (Fan 2010) general introduction to the character system, learners are left with an unchanging routine of whole-of-character stroke sequences—often up to 17 strokes—as the only insight into how to write and consequently how to remember each character. Learners may learn to rely on self-discovery of patterns in form (and, to a limited extent, function) to enhance their learning, or perhaps on efforts by the teacher to provide more explicit instruction on features of the writing system and how to use such orthographic insights to improve learning. However, where such explicit teaching does occur in the three textbooks reviewed, insights are typically focused solely on the occasional use of the semantic radical side rather than on structural arrangements, positional regularity and graphic relationships (similarities and differences) between component parts in characters encountered.

The size of the character practice square, from 8–15 mm in these instances, leaves students with the rather mindless routine of filling in a tiny square with a myriad of up to 17 strokes. The finer details readily get lost in the maze of strokes and the character likely remains hard to write from memory or recognise later. Importantly, the absence of any exploration or discussion of features of the character system may also limit learners' development of metalanguage for talking about their processes of, or experiences with, character learning. It is likely learners do become aware of the presence of recurrent components which appear in new characters, especially those that have also appeared as high frequency, basic characters already.

Components which have occurred as high frequency whole characters in textbooks (such as 口, 人, 子 and 女) would likely be known (and often encountered as radicals as well), but other character-internal components that recur (such as 夂, 夊 and 夕, for example) typically remain 'nameless', and learners' attention is seldom drawn to subtle differences in their stroke configurations. Textbooks seldom draw learners' attention to similarities in form or variations in the configuration of strokes, leaving learners with a degree of ambiguity even with increasingly familiar orthographic data. Ambiguities in stroke type and relationship that emerge but which do not receive attention in textbooks are likely to result in easy confusion with other character components, (as in 小-乐-东-车, 木-未-禾-米 and 住-隹, for example) (Deng and Hu 2022; Švarcová 2023; Yang 2022). Given the absence of this level of attention to finer features of stroke patterns in components and characters in these textbooks, such similarities in form, so readily confused, remain dependent on teacher input to be explored, explained and better understood.

Incorporating a Component-Oriented Approach in Character Learning Routines

Enhancing development of reading and writing skills in Chinese remains a major challenge in school-based CSL contexts (Loh et al. 2018; Orton 2016a; Orton and Scrimgeour 2019). A more conceptual and systematic approach to literacy development in Chinese, providing a clearer conceptual frame and building awareness of the nature of components as the building blocks of Chinese characters may be a useful innovation. An introductory exploration of the range of key stroke types and stroke configurations or sequences, of the range and nature of key, high-frequency components and component families that share these stroke patterns and of the structure types and component configurations in characters may provide the explicit instruction necessary to develop the type of essential orthographic knowledge proposed by Loh et al. (2018). Initial training in learning to write in Chinese, should focus on the lower tiers of the orthographic system; learning to reproduce the most basic stroke patterns that form particular components, and learning how variations in stroke type and stroke intersection alters both form and meaning. Such focused writing practice and attention to detail may provide the necessary initial insights into the nature of and learning challenges inherent in the Chinese writing system. Initially, a general awareness of how to reproduce stroke patterns and how to configure components in a square should be developed. Then, more time and attention should be given to learn to 'read' characters analytically, to decompose each character encountered for communicative purposes, to both identify (and name) new components and relate them to other components of similar form. This means instilling each component in the memory in a systematic manner, as learners develop purposeful reading skills via more holistic text processing that may lead to improvements in both character recognition and more purposeful reading and writing skills over time.

The Challenges of a Component-Oriented Approach

Instituting a component-oriented approach to initial literacy development among school-based CSL learners presents many challenges. Foremost is the inherent complexity of the three key levels of the orthographic system; stroke types, components (stroke patterns) and characters (component configurations). Learning to write a sequence of strokes to make components and to configure them in a square is in itself a great challenge (Deng and Hu 2022; Lu et al. 2019; Švarcová 2023). An inventory of components for novice learners as the second tier of orthographic knowledge outlined by Loh et al. (2018), organised under the first tier of that system—stroke types and basic stroke patterns—may provide some clearer logic to the component system overall. Arranging and presenting components by similarities in form and drawing attention to emerging patterns and relationships within the extended component inventory could be advantageous to novice learners keen to make sense of the orthographic 'logic' of the character system at the earliest opportunity.

The Challenge of Organising Components for Enhanced Orthographic Awareness

Given the rich diversity of stroke patterns used to create components, some sort of organisational logic is essential to facilitate learners' engagement with and understanding of similarities and discrete differences between the strokes and components in characters encountered. Vocabulary lists of characters are typically organised in alpha-order based on their pinyin sounds or perhaps by their English equivalents (meanings). However, neither of these classifications will provide much insight into, for example, the list of 226 components identified in the HSK1 300 list. With such a large inventory, how these components may be best arranged for maximum pedagogical value to introduce learners to patterns and relationships in the system remains a significant challenge.

Examples of ways in which components related by stroke pattern may be organised and displayed to build connections and strengthen recall are provided in Table 6.2. Row A represents the héng-shù (十 ten) stroke pattern family, with each member displaying slight variation by the

6 Enhancing Understanding and Engagement with the Chinese…

Table 6.2 families of related components

A	十	手	牛	半	丰	
B	干	千	午	平	羊	羊
C	土	生	丰	圭	主	生

addition of one or two additional strokes. Some members are high-frequency whole characters, others low-frequency dependent components, but the stroke patterns enable clear connections to be made which may facilitate faster recognition and recall. Row B represents an extension (héng-héng-shù, 干 stem) family group with an initial short héng (or piě) stroke. Row C includes components derived from the héng-shù-héng (土 earth) family group, each with additional strokes added to the source component.

Such displays offer students insights into orthographic patterns, relationships and systems within stroke configurations, providing context for understanding how any individual component 'fits' into that system. It recognises the fact that for novice learners, the visual orthographic demands remain substantial for the alphabetic background learner, but presenting these 17 components in a logical and organised fashion may reduce the memory load and facilitate rapid recognition and recall of individual components represented.

The Challenge of Naming Components

Another challenge of learning to remember each component and store them in the memory requires there to be some form of reference point—a name, or some form of association that helps build connections in the mind of the L2 learner (Jiang et al. 2020). Components which are whole characters are readily named by their sound (in Chinese) or their meaning (in English). Components which are radicals often have a name (in Chinese and English), and some are named by their connection to a compound form (i.e., naming 艹 in as 草 cǎozi tóu, and in 扁 as biǎnzi xīn in the M.O.E. (2009) component list). This is not particularly helpful for younger CSL learners who may not have encountered the original compound character form.

For components to be a central focus of character study via classroom discussion, rather than routine writing practice alone, some bilingual naming strategy providing learners the capacity to name them (in English) and therefore connect them to familiar objects and ideas would be desirable.

'Dependent' components are often left incorporated within other 'components' on the M.O.E. (2009) list and are therefore typically 'nameless', unless described by their presence or position in a common character. It remains pedagogically useful to have a reference point for talking about individual stroke types and individual components that learners encounter in their learning, particularly for promoting classroom discussion about the nature of the relationships between each tier in the orthographic structure. Realistically, single instance or low-frequency components could be learned as 'name-less' stroke patterns in the context of the character in which they appear. However, the value of becoming familiar with (knowing and naming) both recurrent and single use remnant components once they have been encountered may reduce the overall visual processing demands of each new character, allowing for more attention given to less- or un-familiar stroke patterns appearing in each new character.

Conclusion

At present, given the absence of a consistent conceptualisation of the character system for school-based learners, and the absence of an engaging strategy of exploration and discovery of reliable and recursive patterns within that system, what role might there be for new and emerging technologies? One clear advantage of online, interactive platforms is the potential to enhance student interaction with language features at a conceptual level, separate from any predetermined sequence of content typical of a print-based textbook. Another pedagogical advantage may rest in facilitating out-of-hours, exploratory learning opportunities that may foster learner interest and curiosity in features of the character system. Developing a resource base to facilitate access to a consistent, learner-centred conceptualisation of the character system and interactivity within that system may help fill the gap between learners' inherent interest in the nature of Chinese writing and the current routine processes they are expected to use to learn it.

Given the inconsistent introduction to the character system contained in the textbooks analysed in this chapter and the remarkable variation in characters that learners are likely to encounter (through writing practice) in each text, a data source and activity set that is bottom up—focusing on explanation and exploration of the stroke system and component system—may provide the abstracted conceptual frame that can help build learners orthographic awareness and character literacy skills in a consistent manner, irrespective of their vocabulary exposure. The *Cracking the Code: Character Catalogue* and *Teacher Resource* website (Curriculum Corp. 2007) provided an interactive display of character components with interactive links between lists of characters containing a common component and to each individual compound character that could be animated to decompose hierarchically into its constituent sides and components. Essentially, the website was a catalogue still requiring a teacher's pedagogical intervention to make effective use of it as a teaching resource, but the systematic and interactive display of structural and functional properties of components and radical sides in 2000 high-frequency characters in the system provided a useful teaching resource (Scrimgeour 2011). (The website used Adobe Flash operating system and was consequently shut down in 2021.)

A more conceptual, stroke pattern-based, component-oriented, systematic resource for initial literacy development in Chinese for learners in school-based contexts is urgently required. Pedagogically focused online learning objects have great potential in the Chinese literacy context in providing clear pathways for developing conceptual understanding outside of the limited content and process implicit in textbook design. Online interactive resources aimed at facilitating cognitively engaging interactions with characters can serve a range of skills development purposes, focusing on, for example, developing orthographic working memory; component and character discrimination; fine grained discrimination of ambiguous stroke patterns (又夂攵夕 and 土王士壬), while also providing immediate feedback and facilitating tracked progressions in component and character recognition and recall skills, which are an essential step forward in breaking down barriers to 'cracking the code' of the Chinese writing system.

Determining the sequence of character introduction by textbook topic and oral communicative need creates a significant impediment to an orderly introduction to the character system, to the nature of Chinese writing in contrast to English and to a manageable exploration of the range and variety of character components that make up and give logic to the orthographic system. The reality is that textbooks play a significant role in determining what information about the system is provided and what characters are to be learned. At present, students in diverse contexts are likely to develop a somewhat idiosyncratic view of the system and how to best engage with it. An online pedagogical resource which provides access to and interaction with the key tiers of the orthographic system from the CSL learner's perspective (the stroke system and the component system) is sorely needed. This may provide the foundation for all students with a stable, consistent resource in whatever context to explore and interact with these underlying tiers as they engage with Chinese characters in more communicatively oriented contexts. Using online, interactive technologies to assist novice learners to crack the complex code of the Chinese writing system at the earliest opportunity may be one way to break down perceptual barriers and promote a more positive literacy outcome for learners of Chinese in second language contexts.

Competing Interests The author has no conflicts of interest to declare that are relevant to the content of this chapter.

References

Allen, Joseph R. 2008. Why Learning to Write Chinese is a Waste of Time: A Modest Proposal. *Foreign Language Annals* 41 (2): 237–251. https://doi.org/10.1111/j.1944-9720.2008.tb03291.x.

Anderson, Richard C., Yu-Min Ku, Wenling Li, Xi Chen, Xinchun Wu, and Hua Shu. 2013. Learning to See the Patterns in Chinese Characters. *Scientific Studies of Reading* 17 (1): 41–56. https://doi.org/10.1080/10888438.2012.689789.

Araújo, Susana, Miguel Domingues, and Tânia Fernandes. 2022. From Hand to Eye: A Meta-Analysis of the Benefit from Handwriting Training in Visual Graph Recognition. *Educational Psychology Review* 34: 1577–1612.

Curriculum Corporation. 2007. *Cracking the Code: Character Catalogue and Teacher Resource*. Melbourne: Curriculum Corporation.

Deng, Siqi, and Wenhua Hu. 2022. An Examination of Chinese Character Writing Errors: Developmental Differences among Chinese as a Foreign Language Learners. *Journal of Chinese Writing Systems* 6 (1): 39–51.

Everson, Michael E. 2007. Developing Orthographic Awareness among CFL Learners: What the Research Tells Us. In *The Cognition, Learning and Teaching of Chinese Characters*, ed. Andreas Guder, Jiang Xin, and Wan Yexin, 33–50. China: Beijing Language & Culture University Press.

———. 2011. Best Practices in Teaching Logographic and Non-Roman Writing Systems to L2 Learners. *Annual Review of Applied Linguistics* 31: 249–274.

Fan, Melissa H.-M. 2010. *Developing Chinese Orthographic Awareness: What Insights into Characters do Beginning Level Chinese as a Foreign Language Textbooks Provide?* Berlin, Germany: Lambert Academic Publishing.

Fei, Jinchang. 1996. Research on Modern Chinese Character Components [现代汉字部件探究]. *Applied Linguistics [语言文字应用]* 2: 20–26.

Guan, Connie Qun, Ying Liu, Derek Ho Leung Chan, Feifei Ye, and Charles A. Perfetti. 2011. Writing Strengthens Orthography and Alphabetic-Coding Strengthens Phonology in Learning to Read Chinese. *Journal of Educational Psychology* 103 (3): 509–522. https://doi.org/10.1037/a0023730.

Hsiung, Hsiang Yu, Yu Lin Chang, Hsueh Chih Chen, and Yao Ting Sung. 2017. Effect of Stroke-Order Learning and Handwriting Exercises on Recognizing and Writing Chinese Characters by Chinese as a Foreign Language Learners. *Computers in Human Behavior* 74: 303–310.

Isselé, Joanna, Fabienne Chetail, and Alain Content. 2022. The Nature of Perceptual Units in Chinese Character Recognition. *Quarterly Journal of Experimental Psychology* 75 (8): 1514–1527.

Jiang, Song. 2006. Defining the So-Called 'Core Vocabulary': A Case Study of Chinese Textbooks. *Journal of Chinese Language and Computing* 16 (1): 63–71.

Jiang, Chenhao. 2023. *Effects of Handwriting and Keyboarding on Character Recognition*. Paper presented at CASLAR Conference, Beijing, China.

Jiang, Nan, and Lijuan Feng. 2022. Analytic Visual Word Recognition among Chinese L2 Learners. *Foreign Language Annals* 55 (2): 540–558.

Jiang, Nan, Fengyun Hou, and Xin Jiang. 2020. Analytic Versus Holistic Recognition of Chinese Words Among L2 Learners. *Modern Language Journal* 104 (3): 567–580.

Lee, Lucy Chu, and Xia Chen. 2021. *Step Up with Chinese: Textbook 1 and Workbook 1*. 2nd ed. Singapore: Cengage.

Li, Michael. 2020. A Systematic Review of the Research on Chinese Character Teaching and Learning. *Frontiers of Education in China* 15: 39–72. https://doi.org/10.1007/s11516-020-0003-y.

Loh, Elizabeth Ka Yee, Xian Liao, and Shing On Leung. 2018. Acquisition of Orthographic Knowledge: Developmental Difference among Learners With Chinese as a Second Language (CSL). *System* 74: 206–216.

Lu, Xiwen, Korinn S. Ostrow, and Neil T. Heffernan. 2019. Save Your Strokes: Chinese Handwriting Practice Makes For Ineffective Use of Instructional Time in Second Language Classrooms. *AERA Open* 5 (4): 1–15. https://doi.org/10.1177/2332858419890326.

Ministry of Education. 2009. *Specification of Common Modern Chinese Character Components and Component Names* [现代常用字部件及部件名称规范] GF 0014-2009.

———. 2013. *Table of General Standard Chinese characters* [通用规范汉字表] Accessed March 21, 2024. http://www.moe.gov.cn/jyb_sjzl/ziliao/A19/201306/t20130601_186002.html

———. 2021. *Chinese Proficiency Grading Standards for International Chinese Language Education* [国际中文教育中文水平等级标准] GF 0025-2021. http://www.moe.gov.cn/jyb_xwfb/gzdt_gzdt/s5987/202103/W020210329527301787356.pdf

Myers, James. 2019. *The Grammar of Chinese Characters: Productive Knowledge of Formal Patterns in an Orthographic System*. Oxon, UK: Routledge.

Nguyen, Thi Phuong, Hong Li, Jie Feng, and Xinchun Wu. 2023. Component Awareness Facilitates Chinese Character Recognition in Non-Native Chinese

Speakers: Analysis of the Multiple Mediation Effect. *Reading and Writing* 36: 1685–1704.

Orton, Jane. 2016a. Chinese Language Education: Teacher Training. In *The Routledge Encyclopedia of Chinese Language and Culture*, ed. Chan Sin-Wai, 177–197. Abingdon, Oxon: Routledge.

———. 2016b. Issues in Chinese Language Teaching in Australian Schools. *Chinese Education & Society* 49 (6): 369–375. https://doi.org/10.108 0/10611932.2016.1283929.

———. 2016c. *Building Chinese Language Capacity in Australia*. Sydney, Australia: The Australia-China Relations Institute (ACRI).

Orton, Jane, and Andrew Scrimgeour. 2019. *Teaching Chinese as a Second Language: The Way of the Learner*. New York: Routledge.

Osborne, Caitríona, Qi Zhang, and George Xinsheng Zhang. 2018. Which is More Effective in Introducing Chinese Characters? An Investigative Study of Four Methods Used to Teach CFL Beginners. *The Language Learning Journal* 48 (4): 385–401. https://doi.org/10.1080/09571736.2017.1393838.

Scrimgeour, Andrew. 2011. Issues and Approaches to Literacy Development in Chinese Second Language Classrooms. In *Teaching and Learning Chinese in Global Contexts*, ed. Linda Tsung and Ken Cruickshank, 197–212. London: Continuum.

———. 2014a. Dealing with 'Chinese Fever': The Challenge of Chinese Teaching in the Australian Classroom. In *Dynamic Ecologies*, ed. Neil Murray and Angela Scarino, 151–167. Dordrecht: Springer.

———. 2014b. Responding to the Diversity of Chinese Language Learners in Australian Schools. *Babel* 49 (3): 26–37.

———. 2023. *The Dynamics of Chinese Language Education in Australian Schools*. Paper presented at CASLAR Conference, Beijing, China.

Shen, Helen H. 2005. An Investigation of Chinese-Character Learning Strategies among Non- Native Speakers of Chinese. *System* 33 (1): 49–68. https://doi.org/10.1016/j.system.2004.11.001.

Shu, Hua. 2003. Chinese Writing System and Learning to Read. *International Journal of Psychology* 38 (5): 274–285.

Shu, Hua, Xi Chen, Richard C. Anderson, Wu Ningning, and Yue Xuan. 2003. Properties of School Chinese: Implications for Learning to Read. *Child Development* 74 (1): 27–47.

Švarcová, Tereza. 2023. High Dropout Ratesin Secondary Chinese Courses: Are Characters to be Blamed? *The Language Learning Journal*: 1–12.

Tan, Li Hai, John A. Spinks, Guinevere F. Eden, Charles A. Perfetti, and Wai Ting Siok. 2005. Reading Depends on Writing, in Chinese. *Proceedings of the National Academy of Sciences of the United States of America* 102 (24): 8781–8785. https://doi.org/10.1073/pnas.0503523102.

Victorian Curriculum and Assessment Authority (VCAA). 2018. *Victorian Certificate of Education: Chinese Second Language Study Design*. Victorian Curriculum and Assessment Authority.

Xu, Zhengye, Duo Liu, and R. Malatesha Joshi. 2020. The Influence of Sensory-Motor Components of Handwriting On Chinese Character Learning in Second- and Fourth- Grade Chinese Children. *Journal of Educational Psychology* 112 (7): 1353–1366.

Yang, Juan. 2022. Teenage Beginners' Perceptions of learning Chinese Characters: A Case Study. *Journal of Chinese Writing Systems* 6 (1): 3–15.

Ye, Lijuan. 2013. Shall We Delay Teaching Characters in Teaching Chinese as a Foreign Language? *Foreign Language Annals* 46 (4): 610–627.

Yeh, Shao-Ping, Lifen Chen, Jessy Tu, Hugo Wing-Yu Tam, and Daiwei Wei. 2019. *Amazing Chinese [真棒] Textbook and Workbook*. Taiwan: Kang Hsuan Educational Publishing Group.

Yin, Binyong, and John Rohsenow. 1994. *Modern Chinese Characters*. Beijing: Sinolingua.

Zhang, Phyllis Ni. 2021. Typing to Replace Handwriting: Effectiveness of the Typing-Primary Approach for L2 Chinese Beginners. *Journal of Technology and Chinese Language Teaching* 12 (2): 1–28.

Zhang, Qi, and Ge Min. 2019. Chinese Writing Composition among CFL Learners: A Comparison between Handwriting and Typewriting. *Computers and Composition* 54 (December): 102522. https://doi.org/10.1016/j.compcom.2019.102522.

Zhang, Qi, George Zhang, and Yuhui Gao. 2019. A Comparative Study of the Chinese Characters in the Graded List and the EBCL List. *Chinese Language Teaching Methodology and Technology* 2 (2): 20–39.

Zhao, Yang. 2011. A Tree in the Wood: A Review of Research on L2 Chinese Acquisition. *Second Language Research* 27 (4): 559–572.

Zhu, Xiaoming, and Yu Bin. 2011. *Jinbu: Textbook 1 and Workbook 1*. Australia: Pearson Education.

7

Visual Skill and Orthographic Decomposition in Character Learning

Yi Xu

Introduction

While Chinese character instruction has always been a topic of interest for Chinese language teachers, scholars, and applied linguists, there have been increasing discussions on effective teaching and learning strategies in the recent decade. For instance, the compatibility of the traditional rote memorisation approach to learning characters through handwriting has been called into question in the context of online learning, especially after the COVID-19 pandemic (Wang and East 2020). A "penless" approach (i.e., learning Chinese characters without repeated handwriting practice) was proposed decades ago (Xu and Jen 2005), but studies reporting empirical support for the "no handwriting" practice remain scarce, with a few exceptions (Zhang 2021). A crucial question is: If the

---

Y. Xu (✉)
Department of East Asian Languages and Literatures, University of Pittsburgh, Pittsburgh, PA, USA
e-mail: xuyi@pitt.edu

© The Author(s), under exclusive license to Springer Nature Switzerland AG 2024
C. Osborne et al. (eds.), *Teaching Chinese Characters in the Digital Age*, Palgrave Studies on Chinese Education in a Global Perspective,
https://doi.org/10.1007/978-3-031-64784-0_7

traditional rote approach is no longer implemented, what new pedagogical tools do we have to facilitate student learning? Earlier research points to some possible directions, including typing (Guan et al. 2011), radical-based grouping (Xu et al. 2014), and stroke order animation digital flashcards (Zhu et al. 2012), to name but a few. As the field explores evidence-based pedagogical approaches to support Chinese as a foreign language (CFL) students' character learning, this chapter examines the relationship between learners' visual skills and their orthographic awareness and argues that developing Chinese orthography-specific perceptual skills is a fundamental step in students' learning.

The chapter is organized as follows. The first section reports evidence that learners' visual skill is correlated with their character learning performance, especially in the early stages of learning. The second section links visual skills to character decomposition and approaches the topic from the perspective of teachers' and students' perceptions. The last section reports an exploratory study on CFL learners' perceptual decomposition (or chunking) performance across characters' different structural configurations.

Visual Skills in Chinese Reading

Two Types of Visual Skills in Reading

The fundamental and most challenging aspect of reading (at the basic or character level) for Chinese learners is often form recognition, due to the lack of grapheme-phoneme correspondence in Chinese, the sheer number of characters, and the large number of homophones that make it necessary for one to focus on the orthography-to-meaning route of character recognition. Chinese also has the most visually complex orthography in writing systems in the world (Chang et al. 2018). Thus, visual skills are especially important for Chinese reading development. There are at least two distinctive categories of visual skills related to reading acquisition: perceptual visual skills and visual-orthographic skills. Perceptual visual skills as a basic cognitive function are culture-free and involve abilities of visual memory and visual discrimination. These are abilities to process visual representations such as figures, shapes, dots and lines, and they do not rely on one's familiarity or knowledge of any particular script (Li et al. 2012). Studies based on English L1 acquisition show perceptual visual skills, including visual-spatial attention (e.g., Franceschini et al. 2012) and sensitivity towards dynamic visual stimuli (e.g., Talcott et al. 2000), are associated with children's reading development or literacy skills.

Perceptual visual skills can play an even more crucial role in the reading development of Chinese. For instance, the visual-spatial skill of identifying the same form or shape when it is placed in different orientations resembles the skill needed to recognize and utilize character components (e.g., radicals) when they appear in different directions or positions in a character, and visual memory is likely relevant to one's ability to establish links between the character form and meaning or sound when the form itself is visually complex (Zhou et al. 2014). In Tan et al.'s (2001) fMRI study, researchers found that when Chinese L1 adults process Chinese characters, there is peak brain activation in the left lateral middle frontal cortex, an area controlling mediations of visual-spatial working memory. Liu et al. (2006) also found ERP evidence that reading Chinese characters requires more visual processing than reading alphabetic languages for second language (L2) learners in their initial stages of learning, though the difference between visual workload in processing the two different scripts diminished after two semesters of classroom learning.

The second type of visual skill associated with reading is visual-orthographic in nature and is closely tied to the orthographic knowledge specific to a given language (Cassar and Treiman 1997). It involves the ability to detect acceptable and unacceptable grapheme sequences and their relations to positions in words (or characters, in the case of Chinese). This visual-orthographic skill reflects a type of "orthographic awareness" and is crucial in reading in Chinese. Despite the form complexity, Chinese characters have internal structures that are "fairly predictable" and compound characters in Chinese are formed based on sets of orthographic rules (Li et al. 2012, p. 290). For instance, subcharacter components have visual regularity (in terms of their shape or how they are formed by series of strokes) and many radicals also exhibit functional regularity (indicating meaning or sound) and positional regularity when occurring in characters. Position-specific radicals (e.g., 扌, 刂, 艹 and 灬) need to appear in a consistent position and violations of these orthographic constraints will result in a non-character. The knowledge of Chinese characters' orthographic structure constraints and the ability to visually distinguish violations from legal forms constitute such orthographic awareness, and a good grasp of such predictable rules can tremendously help one's learning to read.

Studies on the contribution of visual skills to Chinese reading have been more fruitful in L1 acquisition studies than in the L2 context. In a meta-analysis, Yang et al. (2013) examined 64 independent samples from 34 studies published from 1991 to 2011 and reported that visual perception, speed of processing and pure visual memory had medium correlations with Chinese reading acquisition in the lower grades, with the correlations ranging from 0.34 to 0.44, whereas in the higher grades (second to sixth grade), the correlations decreased to a range between 0.12 and 0.20. Several more recent studies, including Li et al. (2012), Zhou et al. (2018) and Zhou and McBride (2018), confirmed that both the perceptual visual and visual-orthographic skills of L1 Chinese children are closely related to their reading abilities. In comparison, the relationship between visual skills and reading among L2 adult Chinese learners is not yet well understood. In terms of *perceptual visual skills*, only a few studies examined the relationship between visual working memory and L2 adult Chinese character learning. Kim et al. (2015) used a verbal working memory task (reading span) and a visual working memory (WM) task (judgement of letter orientation) and asked participants to learn distinctive characters (i.e., characters formed by bolding, lengthening or changing the size of a particular stroke in a character), regular characters and orthographically similar characters. The authors reported that visual WM correlated with the learning of distinctive characters only and not regular characters, while verbal WM predicted the learning of regular characters. The authors concluded that L2 Chinese adult learners, unlike L1 children, bypassed the visual stage of character learning. On the other hand, an fMRI study by Opitz et al. (2014) reported that visual WM training, compared to the control condition, led to positive outcomes in visual Chinese character learning among their participants.

In terms of visual-orthographic skill, studies by Shen and Ke (2007) and Tong and Yip (2015) both addressed its role at the (semantic or phonetic) radical level. Shen and Ke (2007) noted that adult L2 Chinese learners can visually decompose compound characters into radicals with 54% accuracy after one month of learning approximately 100 characters and participants achieved 73% accuracy after one year of study. These authors argued that the rapid development of visual-orthographic skills at the beginning stages of learning "contributes to character acquisition by reducing the burden of character memorization" (p. 107). In Tong and Yip's (2015) study, they found that CFL learners' sensitivity to semantic and phonetic radicals' positions, i.e., skill on the interaction of form perception and form regularity, predicates learners' reading ability measured by word recognition. Xu and Chang (2014) was one of the few studies that focused on a visual-orthographic skill at a structural level lower than "radicals". They used multimedia presentations that displayed characters chunk-by-chunk and found that when learners learned characters in the radical-grouped sequence (e.g., 姑, 娇, 婚, etc., together as one group and 晾, 喧, 暗 as another group), chunking condition led to better character reproduction accuracy than the handwriting condition. These authors pointed out that the visual chunking learning method leverages learners' visual-orthographic sensitivity so that the cost of memorisation can be reduced by perceiving characters as the composition of a few chunks instead of numerous strokes.

A Correlation Study on Visual Skills and CFL Character Learning

The above studies indicate that visual skills may be involved in L2 learners' character learning, but the evidence was either indirect or controversial. To address the gap, Chang et al. (2014) directly measured the relationship between L2 learners' perceptual visual skill, visual-orthographic skill and their success rate in learning new characters over a short period of time. In the study, we asked two groups of Chinese language students with English-L1 background (Beginner Group: 48;

Intermediate Group: 32) to learn 48 new characters in four days.[1] Before participants' learning sessions, we assessed participants' *perceptual visual skills* in two aspects, their "visual discrimination" skill through pattern discrimination and their visual WM in "position sequence recall". At the end of the learning sessions, we assessed participants' visual-orthographic skills, through lexical decision tasks involving ill-formed characters.

The perceptual visual skill tasks were modified based on Chein and Morrison (2010). Participants encountered pairs of stimuli that consisted of pattern discrimination (i.e., judging whether two patterns were both symmetrical or asymmetrical within 3 seconds) followed by a position memory stimulus in which participants needed to remember the location of dots and their sequences on a four-by-four grid. After four pairs (of pattern discrimination and position memory stimuli presentation, illustrated in Fig. 7.1), participants had to report the sequence of locations of the red dots by clicking the mouse in the grid. To assess learners' visual-orthographic skills, we followed previous studies (e.g., Li et al. 2012) and used both ill-component characters and ill-structured characters in a lexical decision task. The ill-component characters (e.g., 唱) were created by adding, removing, or changing the position of a stroke from a component in a real, familiar character so that participants' judgement of those ill-component characters reflected their sensitivity towards the subtle differences in stroke patterns (e.g., 口 vs. 日). The ill-structured characters (e.g., 怀) were created from novel characters by moving the positions of radicals to form non-characters so that participants' judgement of this type of stimuli reflects their visual-orthographic awareness regarding the radicals' positional specificity (Tong and Yip 2015).

Given the above, there were seven key measures in the study. Participants' *pattern discretion* skill was measured by participants' accuracy in pattern discrimination shown in Screen 1 in Fig. 7.1; their *perceptual location memory* was measured by their accuracy in reporting the locations of the red dots and the sequence of such locations. Participants'

---

[1] The beginner group participants were in their first-semester college Chinese classes and had learned approximately 180 characters, whereas the intermediate group participants were in their third-semester Chinese classes, with approximately 240 hours of classroom instruction and 530 characters under their belt. The 48 characters as learning materials were the same as the ones reported by Xu et al. (2014).

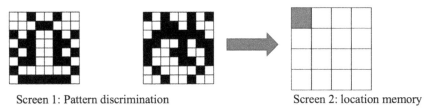

Fig. 7.1 One pair of pattern discrimination and location memory stimuli

stroke pattern discrimination was measured by participants' accuracies in judging ill-component characters (e.g., 唱), and their awareness of *radical position specificity* was measured by accuracies in judging ill-structured characters (e.g., 怅). Scoring was based on accuracies of illegal characters only (e.g., 唱 and 怅) in these two measures. As for participants' gains in learning new characters, participants engaged in a pretest to write down the pinyin and English translation for the 48 new characters (when the character form is provided) and they completed two post-tests, including a pinyin and meaning test (i.e., writing down pinyin and translation based on the form provided) and a form production test (i.e., handwriting characters based on the English meaning). The pretest and post-tests were conducted with paper and pencil. Each participant's score differences between their post-tests and pretest in pinyin and meaning productions were used as pinyin and meaning gains. Participants' scores in form production in the post-test were the measure of their form learning gain.

Chang et al. (2014) found that for beginner-level learners, their *visual pattern discrimination* skill but not *visual WM* (assessed by participants' accuracies in the location memory task) moderately correlated with gains in character form learning (i.e., accuracy score in handwriting production) and character meaning learning. Their visual-orthographic skill in judging ill-formed structures and ill-formed subcharacter components both correlated with their learning success in character form and meaning. While the lack of significance in the *location sequence memory* measure may be attributed to task difficulty—such kind of visual WM tasks may be sensitive enough for children but could arguably be too easy for adults to lead to enough variations—these results confirmed that both perceptual visual skills and visual-orthographic awareness play important roles in beginning CFL students' character learning. On the other hand, visual skills in general (perceptual or orthographic) were found to be unrelated to intermediate-level participants' character learning in the study, since no significant correlation was found between visual skills and participants' character learning outcomes. See Table 7.1 for the correlation result.

These findings show that, for Chinese adult learners in their initial stage of learning, both *perceptual visual* skills and *visual-orthographic* skills were related to their character learning success. In some cases, their successful learning in form reproduction also transferred to better performance in making form-meaning associations. There are at least two interesting points worth noting when the results are interpreted in comparison with findings from earlier studies. First, the magnitude of these correlations (0.29 to 0.42) matched correlations of visual skill and reading ability among L1 Chinese children (Yang et al. 2013). This suggests that visual skills are important in the beginning stages of character learning, independent of other cognitive function development associated with age. Second, the difference between beginner- and intermediate-level learners corresponded to developmental patterns in both L1 studies among children and L2 adult studies. This mirrored the diminished correlation between children's perceptual visual skill and their reading acquisition in higher grades reported by Yang et al. (2013) and the decreased reliance on visual workload in Chinese L2 reading as CFL learners gained more experience with the writing system (e.g., Liu et al. 2006).

Related, Xu et al. (2014) found that L2 Chinese students in first-year classes benefited from a radical-based grouping method in character presentation sequence, but grouping had no effect for second-year students, suggesting that novice and experienced learners employ different mechanisms and processes in character learning. Novice L2 Chinese learners tend to process character forms as a whole, and intermediate-level learners habitually decompose characters for learning (e.g., Jackson et al. 2003). In the holistic perception of characters by novice learners, superior visual skills in differentiating graphemic patterns can enable one to memorize character forms more accurately. For experienced learners, however, character learning could be less or seldom reliant on

Table 7.1 Correlations between visual skills and participants' gain scores in character learning

	1. Pattern	2. Loc. memory	3. Stroke discrimination	4. Radical position	5. Form production	6. Pinyin	7. Meaning
1. Perceptual: Pattern discrimination	–	0.62**	-0.16	-0.20	0.25	0.20	0.22
2. Perceptual: Location memory	0.08	–	-0.15	-0.27	-0.03	0.06	0.03
3. Orthographic: Stroke pattern discrimination	0.13	0.20	–	0.50*	-0.08	-0.23	-0.06
4. Orthographic: Radical position specificity	0.07	0.01	0.41*	–	0.03	-0.06	-0.05
5. Character form production	0.36*	0.01	0.29*	0.39**	–	0.82**	0.84*
6. Character pinyin gain	0.19	-0.07	0.23	0.37*	0.65**	–	0.89*
7. Character meaning gain	0.35*	-0.03	0.32*	0.42**	0.83**	0.77**	–

Note: Correlations for beginner-level participants (n = 48) are presented below the diagonal, and correlations for intermediate-level participants (n = 32) are presented above the diagonal. *$p < 0.05$, two-tailed; **$p < 0.01$, two-tailed memorizing the grapheme as a whole and rely instead on using one's orthographic awareness (e.g., metalinguistic knowledge regarding principles of character formation) in learning.

The above shows that prior to learners' development of sufficient radical knowledge to habitually decompose characters to learn, visual skills to perceive characters as the principled composition of small components are helpful for form recognition and character learning. This can be especially so for beginner-level learners. In CFL research, learners' visual-orthographic awareness has mostly been discussed at the level of radicals, i.e., character components bearing semantic or phonetic functions. The rest of this chapter argues that an effective radical-based approach should integrate the (potentially) smaller perceptual unit of chunks (*bujian*). Chunks are visually integral components that form patterns in between the level of strokes and radicals. They may incidentally overlap with a stroke or a radical but differ from these component levels in definition. For instance, stroke combinations such as 丷, 又, 乂, 冖, 厶 and 也 are frequently occurring patterns (or chunks) with no meanings. In addition, an orthographic form that constitutes a radical often occurs in positions not associated with meaning or sound and can thus actually be a chunk in those characters. For instance, at the visual perceptual level, being able to identify 女 or 贝 as one component in characters like 案 or 樱 is as important as being able to recognize the 木 component or radical in 案. The next section focuses on "chunking", i.e., decomposing characters into the smallest visually integral unit, as chunks are the basic unit (above strokes) that compose the visual forms of characters.

Character Decomposition and Chunking

A Chunking-Based Approach

Character handwriting and radical learning are some of the most frequently discussed character learning strategies in the literature. In addition, scholars have reported on the teaching effectiveness and students' learning strategies of using etymological information (e.g., Jin 2003), making up a story (e.g., McGinnis 1999), and using visuals or ideographs (e.g., Shen 2010). It is relatively recent that CFL researchers started paying attention to the orthographic unit of chunks. In a character, each chunk is "separated by a visible diminutive space from other units" (Shen and Ke 2007, p. 99). Unlike "radicals", a chunk as the recurring graphic component is not constrained to a particular semantic or phonetic function. Its function is only at the visual representation level. Because the vast majority of Chinese characters are compounds (e.g., *Dictionary of Chinese Character Information* 1988), applying one's familiarity with chunks should facilitate memories associated with character forms. Different sources refer to anywhere between 440 and 600 chunks that can form 7000–8000 characters according to Chen et al. (2011) based on the traditional Chinese script and National Language Commission (2009) based on the simplified script. Chunks can be highly productive. The most frequently occurring chunks (口, 日, 木 and 氵) each from 200 to 500 characters and the top 13 productive chunks each form more than 100 characters (National Language Commission 2009).

The theoretical foundation for "visual chunking" (i.e., perceiving characters as the composition of several visually integrative units and memorizing the character's form through such compositions) stems from Miller (1956), who argued that short-term memory could hold anywhere from five to nine chunks of information and memory can be facilitated if information is organized into these small number of items. Several studies in English word learning have illustrated the benefit of "chunking" in alphabetic letter strings (e.g., Rastle et al. 2000; Taft and Forster 1975). Linguists have pointed out the potential role of chunking in Chinese. In simplified Chinese, a character contains on average 10.15 strokes and is typically composed of five or fewer chunks (Cao et al. 2013). The traditional Chinese script has more stroke numbers than simplified Chinese, but they still typically (93%) consist of five or fewer chunks (Chen et al. 2011, p. 280). In other words, in both the simplified and the traditional scripts, learning through chunking will greatly reduce students' visual memory load.

Empirical studies on learning through chunking remain scarce. Pak et al. (2005) discussed children's chunking perception of characters by analysing their errors in delayed copying tasks. Through error analysis, they confirmed that higher-graders have more advanced visual chunking skills than lower-graders. In Cao et al.'s (2013) ERP study, the researchers recruited 30 Chinese L2 learners to learn 120 characters using three different encoding approaches: passive viewing (reading), writing, and visual chunking (where the monitor showed participants how the character is composed of chunks). Although their study did not find a learning outcome difference across the three training groups, they reported that N170 amplitude, an indicator of enhanced orthographic representation, was greater for the visual chunking group than the other two groups combined. The researchers suggested that visual chunking training directed learners' attention to the local features of the character components, and it refined and optimized the character form representation.

Two studies reported behavioural evidence for the benefit of learning through chunking. Xu and Chang's (2014) participants learned 48 characters in four sessions and all participants experienced four learning conditions: chunking, handwriting, reading and stroke-reporting. It was found that for the 24 participants who learned characters sequenced by their radical groups (e.g., characters in the 女 radical group were sequenced together in participants' learning), learning through chunking led to higher accuracies than the handwriting and stroke-reporting methods in character form reproduction post-test. On the other hand, for a matching group of another 24 participants who learned the same set of characters through a distributed sequence (i.e., characters in the same radical group were learned on different days), the chunking condition did not lead to an advantage. This indicates that the benefit of visual chunking may be enhanced when students learn in a character form-focused curriculum. The joint facilitation of radical-based grouping and chunking helped students the most. In a different study, Xu and Padilla (2013) implemented a "meaningful-interpretation and chunking (MIC)" instructional approach among novice-level high school students. In their MIC treatment, instructors gave explicit instructions including character-forming principles, radical knowledge, and character decomposition into chunks. The treatment group had better performances in immediate post-tests of pinyin, meaning and form production than the control group, which used the traditional approach of stroke-order memorisation.

Pedagogical experts acknowledged that chunking-based character instruction (部件教学) was a feasible and efficient approach decades ago (Xing 2005). In today's context where the traditional handwriting approach is being challenged due to its lack of practicality in the digital world, exploration in the chunking-based direction should be especially relevant. Notably, in both Xu and Chang (2014) and Xu and Padilla (2013), the chunking-based approach led to more advantageous results than the handwriting approach in certain situations. These studies point to the potential of implementing form-focused instructions that accentuate the recurring perceptual units in characters. The "chunking-based" approach proposed here is not in contradiction with the radical-based approach. Rather, similar to Xu and Padilla's (2013) approach, both chunks and radicals (i.e., semantically or phonetically functional chunks) are considered to be important subcharacter components meriting pedagogical attention here. It should be noted that, despite the cognitive basis and empirical evidence that supports the benefit of visual chunking, we know little about language practitioners' or the students' perceptions or practices of using visual subcharacter components in the language classroom. Do teachers and students consider chunking a beneficial strategy for learning? In practice, how do teachers incorporate chunking in their character instructional method? Do students actively apply chunking skills to learn? While many survey studies have reported on students' general character learning strategies (e.g., Ke 1998), teachers' perceptions (e.g., Xu et al. 2021) often included discussions of radical-based learning, no earlier published research addressed these questions specifically related to visual chunking. Below, I try to fill the gap by providing preliminary discussions based on results from a survey study.

Teacher and Student Perceptions: Evidence from a Survey Study

This section reports data from a survey study that aimed to investigate teachers' and students' perceptions and practices regarding chunking-based character learning. The data were drawn from part of a bigger survey on Chinese character instruction by Yee (2019)[2] and were reorganized and re-analysed to address the questions listed at the end of the previous section, including how teachers and students perceived the benefit of chunking, their practices in using visual chunking to teach or learn and their opinions on when and how the concept should be introduced.

Participants

The survey was conducted in spring 2019 with two different versions of online questionnaires, one designed for Chinese language instructors and the other for students. Forty college-level Chinese language instructors in different institutions and regions in the US completed the instructor version of the questionnaire. Forty-six students (first-year: 24; second-year: 8; third-year: 7; heritage language students: 7) enrolled in language classes in a Chinese programme in the U.S. completed the student version of the survey.

Instrument

A series of survey questions appeared in both the teacher and student surveys. This enables us to make side-by-side comparisons of students' and teachers' responses.

The key survey questions pertaining to the current discussion are listed in Table 7.2. For Question 2 (Q2), options include (1) Historical Etymology; (2) Self-made Stories; (3) Chunking (i.e., break down characters into smaller pieces to more easily remember characters e.g., 疑 = 匕 +矢 +厶+ 疋); (4) Radicals (i.e., Use semantic or phonetic radicals to remember characters and infer a character's meaning); (5) Visual (i.e., Use pictures corresponding to a character's meaning); (6) Rote Memorisation (i.e., Copying characters line by line); and (7) "Others (Please explain)".

---

[2] Yee (2019) was an unpublished BA Honours project. With the author's permission, a small proportion of the data in that project was reorganized and analyzed here, independent of the results reported in Yee (2019).

7 Visual Skill and Orthographic Decomposition in Character... 177

Table 7.2 Participants' responses to "chunking" survey questions

Survey question		Teachers (N = 40)	Students (N = 46)
Q1: Do you think it is important for students/you to chunk characters into small parts in order to remember characters easily?	Yes No	27 (67.5%) 11 (27.5%)	38 (82.6%) 8 (17.4%)
Q2: Which character teaching/learning strategies do you use?		Radicals: 36 (90%) Visuals: 28 (70%) Chunking: 25 (62.5%)	Rote memorization: 31 (67.4%) Chunking: 30 (65.2%) Radicals: 27 (57.4%)
Q3: How often should chunking be explicitly taught?	a. Frequently emphasized when students FIRST learn characters	13 (32.5%)	3 (6.5%)
	b. Emphasized from time to time AFTER a few hundred characters are learned	14 (35%)	18 (39.1%)
	c. Once or twice a semester in workshops	3 (7.5%)	15 (32.6%)
	d. Once to introduce the concept	3 (7.5%)	4 (8.7%)
	e. Never	2 (5%)	0 (0%)
	f. No opinion	1 (2.5%)	5 (10.9%)

Note: For Q2, only the three most frequently chosen strategies are listed here

In addition, the teacher's survey also contains a question about teaching strategy ("How do you teach chunking strategies?"). Participants were asked to choose all that apply, and options include "Quizzing students on their chunking ability (e.g., What are the chunking components in 疑? Answer: 匕+矢+マ+疋)", "Introducing groups of characters based on shared chunks" and "Others (please explain)".

Results

For the first three identical survey questions on the teacher and student surveys, a summary of participants' responses is included in Table 7.2.

For the teacher's survey question "How would you teach chunking?", 10 participants selected "quizzing the students" and 29 selected "introducing groups of characters based on shared chunks". Text responses of teachers' strategies include the following categories: (a) cueing students to raise awareness (e.g., "Ask students what they notice about the characters"); (b) delegating tasks to students for chunk-based character grouping (e.g., "Have students summarize their own chunking list like putting learned characters into a chunk-grouped list"); (c) incorporating chunk-learning when making connections between new and familiar characters (e.g., "Reflect learned characters with the chunk when introducing a new character"; "学新词的时候顺便复习有相同部件的旧字"); (d) visual form comparisons (e.g., "Compare chunks that look similar") and (e) context-based instruction (e.g., "Teach in very short bursts when dealing with texts"). The most frequently referred to approaches were character form grouping and comparisons.

Discussions

Most teachers and students agreed to the importance and benefit of chunking in character learning, although a lower percentage of the teachers considered the strategy helpful compared to students. When asked about their practices of using different strategies (Q2), chunking was also one of the most frequently chosen approaches for both teachers and students.

On the other hand, there were more varying opinions among the teachers than students regarding the importance of chunking. When teachers' responses to Q1 and Q3 were analysed together, we see that approximately 67.5% of teachers considered chunking helpful, and this subgroup of teachers believed in repeated explicit instructions either at the beginning stages of learning (32.5%) or after students have had some exposure to the Chinese writing system (35%). Meanwhile, more than a quarter of the teacher participants did not acknowledge the benefit of chunking. Two teachers, who claimed to exclusively use the "cold character reading" or "student self-made stories", believed that chunking should "never" be explicitly taught. Some teachers believed that when it comes to character learning, students' self-learning precedes explicit instruction. A teacher stated that students' "self-discoveries … about character forms" were "better for their learning and memory" and that she did "not find a lot of attention and time necessary [from the teachers] for them [students] to be good readers". Another rationale for not teaching chunks was that chunks, unlike radicals, lack semantic function. A teacher who acknowledged using radicals but not chunks in her teaching felt that chunks "don't have a concrete meaning" and thus "may be just random strokes". By decomposing radicals further into chunks, she felt that "meaningful parts were lost as a result of simplification". This remark on the differences between "chunks" and "radicals" appears to reflect teachers' views on "radicals" versus chunks: Seen from teachers' responses to Q2, an overwhelming majority of the teacher group was in favour of using radicals to teach characters, but their stance varied on the usefulness of chunking.

There was a higher percentage of students than teachers who believed in the importance of chunking. A majority of the student participants also acknowledged the use of chunking in their learning, next only to "rote memorisation", the most recognized traditional way of character learning. When participants' responses were examined in relation to their language background, we found that the heritage language learners subgroup and the advanced-level subgroup valued chunking more than other subgroups. All seven heritage language students and seven third-year students responded positively to the usefulness of chunking in their learning (Q1), and five students among both of these subgroups (71.4%) acknowledged the active use of chunking in their learning (Q2), showing a higher percentage of "chunking usage" compared to other student subgroups. In other words, the two learner subgroups with the most experience in Chinese language use valued the chunking strategy more than others.

Regarding the timing and frequency of explicit chunk instruction, most students felt that receiving instructions from time to time or a few times in workshops would be sufficient. Only three students believed that early and "frequent emphasis" on chunking right from the start of character learning was necessary. These three students came from the advanced-level (2) and the heritage language student subgroups. Students' responses to this question differed from the pattern observed from the teacher group. Although teachers appeared divergent in their opinions on the importance of chunking, a higher percentage of the teachers compared to students believed that chunking should be emphasized early on in the curriculum.

Taken together, students' and teachers' expectations of chunking instruction do not always align. Teachers had more variations of opinions on the usefulness of chunking. Some were supporters who believed in repeated emphasis on the approach, but more than a quarter of the teacher participants held doubts. Teachers also differed in their beliefs of learning characters through "self-discoveries" versus teacher-led discoveries or direct instructions, and a few teachers admitted to not applying the chunking technique at all. For the student group, two patterns may be worth noting. First, most students believed that chunking would be most helpful when the concept or practice is introduced *after* they have had some exposure to the Chinese language. Second, students' perceptions of chunking and practices differed depending on their language experiences. Those who have had more language learning experience (i.e., heritage language students and third-year students) gave more positive responses to chunking. Although the sample size in this study was small, these observations point to potential areas of future exploration. For instance, the different beliefs, practices, and preferences of teachers indicate the need for experience sharing among and professional development opportunities for teachers. The potentially different perceptions between experienced versus novice, and heritage versus non-heritage learners echoed earlier studies (e.g., Ke 1998) and suggest that our pedagogical approach of chunking may also need to differ depending on the student population.

A Perceptual Decomposition Study

Background of the Study

Earlier research has pointed out that chunks and radicals are associated with various types of prototypical and permissible positions in specific character configurations. For instance, 女, 山 and 日 can occur in various configurations and permissible positions, but there are often regularities to follow, once a character configuration is determined. 女 occurs in the left-right configuration 60% of the time, and when it occurs in the left-right configuration, it predominantly occurs on the left; 山 is associated with the up-down configuration 60% of the time, and it predominantly occurs at the bottom in that configuration (Chen et al. 2011). Some other chunks, such as 日, can be productive in various configurations (e.g., 旬, 间, 旭 and 者). Understanding character configurations, in addition to familiarity with the chunk's graphic forms, can enhance learners' character learning. Some studies assessing CFL learners' visual-orthographic skills intentionally included a variety of character configurations in their component perception tasks (e.g., Shen and Ke 2007), but to date, investigations on learners' awareness of character configurations are scarce.

In the literature based on simplified Chinese (e.g., Xing 2005), compound characters may be in one of the following 12 configurations: left-right up-down; left-middle-right; up-middle-down; fully enclosed; three-side enclosed (with three different variations); two-side enclosed (with three different variations) and an "overlaid" structure with overlapping parts or a left-right surrounding (夹击) structure.

In empirical studies on Chinese character learning, more detailed classifications of character configurations are often considered. For instance, in Shen and Ke's (2007) radical perception test, their materials included five types of left-right structures and eight types of top-bottom structures. As learners' ability to perceive chunks in a character should be closely related to their awareness of the character's internal configurations, I conducted an exploratory study to examine beginner-level CFL students' perceptual decompositions of unfamiliar characters. The study aimed to investigate students' familiarity with various character configurations and their performance in visual chunking (i.e., identifying and reproducing chunks in a character).

Methodology

Participants

Thirty-five non-heritage students enrolled in a second-semester Chinese language class at a university in the United States participated in the study. Before the experiment, participants had received approximately 140 hours of instruction in Chinese and had learned about 250 characters.

Materials

The key materials were 60 characters in different structural configurations. Those configurations include the 12 structures in Fig. 7.2, 7 configurations with different combinations of left-right and up-down sub-structures, and other combinations involving a (semi-)enclosed intermediate-level component (e.g., 娴 and 菌) or more complex left-right, up-down combinations (e.g., 睦, in which the intermediate-component consists of three chunks, and 樱, in which the intermediate-level component itself is a combination of left-right and up-down structure). The full list of the 60 characters and their configurations can be found in Table 7.3.

The characters were chosen based on the following criteria to maximize the study's validity in character teaching practice:

(a)杖 (b)杏 (c)梆 (d)案 (e)回 (f)同 (g)凶 (h)区 (i)居 (j)句 (k)过 (l) 乘

Fig. 7.2 12 Configurations of compound characters

7 Visual Skill and Orthographic Decomposition in Character...

Table 7.3 Participants' chunking performance on different characters and configurations

No.	Configuration	Configuration	Character	Accuracy (%)	Character	Accuracy (%)
1	Horizontally		杖	94.3	枚	100.0
2	oriented		桔	97.1	格	94.3
3			静	74.3	韵	85.7
4			嫩	97.1	梆	100.0
5			撤	94.3	撅	97.1
6	Vertically		杏	97.1	呆	100.0
7	oriented		荫	94.3	药	100.0
8			翁	80.0	聂	60.0
9			染	97.1	婆	94.3
10			盟	100.0	怒	100.0
11			宣	45.7	宴	100.0
12			案	97.1	章	60.0
13			苹	91.4	煎	85.7
15			蓿	80.0	菀	91.4
16	2-side-		右	88.6	石	100.0
17	enclosed		肩	91.4	居	100.0
18			述	100.0	赵	100.0
19			赶	94.3	迷	100.0
20			句	100.0	旬	100.0
21			栽	91.4	哉	91.4
22	3-side enclosed		闯	97.1	闭	100.0
23			匹	100.0	巨	94.3
24			齿	91.4	画	62.9
25	Fully enclosed		囡	94.3	困	100.0
26	overlaying		巫	91.4	乘	100.0
27	Mixed 1		娴	97.1	润	100.0
28	Mixed 2		茴	88.6	菌	100.0
29	Mixed 3		堰	91.4	恼	57.1
30	Mixed 4		睦	42.9	樱	77.1

Notes: Low-accuracy characters (accuracy < 80%) are underlined.
画 is considered to have a ⊔ configuration by Xing (2005) but grouped as an up-down configuration character in the *Comprehensive Resource Application System* (Laboratory for Chinese Character Research and Application 2019). 齿 and 画 were chosen as the representative characters for the ⊔ configuration here due to the saliency of their semi-enclosed structure, as other character candidates in this configuration either have too few numbers (凶) or primarily contain chunks that are unfamiliar to participants (凿).

1. All characters are unfamiliar to the participants. Participants had no exposure to these characters in their Chinese language classroom materials. Pilot studies with five students in the same second-semester class as the participants confirmed that those were new characters to the participant population.
2. Most of these characters are formed with a familiar chunk chosen from a list of chunks most familiar to students, including 木, 女, 心 (忄), 人, 月, 目, 日 and 口. To include characters in different configurations that satisfy all the requirements, other familiar chunks such as 走/辶, 目, 艹 and 又 are also used. The familiarity of chunks was defined in terms of the participants' Chinese language course curriculum. These were constituents of characters explicitly taught prior to the study.
3. To control the visual complexity of the characters while allowing variation, all chosen characters have 5 to 15 stroke numbers (M = 9.3, SD = 2.9). All the characters have two to four chunks.
4. At least two characters with orthographically similar chunks were chosen for each configuration (e.g., 枚 and 杖, 句 and 旬, 右 and 石, 茴 and 菌). Aside from controlling the visual complexities of characters, this design enables us to tease apart participants' errors with stroke features and their errors resulting from structural configurations.

With the pairs of characters chosen for each configuration, two versions of chunking test papers were designed and were given to participants at two different time points (with 30 minutes in between, so that participants would not be able to directly compare the orthographically similar pairs like 枚 and 杖). Characters were randomized in order in each version. The two versions of the test were also used to calculate the internal consistency of the task. Cronbach's alpha was 0.71, indicating acceptable internal reliability.

Procedures

Participants completed the task in a Chinese language class. The test was administered with paper and pencil. Participants were asked to write out the constituting chunks of a character. They were given definitions of "chunks" (i.e., "visually integral units which may occasionally contain just one stroke but often more than that" and "building blocks of characters"). They were also given examples of chunks (e.g., 氵, 十, 亻, 纟, 厶 and 灬) and were reminded that chunks "may also be radicals at the same time". Several examples of character decomposition into chunks were given (e.g., 忠—中+心; 妍—女+开). Participants were given opportunities to ask clarification questions before they began the task. Participants completed each version of the test within 10 minutes.

Scoring

For each character, the correct chunk breakdown was assigned a score of 1. A response with incorrect structural decomposition or inaccurate or incomplete chunk reproductions was assigned a score of 0. The PI and a research assistant independently scored participants' responses. *Character Components and Component Names* by the National Language Commission (2009) was used as the reference to determine what constitutes a chunk. Discrepancies in scoring were resolved in discussion until a full agreement was reached.

Result and Analysis

The accuracy rates for each character were calculated based on the percentage of participants who were able to correctly break down the characters. The results are in Table 7.3.

The mean accuracy of all items is 90.0% (SD = 0.14), suggesting that beginner-level students generally had high performance in this visual-orthographic task. Characters composed entirely with high-frequency familiar chunks such as 怒, 宴, 案, 娴, 菌 and 堰 had especially high accuracies, regardless of their structural configuration. Further, there were very few errors associated with stroke features. For instance, participants were clearly able to differentiate 杖 from 枚, 石 from 右, etc., and reproduced them in copying the chunk components accurately. That is, beginner-level learners had developed fine-grained stroke representations and were sensitive towards nuanced stroke features. Participants' high performance in reproducing chunks with accurate stroke features and general familiarity with different configurations corresponded to earlier findings in Shen and Ke (2007), in which rapid development in CFL students' radical perceptual skills within their first year of study was reported.

As earlier studies suggest that stroke numbers—an indicator for a character's visual complexity—may affect processing (Peng and Wang 1997), a correlation analysis was conducted with stroke number as the independent variable and characters' accuracy rates as the dependent variable. Results showed a median correlation between the variables (Pearson's r = 0.27, t = 2.10, p = 0.04). Higher stroke density in the square space contributed to difficulties in this task. This confirms that, for beginner-level learners, character decomposition or chunking remains tied to their visual-perceptual skills.

In this study, the stroke numbers and chunk numbers in characters in each configuration are not matched. This is primarily due to the limitation of character choices when the study used a specific set of high-frequency chunks familiar to learners. Thus, we cannot claim statistical significance in accuracy comparisons across different configurations. Nevertheless, it is useful to note that accuracies in the semi-enclosed or fully enclosed configurations were high (M = 0.95, SD = 0.09), even though these configurations have very low frequencies in character databases in general (8.85% according to Xing (2005)). Aside from the possible facilitation of having few stroke numbers in this set of characters (M = 7.05, SD = 1.9) or fewer chunks in this group of characters, (semi-)enclosed configurations may be easier for perceptual decomposition tasks because the enclosed structures give clear boundaries to chunks, thus facilitating the visual decomposition for beginner-level Chinese learners. Similarly, characters in the "overlying" configuration are extremely rare (0.55% based on Xing (2005)), but the two characters in this configuration both had high accuracies. It is likely that familiar chunks, 工 and 人 in 巫 and 禾 (which occurs in the high-frequency character of 和) in 乘, contributed to participants' successful task completion.

Representative examples of errors associated with characters of low accuracy (i.e., < 80% accuracy) are shown in Table 7.4. Among the

7 Visual Skill and Orthographic Decomposition in Character...

Table 7.4 Participants' error samples in low-accuracy chunking characters

Error type	Character		Error samples
Mix-configuration errors	恼	(1)	忄 卤 __
		(2)	忄 亠 凶
		(3)	忄 卤 乂
	樱	(4)	扌 ՈՈ 丬丬 女
	睦	(5)	且 土 儿 土
		(6)	且 ナ 土 __
		(7)	且 十 一 土
Under-decomposition errors	章	(8)	立 早 __
	聂	(9)	耳 又又 __
Horizontal bar errors	画	(12)	凵 田 __
		(13)	囼 凵 __
	宣	(14)	宀 旦 __ __
		(15)	宀 亘 __ __
		(16)	宀 亘 __
Unfamiliar and complex chunk	静	(17)	土 月 __ __
		(18)	土 月 亅 __
		(19)	土 月 ⁊ 亅 ⼅ 一

characters with an intermediate-level (semi-)enclosed structure, 恼 had a different pattern from 娴, 涧, 茴, 菌 and 堰, and had a low accuracy (57.1%). Upon a closer look, the semi-enclosed structure (凶) in 恼 is more embedded than the enclosed structures in others. For instance, although both 堰 and 恼 have four chunks, the former has two levels of decomposition, whereas the latter has three. Once participants decomposed 堰 into two left-right components, the semi-enclosed structure 匽 with the 日 and 女 components inside would be evident. For 恼, participants had to perform two steps of decomposition, first in the left-right direction to tease apart 忄 and 卤, and then perform up-down decomposition to separate 亠 from 凶 to retrieve the semi-enclosed structure. As errors of 恼 in Table 7.4 show, participants tended to stop in the first or second step of decomposition. The difficulties associated with 樱 were similar. This character needs to be decomposed in three layers, first left-right (木-婴), then up-down (贝贝-女) and finally left-right again (贝-贝). Participants' errors indicated that decomposing the embedded level component (贝贝) was challenging. The challenges in decomposing

睦, on the other hand, appear to be induced by the vertically oriented structure on its right side; all errors were associated with decomposing the intermediate-level component of 坴. While all participants were familiar with the chunk of 土, they still struggled with how other strokes combine to make patterns. The challenges with decomposing a visually complex vertical structure were also seen in 章, 聂, 画 and 宜.

Errors in 章 and 聂 were predominantly due to lack of full decomposition. In these characters, a subcharacter component forms a familiar orthographic form: 早 in 章 and 双 in 聂 both form high-frequency stand-alone characters with concrete meanings. Participants' familiarity with these forms could have led to holistic perceptions of 早 and 双 as integral single units.

Frequent errors in 画 and 宜 indicated that participants lacked awareness that 一 (a horizontal bar) is an integral chunk. The vertically oriented structure likely has induced more difficulties. 一 is one of the most productive primitive chunks in Chinese and appears in 161 characters (National Language Commission 2009). Without this metalinguistic awareness, many participants attempted to group 一 together with other stroke patterns and sometimes completely missed the 一 chunk in 画 and 宜.

The only horizontally oriented character that imposed difficulties was 静, where its subcharacter component 争 was both unfamiliar to participants and visually complex. Participants had difficulty reproducing this chunk. Even though they had constant access to the character's form to copy it, several participants decomposed the component into random strokes or gave up trying.

Discussions of Character Decomposition

The findings confirmed that students' perception and successful structural decomposition are related to characters' visual complexity measured by stroke numbers. The relative ease or difficulty in perceiving chunks may also be relevant to different character configurations. Although low-frequency configurations are not necessarily more difficult to decompose, deeply embedded subcomponents can be harder for students to extract.

Numerically, accuracy rates in vertically oriented configurations were lower than in horizontally oriented configurations. A possible explanation is that native speakers of alphabetic languages are more accustomed to orthographic units (e.g., letters) arranged in the left-to-right linear order, and a vertically oriented configuration can be thus more visually demanding in decomposition tasks. As characters in various configurations in this study involve different chunks and stroke numbers, this speculation remains tentative, but the preliminary patterns observed indicate the need for further research on the effect of character configuration on perceptual challenges for learners from an L1 background with a linearly organized orthography.

Errors of under-decomposition occurred more often than over-decomposition in participants' performances in this task. It is easier for students to perceive characters in higher-level components than in primitive chunks. These errors suggest that our participants were progressing in their orthographic awareness development. They were no longer seeing characters as a combination of random strokes and were generally able to use intermediate-level character components to understand new character structures, and they used learned meaning- and sound-bearing orthographic forms as a crutch (e.g., 早, 双). Such a tendency has its benefits. Xing (2005) pointed out that among the approximately 500 chunks in simplified Chinese, 285 are chunks overlapping with an independent character in their orthographic forms (成字部件) (e.g.,末, 丁 and 甘). In other words, learners would be able to use these "meaningful" chunks to acquire new characters. Nevertheless, many chunk combinations, especially in simplified Chinese, are not meaning- or sound-bearing orthographic components, and the ability to decompose phonetic or semantic radicals further into primitive chunks is needed for students to use small units to build substantial quantities of combinations. Most of the "character-form" chunk examples (成字部件) listed in Xing (2005) (e.g.,卵, 隶, 兼, 甲 and 谷) do not occur in typical CFL textbook curricula for beginner-level learners. That is, using independent character forms as the chunking unit is not a productive way to learn for beginner to intermediate-level learners. According to the National Language Commission (2009), chunks that form more than 70 characters include 一, 十, 土, 又, 贝, 八, 亠 and 冖, among others. Many of them do not receive much attention in character instruction because they are not meaning-bearing radicals. Others (e.g., 土) can function as radicals but occur earlier or more frequently as "meaningless" chunks in high-frequency characters in Chinese language students' curriculum (e.g., 在, 去). Other productive chunks that form more than 50 characters include 勹, 乂 and 厶. Thus, while we leverage learners' radical knowledge and learned character forms (e.g., 口, 日, 木 and 氵) to facilitate their learning, due pedagogical consideration should also be given to frequently used chunks, even if they are "meaningless", as those constitute visual form building blocks to support beginner-level learners' orthographic awareness development.

As an exploratory study, the above attempt to examine students' performance in character decomposition has several limitations including its small sample size both in participant number and in experimental materials. Among many questions that need addressing, some key foci include exploring how novice-level Chinese language learners' perceptual decompositions of characters in varying configurations differ from native speakers or experienced learners, and whether students' ability to visually decompose characters or their use of the chunking strategy correlates with their character learning outcome.

Conclusion

Developing visual-orthographic skills is the foundation of perceiving characters as the structured composition of smaller units. This chapter argues for this position by establishing the correlation between learners' perceptual skills with their character learning, studying teachers' and students' perceptions of the chunking strategy, and reporting students' performances in chunking unfamiliar characters. Finding ways to support students' use of subcharacter components and help them develop the metalinguistic knowledge of their graphic forms, positions and regularities will facilitate students' learning. This can be an especially fruitful direction when instructors experiment with a "penless" curriculum in the present-day context.

Currently, stable and readily accessible open-resource databases suitable for chunk- or radical-based character instruction are still lacking. But a notable development highlighting the field's ongoing effort in this domain is the 汉字全息资源应用系统 by the Laboratory for Chinese Character Research and Application (2019), which offers character lists categorized by their constituent chunks and structural configurations, in addition to giving comprehensive etymology information to each character. There remains considerable scope for advancement in our pedagogy to facilitate students' perceptual and chunking skill development to improve their orthographic awareness.

Acknowledgement The author wishes to thank Dr Li-Yun Chang for her approval to include partial results from Chang et al. (2014) in this chapter. The author also thanks Brandon Yee for sharing his data in Yee (2019) for reanalysis in this chapter.

Ethical Approval For the research projects referred to in this chapter, including the visual skill correlation study, the teacher and student perception survey study, and the character decomposition study, informed consent was obtained from individual participants.

Competing Interests The author has no conflicts of interest to declare that are relevant to the content of this chapter.

References

Cao, Fan, Ben Rickles, Vu Marianne, Ziheng Zhu, Derek Ho Lung Chan, Lindsay N. Harris, Joseph Stafura, Yi Xu, and Charles A. Perfetti. 2013. Early Stage Visual-Orthographic Processes Predict Long-Term Retention of Word Form and Meaning: A Visual Encoding Training Study. *Journal of Neurolinguistics* 26 (4): 440–461.

Cassar, Marie, and Rebecca Treiman. 1997. The Beginnings of Orthographic Knowledge: Children's Knowledge of Double Letters in Words. *Journal of Educational Psychology* 89 (4): 631–664.

Chang, Li-Yun, Yi Xu, Alison M. Tseng, and Charles A. Perfetti. 2014. *Basic Visual Skills Modulate Chinese Character Reading Acquisition in Learning*

Chinese as a Foreign Language: An In-Vivo Study. Paper presented at the annual meeting of the American Association for Applied Linguistics, Portland, OR.

Chang, Li-Yun, Yen-Chi Chen, and Charles A. Perfetti. 2018. GraphCom: A Multidimensional Measure of Graphic Complexity Applied to 131 Written Languages. *Behaviour Research Methods* 50: 427–449.

Chein, Jackson M., and Alexandra B. Morrison. 2010. Expanding the Mind's Workspace: Training and Transfer Effects with a Complex Working Memory Span Task. *Psychonomic Bulletin and Review* 17 (2): 193–199.

Chen, Hsueh-Chih, Li-Yun Chang, Yu-Shiou Chiou, Yao-Ting Sung, and Kuo-En Chang. 2011. Chinese Orthography Database and Its Application in Teaching Chinese Characters [中文部件组字与形构资料库之建立及其在识字教学的应用]. *Bulletin of Educational Psychology [教育心理学报]* 43: 269–290.

Dictionary of Chinese Character Information [汉字信息字典]. 1988. Shanghai, China: Science Press.

Franceschini, Sandro, Simone Gori, Milena Ruffino, Katia Pedrolli, and Andrea Facoetti. 2012. A Causal Link between Visual Spatial Attention and Reading Acquisition. *Current Biology* 22 (9): 814–819.

Guan, Connie Qun, Ying Liu, Derek Ho Leung Chan, Feifei Ye, and Charles A. Perfetti. 2011. Writing Strengthens Orthography and Alphabetic-Coding Strengthens Phonology in Learning to Read Chinese. *Journal of Educational Psychology* 103 (3): 509–522. https://doi.org/10.1037/a0023730.

Jackson, Nancy Ewald, Michael E. Everson, and Chuanren Ke. 2003. Beginning Readers' Awareness of the Orthographic Structure of Semantic-Phonetic Compounds: Lessons from a Study of Learners of Chinese as a Foreign Language. In *Reading Development in Chinese Children*, ed. Catherine McBride-Chang and Hsuan-Chih Chen, 141–153. Connecticut: Greenwood Publishing Group.

Jin, Hong Gang. 2003. Empirical Evidence on Character Recognition in Multimedia Chinese Tasks. *Concentric: Studies in English Literature and Linguistics* 29: 36–58.

Ke, Chuanren. 1998. Effects of Strategies on the Learning of Chinese Characters among Foreign Language Students. *Journal of the Chinese Language Teachers Association* 33 (2): 93–112.

Kim, Sun-A, Kiel Christianson, and Jerome Packard. 2015. Working Memory in L2 Character Processing: The Case of Learning to Read Chinese. In *Working Memory in Second Language Acquisition and Processing*, ed. Edward

Zhisheng Wen, Mailce Borges Mota, and Arthur McNeill, 85–104. Bristol: Multilingual Matters.

Laboratory for Chinese Character Research and Application [汉字研究与现代应用实验室]. 2019. *Comprehensive Resource Application System for Chinese Characters [汉字全息资源应用系统]*. Accessed March 21, 2024. https://qxk.bnu.edu.cn/#/

Li, Hong, Hua Shu, Catherine McBride-Chang, Hongyun Liu, and Hong Peng. 2012. Chinese Children's Character Recognition: Visuo-Orthographic, Phonological Processing and Morphological Skills. *Journal of Research in Reading* 35 (3): 287–307.

Liu, Ying, Charles A. Perfetti, and Min Wang. 2006. Visual Analysis and Lexical Access of Chinese Characters by Chinese as Second Language Readers. *Linguistics and Language* 7 (3): 637–657.

McGinnis, Scott. 1999. Student's Goals and Approaches. In *Mapping the Course of the Chinese Language Field: Chinese Language Teachers Association Monograph Series*, ed. Madeline Chu, vol. III, 151–168. Kalamazoo, Michigan: Chinese Language Teachers Association, Inc.

Miller, George A. 1956. The Magical Number Seven, Plus or Minus Two: Some Limits on our Capacity for Processing Information. *Psychological Review* 63: 81–97.

National Language Commission. Department of Education, P.R. China [中华人民共和国国家语言文字工作委员会]. 2009. *Specification of Common Modern Chinese Character Components and Component Names [现代常用字部件及部件名称规范]*. Accessed March 21, 2024. http://www.moe.gov.cn/jyb_sjzl/ziliao/A19/201001/t20100115_75696.html

Opitz, Bertram, Julia A. Schneiders, Christopher M. Krick, and Axel Mecklinger. 2014. Selective Transfer of Visual Working Memory Training on Chinese Character Learning. *Neuropsychologia* 53: 1–11.

Pak, Ada K.H., Alice Cheng-Lai, Ivy F. Tso, Hua Shu, Wenling Li, and Richard C. Anderson. 2005. Visual Chunking Skills of Hong Kong Children. *Reading and Writing* 18: 437–454.

Peng, Danling, and Chunmao Wang. 1997. Basic Processing Unit of Chinese Character Recognition: Evidence from Stroke Number Effect and Radical Number Effect. *Acta Psychologica Sinica* 29 (1): 9–17.

Rastle, Kathleen, Matt H. Davis, William D. Marslen-Wilson, and Lorraine K. Tyler. 2000. Morphological and Semantic Effects in Visual Word Recognition: A Time Course Study. *Language and Cognitive Processes* 15: 507–538.

Shen, Helen H. 2010. Imagery and Verbal Coding Approaches in Chinese Vocabulary Instruction. *Language Teaching Research* 14 (4): 485–499.

Shen, Helen H., and Chuanren Ke. 2007. Radical Awareness and Word Acquisition among Nonnative Learners of Chinese. *The Modern Language Journal* 91 (1): 97–111. https://doi.org/10.1111/j.1540-4781.2007.00511.x.

Taft, Marcus, and Kenneth I. Forster. 1975. Lexical Storage and Retrieval for Prefixed Words. *Journal of Verbal Learning and Verbal Behavior* 14: 638–647.

Talcott, Joel B., Caroline Witton, Maggie F. McLean, Peter C. Hansen, Adrian Rees, Gary G.R. Green, and John F. Stein. 2000. Dynamic sensory Sensitivity and Children's Word Decoding Skills. *Proceedings of the National Academy of Sciences* 97 (6): 2952–2957.

Tan, Li Hai, Ho-Ling Liu, Charles A. Perfetti, John A. Spinks, Peter T. Fox, and Jia-Hong Gao. 2001. The Neural System Underlying Chinese Logograph Reading. *NeuroImage* 13: 836–846.

Tong, Xiuli, and Joanna Hew Yan Yip. 2015. Cracking the Chinese character: Radical Sensitivity in Learners of Chinese as a Foreign Language and Its Relationship to Chinese Word Reading. *Reading and Writing* 28: 159–181.

Wang, Danping, and Martin East. 2020. Constructing an Emergency Chinese Curriculum during the Pandemic: A New Zealand Experience. *International Journal of Chinese Language Teaching* 1 (1): 1–19. https://doi.org/10.46451/ijclt.2020.06.01

Xing, Hongbing. 2005. A Statistical Analysis of Components of the Character Entries in the HSK Graded Character List [《汉字水平汉字等级大纲》汉字部件统计分析]. *Chinese Teaching in the World* 2: 49–55.

Xu, Yi, and Li-Yun Chang. 2014. Computer-Assisted Character Learning using Animation and Visual Chunking. In *Engaging Language Learners through Technology Integration: Theory, Applications, and Outcomes*, ed. Shuai Li and Peter Swanson, 1–22. USA: IGI Global.

Xu, Ping, and Theresa Jen. 2005. Penless Chinese Language Learning: A Computer-Assisted Approach. *Journal of the Chinese Language Teachers Association* 40 (2): 25–42.

Xu, Xiaoqiu, and Amado M. Padilla. 2013. Using Meaningful Interpretation and Chunking to Enhance Memory: The Case of Chinese Character Learning. *Foreign Language Annals* 14 (3): 402–422.

Xu, Yi, Li-Yun Chang, and Charles A. Perfetti. 2014. The Effect of Radical-Based Grouping in Character Learning in Chinese as a Foreign Language. *The Modern Language Journal* 98 (3): 773–793.

Xu, Yi, Li Jin, Elizabeth Deifell, and Katie Angus. 2021. Facilitating Technology-Based Character Learning in Emergency Remote Teaching. *Foreign Language Annals* 55 (1): 72–97.

Yang, Ling-Yan, Jian-Peng Guo, Lynn C. Richman, Frank L. Schmidt, Kathryn C. Gerken, and Yi Ding. 2013. Visual skills and Chinese Reading Acquisition: A Meta-Analysis of Correlation Evidence. *Educational Psychology Review* 25 (1): 115–143.

Yee, Brandon. 2019. *Chinese Character Acquisition among Chinese as a Foreign Language Learners: Teaching and Learning Strategies and the Implications*. PhD diss: University of Pittsburgh.

Zhang, Phyllis Ni. 2021. Typing to Replace Handwriting: Effectiveness of the Typing-Primary Approach for L2 Chinese Beginners. *Journal of Technology and Chinese Language Teaching* 12 (2): 1–28.

Zhou, Yanling, and Catherine McBride. 2018. The Same or Different: An Investigation of Cognitive and Metalinguistic Correlates of Chinese Word Reading for Native and Non-Native Chinese Speaking Children. *Bilingualism: Language and Cognition* 21 (4): 765–781.

Zhou, Yanling, Catherine McBride-Chang, and Natalie Wong. 2014. What is the Role of Visual Skills in Learning to Read? *Frontiers in Psychology* 5: 776.

Zhou, Yanling, Catherine McBride, Judy Sze Man Leung, Ying Wang, Malatesha Joshi, and JoAnn Farver. 2018. Chinese and English Reading-Related Skills in L1 and L2 Chinese-Speaking Children in Hong Kong. *Language, Cognition and Neuroscience* 33 (3): 300–312.

Zhu, Yu, Andy S.L. Fung, and Hongyan Wang. 2012. Memorization Effects of Pronunciation and Stroke Order Animation in Digital Flashcards. *CALICO Journal* 29 (3): 563–577.

8

Psycholinguistic Research Related to Chinese Character Recognition: Implications for CFL Teaching

Xi Fan and Ronan Reilly

Introduction

The complexity and opacity of the Chinese character system have consistently posed a significant challenge for Chinese as a foreign language (CFL) learners in the realm of character recognition. Becoming a fluent Chinese reader requires a substantial investment of time and cognitive effort (Chen et al. 2023; Wong 2017). The Simple View of Reading (SVR) posits that reading consists of two relatively independent core components: word decoding and (oral) language comprehension (Hoover

---

X. Fan (✉)
School of Health Management, Guangzhou Medical University, Guangzhou, China
e-mail: gyfanxi@gzhmu.edu.cn

R. Reilly
Department of Computer Science, Maynooth University, Maynooth, Ireland
e-mail: ronan.reilly@mu.ie

and Gough 1990). Specifically, it involves bottom-up lexical decoding starting from word recognition and top-down language comprehension based on individual oral experiences. This theory provides a relatively concise model for understanding reading development and has been widely validated across different languages and writing systems (Peng et al. 2021). Recent studies indicate that SVR is applicable to both Chinese native speakers and CFL learners. In both contexts, word decoding and auditory comprehension play unique and crucial roles in Chinese reading comprehension, with word decoding even surpassing auditory comprehension in its impact (Chen et al. 2023; Wong 2017). Consequently, accurate recognition of Chinese characters stands as the primary task for CFL learners in developing their reading abilities.

Decoding refers to the cognitive process of transforming written symbols into sound and meaning, involving accurate visual recognition of Chinese characters and mastery of its orthographic phonological mapping rules. Character reading and orthographic knowledge constitute decoding ability. In the context of the Chinese language, orthographic knowledge is commonly characterised as the comprehension of legal components in written or printed words, including strokes, radicals and entire characters, along with awareness of their positional and functional constraints (Ho et al. 2003). However, unlike Chinese native speakers who learn characters after mastering most phonetic and semantic representations, CFL learners, especially at the initial stages, must acquire orthographic knowledge while concurrently developing oral proficiency in the Chinese language. Therefore, in the learning of Chinese characters by CFL learners, orthographic knowledge is particularly crucial for character decoding. In fact, orthographic knowledge has been found to have a significant predictive role in L2 Chinese word decoding (Chen et al. 2023; Tong and Yip 2015; Wong 2017).

Given the practical challenges of Chinese character recognition and the theoretical importance of accurate visual Chinese character reading, this chapter will focus on investigating psycholinguistic research in the field of graphic information processing. It aims to explore insights provided by these studies for CFL teaching and contribute to addressing challenges in learning Chinese characters.

The Challenges of Learning Chinese Characters

It is necessary first to examine the characteristics of Chinese characters to understand why the recognition of Chinese characters poses a challenging task for CFL learners.

First, the structure of Chinese characters is intricate, involving strokes, radicals and characters. Strokes (such as dot, horizontal, vertical, throw, pressing, rise, bend and hook) constitute the smallest units forming Chinese characters, each with a distinct shape. Chinese characters can be composed of different strokes in various combinations, ranging from simple characters with only one stroke to complex characters with up to 36 strokes (*Dictionary of Chinese Character Information* 1988).

According to Chen (1993), characters with six to nine strokes account for approximately 50% of the 1000 most frequently used characters, while in the 7000 commonly used characters, this ratio is 33.64%. Radicals, which are composed of strokes, play a crucial role in character formation. A Chinese character can be formed by combining one or more radicals. English words are formed by linear combinations of 26 letters, whereas there are up to 514 distinct radicals, the combination of which is constrained by the square form of Chinese characters (Leong et al. 2011). The complex structure of Chinese characters imposes higher demands on CFL learners for accurate character recognition and memorisation compared to alphabetic languages.

Second, the orthographic regularity of Chinese characters plays a significant role in recognition (Hong et al. 2016; Tong and McBride 2014). It is essential to combine different strokes or radicals in accordance with orthographic rules to construct valid Chinese characters.

For instance, taking the radicals "月" (moon), "几" (table) and "又" (again) as examples, there are more than 20 (3*3*3 = 27) different combinations possible on a two dimensional plane. However, only one specific combination with the permitted positional arrangement forms the familiar character "股" (stocks). Note that such positional arrangements are dictated by tradition and practice rather than any specific rules. Moreover, the combination of strokes or radicals is constrained by the square form of Chinese characters, and changing the position of a single radical can alter the character's meaning, such as in the case of "人" (person) and "八" (eight). This aspect contributes to the complexity of character recognition and particularly poses challenges for CFL learners.

Third, the large number of Chinese characters—3500 in common use according to the *Dictionary of Chinese Character Information* (1988)—necessitates that learners master a multitude of character forms and meanings. This requirement demands significant time and effort from CFL learners to individually study and memorise each character, presenting a substantial challenge.

Fourth, the complexity of character recognition in Chinese is heightened by the unclear relationship between pronunciation and character form (Perfetti and Zhang 1995). Unlike in alphabetic writing systems, Chinese characters prioritise semantic features over phonetic ones, lacking a direct visual-to-pronunciation correspondence. This absence of systematic grapheme-phoneme correspondence makes direct phonetic reading impossible. Therefore, phonological activation of Chinese characters may be slower than in alphabetic systems, but their semantic function may facilitate faster and more explicit semantic extraction (Perfetti and Tan 1998; Tan et al. 1995). Additionally, while phonetic radicals primarily indicate the pronunciation of phonetic-semantic characters, mastering their pronunciation requires proficiency in numerous phonetic radical pronunciations. All of these factors make it difficult for CFL learners to remember the pronunciation of Chinese characters, thereby increasing the learning difficulty.

In conclusion, learning Chinese characters is a complex and challenging task for CFL learners. Their intricate configuration, vast quantity, numerous orthographic regularity rules and non-transparent correlation between pronunciation and character morphology collectively impose a substantial cognitive load.

Research on Chinese Character Recognition

The unique characteristics of Chinese characters can potentially provide valuable contributions to psycholinguistic research, especially in terms of deepening our understanding of language information processing.

Over the past century, numerous experimental methodologies have been devised to examine word identification processes, predominantly employing paradigms such as perceptual identification, lexical decision and naming (Reichle 2021). In perceptual identification, words undergo visual degradation via techniques, such as masking or brief presentations. Participants are subsequently tasked with recognising these visually modified words with the accuracy of identification serving as the dependent variable. Researchers also rely extensively on two simpler tasks, namely lexical decision and naming, to investigate isolated word recognition. In lexical decision, participants are asked rapidly to differentiate between real words and non-words, while in naming, they must promptly articulate the visually presented words. The primary emphasis is on comprehending the expeditious execution of these tasks by individuals across diverse conditions, based on the assumption that response latencies reflect the underlying processes associated with accessing lexical representations.

The following sections review some of the key findings associated with Chinese character orthographic representations and processing that have been documented to date, using the tasks described. Considering the extensive scope of the literature on word identification, we will limit our focus to empirical research results from both native speakers and CFL learners that contribute to our understanding of orthographic processing in Chinese character recognition. Our emphasis is on findings that hold theoretical significance and practical value in constructing theories of Chinese character recognition that may have pedagogical implications.

The Stroke Count Effect

Researchers have extensively explored the impact of stroke count on the recognition of Chinese characters by native speakers, indicating a positive correlation between stroke count and processing time as well as error rates (Liu et al. 2007; Peng and Wang 1997; Su and Samuels 2010; Yu and Cao 1992; Zhang and Feng 1992). Zhang and Feng (1992) found that characters with more strokes exhibited relatively slower naming speeds, and this trend was consistent for both high-frequency and low-frequency characters. Experimental results further supported this finding (Peng and Wang 1997; Yu and Cao 1992). Su and Samuels (2010) compared the stroke-count effect in lexical decision tasks among second-grade, fourth-grade and university students, revealing its presence only in the second-grade participants, suggesting that it is probably relatively more pronounced in novice learners.

There are divergent views on whether CFL learners' recognition of Chinese characters is influenced by stroke count. You (2003), using a lexical decision task, investigated the stroke-count effect on CFL learners' recognition of Chinese characters, finding a significant effect but with no significant interaction with character frequency. Zhang (2008) obtained similar results in a comparable lexical-decision task. Hao (2018), using a naming task with advanced-level CFL learners, observed a subtle stroke-count effect, suggesting that as learners' proficiency in Chinese increases, its impact on character naming gradually diminishes. In contrast, Liu (2008) found no impact of stroke count on Chinese character recognition in a phonetic annotation task.

The divergence in findings may stem from the adoption of different experimental methods. Liu (2008) employed a phonetic annotation task under non-speeded conditions, differing from other research that utilised speeded conditions with lexical decision tasks. Non-speeded conditions typically refer to tasks without time constraints, aiming to simulate a more natural learning environment. However, when investigating language processing stages, this experimental design might not specifically focus on the earlier pre-lexical stage. Non-speeded conditions tend to emphasise overall language processing rather than addressing details of the pre-lexical stage. This characteristic may result in the effects observed in Liu's study not fully reflecting influences at the pre-lexical stage. Nevertheless, the stroke count of Chinese characters may significantly impact the early perceptual stages of lexical processing. This viewpoint finds support in research of Zhu et al. (2019).

Overall, stroke count appears to be a fundamental processing unit for Chinese character recognition among both native speakers and CFL learners—particularly those with lower proficiency—across both low- and high-frequency words. However, there is inconsistency in researchers' conclusions regarding the universality of the stroke count effect among CFL learners, with its stability varying and influenced by experimental paradigms. Future studies could focus on exploring the conditions under which this effect manifests in different experimental tasks. It is noteworthy, for example, that studies find an impact of stroke count on Chinese character handwriting among CFL learners (Liu 2008; You 2003; Zhang and Reilly 2015).

Building on the perspectives reviewed above, we propose potential enhancements to the teaching of Chinese characters in the context of CFL. During the initial phase of learning, or for CFL learners with lower proficiency where stroke appears to be a crucial processing unit, the focus could be on introducing characters that have fewer strokes and then progress to those with more. Secondly, in courses primarily focused on writing, the incorporation and emphasis on stroke teaching could be introduced to facilitate character recognition.

The Radical-Level Effects

Not all radicals offer clear cues to the meaning and/or pronunciation of the entire character. As a result, placing greater emphasis on the constructional roles of radicals in processing characters contributes to understanding the processing of characters (Tsang and Chen 2009).

The Radical Count Effect

In addition to stroke count, the number of radicals serves as another indicator of the visual complexity of characters. Zhang and Sheng (1999) discovered an order of difficulty in character naming: single-radical characters; two-radical characters and three-radical characters. Ensuring a relatively balanced stroke count, Zhang and Feng (1992) instructed participants to name characters with either one or two radicals. Their research revealed that under high-frequency conditions, single-radical characters were easier to name than two-radical characters, but there was no difference under low-frequency conditions. However, in the study conducted by Peng and Wang (1997), a naming task was employed, and the number of radicals played a role in low-frequency characters but not in high-frequency characters, which contrasts with the results of Zhang and Feng (1992). Similar results were obtained in a lexical decision task they conducted.

In the above research, we observed that the number of radicals influences Chinese character recognition in native speakers. There is typically a correlation between the stroke count and the number of radicals in a Chinese character, where characters with more strokes often include a greater number of radicals. Therefore, this finding is not surprising given the existence of a stroke effect. Secondly, the influence of the number of radicals is not independent of character frequency, although the results in high- and low-frequency characters are inconsistent. Furthermore, it remains unclear whether characters with more radicals are relatively more difficult to recognise compared to characters with fewer radicals. There is some controversy regarding whether the recognition of Chinese characters by CFL learners is influenced by the number of radicals. Feng (2002) found a significant effect of the number of radicals on the recognition of Chinese characters among CFL learners, with the quantity of radicals inversely related to recognition accuracy. You (2003), using a lexical decision task, observed a significant main effect of radical number on response time. Interestingly, the response time did not increase with an increase in the number of radicals. Instead, the response time was longest for characters with two radicals. The error rates for different radical numbers did not reach significance in high-frequency characters, while in low-frequency characters, the error rate increased with the number of radicals. Therefore, You (2003) proposed that learners process high-frequency Chinese characters through only two levels: strokes and characters. In contrast, low-frequency characters are processed through three levels: strokes; radicals and characters. Additionally, their processing method is primarily sequential, unlike the parallel processing observed in native speakers. However, Liu (2008) found that the influence of radical count is only apparent in a handwriting task and does not affect character recognition in a phonetic annotation task. Moreover, Hao (2018), through a naming task, did not observe the radical count effect in advanced-level CFL learners.

Similar to the stroke count effect in CFL learners, the controversy in findings may stem from the adoption of different experimental methods. In general, the literature indicates that the radical count effect on CFL learners' character recognition displays a certain degree of instability. The stability is influenced by experimental paradigms and proficiency levels. This effect is not significant in advanced-level CFL learners. Moreover, CFL learners likely process high-frequency Chinese characters at two levels (strokes and characters) and low-frequency characters at three levels (strokes, radicals and characters).

To enhance the teaching of Chinese characters to CFL learners, certain aspects can be considered. Firstly, given that the processing of low-frequency Chinese characters likely involves stroke, radical and character levels, whereas high-frequency characters are processed at the stroke and character levels, instructional emphasis on teaching radicals of low-frequency characters could be intensified. Secondly, in courses primarily focused on writing, emphasising radical instruction is also a beneficial strategy.

The Radical Position Effect

In word recognition involving alphabetic scripts, researchers widely acknowledge the importance of letter position (Wu et al. 2016). When comparing Chinese and English, the position of radicals can be considered equivalent to the role of letter position in English. The exploration of how the positions of radicals affect Chinese word recognition has been a primary focus of research. Multiple studies have indicated that radical position information can significantly impact the processing of Chinese characters for both native speakers and CFL learners (Ding et al. 2004; Hong et al. 2016; Lei and Wang 2023; Tong and Yip 2015; Wu et al. 2016).

Ding et al. (2004) investigated the radical priming effect on Chinese characters through a lexical decision task. The results demonstrated a significant facilitation effect when the priming stimulus and the target stimulus shared the same radical position, as in the case of "躯" and "枢". Conversely, no such effect was observed when the radical positions were different, as in the case of "欧" and "枢". This suggests that the psychological representation of radicals involves not only their identity but also accurate spatial location. Therefore, the priming effect manifests only when both the accurate positional and identity representations of radicals are activated based on perceptual features.

In alphabetic scripts, transposition effects are a common phenomenon. A transposed stimulus (e.g., "jugde") is perceived as more similar to its base word ("judge") compared to an orthographic control (i.e., a stimulus with replaced letters, such as "junper"). In contrast to the linear arrangement of letters in an alphabetical writing system, the arrangement of radicals in Chinese characters is more flexible, with many radicals capable of appearing in any position within a character. This flexibility introduces more possibilities for transposition effects, including the swapping of two vertically arranged radicals. In this context, Ding et al. (2004) further explored the transposition priming effect in Chinese character recognition, where the priming stimulus is either a transposed version of the target character or entirely unrelated. For instance, the target character "杏" might have been preceded by a priming character "呆" (where the two radicals of the target character swap positions) or a priming character "垂" (where the radicals are entirely different). The experiment revealed that in cases with identical radicals but different positions, such as transposable characters "杏" and "呆", an inhibitory effect is triggered, particularly for low-frequency target characters. This suggests that changes in the positions of radicals in characters hinder their recognition, revealing the key role of radical position in word processing.

The positioning of radicals within characters significantly impacts CFL learners' recognition of Chinese characters. In a study by Tong and Yip (2015), CFL learners tended to select pseudo-characters containing correct semantic/phonetic radicals in correct positions over non-characters and unrelated visual-orthographic controls, suggesting that CFL learners encode positional radicals during character learning. Moreover, Hong et al. (2016) found that providing a radical position cue before a test resulted in no difference in the word recognition performance of CFL learners, irrespective of their proficiency level, highlighting the significance of positional regularities. More recently, Lei and Wang (2023) revealed that beginner CFL learners perform better in analysing top-bottom structures compared to left-right structures. They attribute this to the consistent positional regularity of radicals in top-bottom structures, which facilitates easier identification of correct positions and leads to higher accuracy rates. The findings highlight how beginner CFL learners have developed the ability to recognise positional regularities, emphasising the importance of radical positions in character recognition for them.

Overall, research findings from both native speakers and CFL learners support the importance of radical position information on Chinese characters recognition. This knowledge influences the recognition process in a top-down manner, serving as a form of orthographic knowledge. Therefore, improving CFL learners' comprehension of radical position regularities may enhance their proficiency in recognising Chinese characters. Considering the presence of both position-general and position-specific radicals (Myers 2019), addressing the challenges posed by position-general radicals, especially for learners without prior experience of Chinese characters, is crucial. Instruction on radicals could encompass their shapes, functions and positional characteristics.

The Word-Superiority Effect

The word-superiority effect is a prevalent phenomenon in language learning. It suggests the coexistence of both bottom-up and top-down processes in word processing (Carreiras et al. 2014). Bottom-up processing refers to the impact of orthographic information on higher-level language representations (such as phonological and semantic information), while top-down processing involves the influence of higher-level language information on visual-orthographic processing. When letters appear in words, the processing of letters involves both bottom-up visual information processing and top-down processing from the word level. This top-down processing from the word level enhances the perceptual processing speed of letters, resulting in the word-superiority effect (Carreiras et al. 2014).

Research has shown the existence of a word-superiority effect in the Chinese lexical processing of native speakers. Specifically, Chinese characters presented within words are recognised more easily compared to when presented in pseudo-words or in isolation (Shen and Li 2012). Studies indicate that word frequency influences the word-superiority effect, with higher-frequency words exhibiting a more pronounced effect. This is because high-frequency words frequently appear, making them easier for holistic processing. As a result, the top-down word-level information activates more quickly, thereby effectively enhancing Chinese character recognition and resulting in the word-superiority effect (Mok 2009). Character frequency is also a crucial factor influencing the magnitude of the word-superiority effect. Shen and Li (2012) found the word-superiority effect in Chinese only under low character frequency. When character frequency is high, character processing is less influenced by words. This is due to differences in character frequency affecting the speed of Chinese character processing, thereby influencing the strength of the word-superiority effect. Compared to high-frequency characters, low-frequency characters are processed slower, making them more reliant on word-level activation, leading to a stronger word-superiority effect in low-frequency character processing.

The word-superiority effect has also been observed in the Chinese character recognition of CFL learners. A study compared the influence of character frequency on the word-superiority effect between native Chinese speakers and non-proficient Chinese learners (native Thai and Indonesian speakers) (Chen et al. 2018). The results showed that character frequency affected the word-superiority effect for native Chinese speakers. Compared to high-frequency characters, native Chinese speakers exhibited a larger word-superiority effect in low-frequency character recognition, consistent with the finding of Shen and Li (2012). Interestingly, character frequency did not impact the word-superiority effect in CFL learners. Both Thai and Indonesian speakers exhibited a word-superiority effect in both high- and low-frequency characters, with no significant difference in the magnitude of the word-superiority effect. Researchers suggested this is because non-proficient Chinese learners rely more on top-down word-level activation than bottom-up character activation in Chinese character recognition. Chen et al.'s (2017) study on non-proficient Korean CFL learners' word-superiority effect found that character frequency similarly did not affect the word-superiority effect. Non-proficient Korean learners exhibited a word-superiority effect in both high- and low-frequency character recognition, with no significant difference in the magnitude of the word-superiority effect. The research findings suggest that the influence of character frequency on the word-superiority effect among non-proficient Chinese learners may exhibit cross-linguistic commonality. In other words, in the Chinese recognition of non-proficient Chinese learners, character frequency does not impact the word-superiority effect, leading to similar-sized effects in the recognition of both high-frequency and low-frequency characters. Overall, the experimental results above reveal the existence of the word-superiority effect in both native Chinese readers and CFL learners from different linguistic backgrounds. Native Chinese readers tend to rely more on lexical information when processing low-frequency characters compared to high-frequency ones. On the other hand, non-proficient CFL learners require word-level information assistance in recognising both high-frequency and low-frequency characters. This emphasises the universal significance of vocabulary size in Chinese reading across various proficiency levels.

According to research findings, in the initial phases of learning, non-proficient Chinese learners tend to prefer whole-word representations. As their vocabulary expands, they progressively cultivate morphemic awareness, constructing character representations for compound words. Consequently, non-proficient Chinese learners demonstrate a comparatively slower bottom-up processing speed for Chinese characters. In teaching environments that prioritise vocabulary over individual characters, CFL learners' knowledge of Chinese characters may develop more slowly.

The Neighbourhood Size/Frequency Effect

The orthographic neighbourhood effect is an extensively studied phenomenon in word recognition research within alphabetic systems. A word's recognition is enhanced when it has numerous neighbours compared to a few, indicating a facilitatory neighbourhood size effect. Conversely, words with higher frequency neighbours pose greater processing challenges than those without higher frequency neighbours, indicating an inhibitory neighbourhood frequency effect (Coltheart et al. 2022; Yao et al. 2022).

Due to script differences, the definition of orthographic neighbours varies between alphabetic languages and Chinese. In alphabetic languages, orthographic neighbours involve words formed by changing one letter while keeping others intact, whereas in Chinese, orthographic neighbours can be defined in multiple ways. According to different levels of Chinese character orthographic structure, there are potentially multiple definitions of an orthographic neighbour. One is based on the stroke level, where neighbours are formed by replacing, adding or deleting one or more strokes (e.g., 习-勺, 响-响). Another is based on the radical level, where neighbours consist of characters sharing the same radicals. This can be further categorised into phonetic radical neighbours (e.g., 躯-驱) and semantic radical neighbours (e.g., 桃-椎). There is also a definition based on the character level, where neighbours are composed of words that differ from a target word by a single character (e.g., 华丽-华美).

Orthographic neighbourhood effects have been extensively studied in Chinese native speakers. In neighbourhood effects based on stroke level, experiments yielded mixed results using masked priming paradigms. Masked priming paradigms involve participants making responses (e.g., naming) to target characters that are preceded by briefly displayed prime characters, which may or may not be stroke neighbours of the target.

Some research found facilitation of target processing with stroke neighbour primes (Shen and Forster 1999), while others observed inhibitory effects (Wang et al. 2014). Recent research (Yu et al. 2022) suggests that stroke neighbour priming is perceptual in origin, primes with one less stroke facilitated processing, but those with one more stroke slowed target identification. Priming was not influenced by prime frequency, indicating that individual strokes contribute to whole character perception. In orthographic neighbourhood effects based on radical sharing, experimental findings (Li et al. 2011, 2015) show facilitation in naming tasks when characters have a large neighbourhood size when higher-frequency neighbour characters are absent (Li et al. 2011). There is also an inhibitory neighbourhood frequency effect in Chinese character naming when neighbour size is controlled (Li et al. 2011). In orthographic neighbourhood effects based on character level, research has found a robust effect that words with a larger neighbourhood size produced shorter reaction time than those with a smaller neighbourhood size, irrespective of the word frequency and the tasks, while the presence of a higher-frequency neighbour has an inhibitory effect (Li et al. 2015, 2017).

In the context of CFL learners, research on the orthographic neighbourhood effect is limited and primarily focuses on the character-level orthographic neighbourhood effect. Moreover, the results of different studies are not entirely consistent. Two studies employing phonetic annotation and word formation tasks found evidence of an orthographic neighbourhood size effect in the Chinese character learning of CFL learners from alphabetic language backgrounds (Jiang 2006; Zhao 2003). The effect suggests that the number of orthographic neighbours within their textbooks influences the accuracy of Chinese character recognition. Specifically, a higher number of orthographic neighbours is associated with better Chinese character recognition performance. Hao and Liu (2007), using similar tasks, observed that Chinese characters with a higher number of orthographic neighbours are less influenced by character frequency in learning effects, while characters with fewer orthographic neighbours are more affected by character frequency. However, Feng and Song (2004), in their study utilising a lexical decision task, discovered that the impact of orthographic neighbourhood size on Chinese character processing is constrained by the morphemic features encoded in the characters (adhesive or free) and is also influenced by the native language background of CFL learners. For Korean students, the size of orthographic neighbours affects the recognition of Chinese characters as adhesive morphemes but not as free morphemes. In contrast, for western students, the size of orthographic neighbours does not significantly impact the recognition of Chinese characters.

The findings from these studies are not entirely consistent and this inconsistency may be attributed to variations in the calculation methods for orthographic neighbours and frequency. The first three investigations (Hao and Liu 2007; Jiang 2006; Zhao 2003) computed the character frequency and orthographic neighbour quantity based on textbooks actually used by students, reflecting the frequency and number of orthographic neighbours encountered by students. In contrast, Feng and Song (2004) employed native speakers' frequency data for character frequency and defined orthographic neighbour quantity based on the Chinese language teaching syllabus vocabulary list. This approach does not necessarily represent the features of the language materials students encounter in reality. The divergence in research outcomes may also stem from differences in experimental tasks. In summary, current research on orthographic neighbourhood effects in CFL learners regarding Chinese characters is relatively limited. The precise nature of these effects remains unclear, highlighting the necessity for further in-depth investigation.

Based on the limited experimental results (Hao and Liu 2007; Jiang 2006; Zhao 2003), these findings provide some practical guidance for more effectively designing the repeated presentation of newly introduced characters in textbooks. For characters with a higher number of orthographic neighbours, there is no need to significantly increase their repetition frequency. Instead, achieving better learning outcomes can be accomplished by increasing the number of compound words containing them. Conversely, for characters with fewer orthographic neighbours, to enhance learning outcomes, it is advisable to increase the frequency of occurrences of that character and words composed of that character.

Conclusion

The research reviewed in this chapter indicates both similarities and differences in Chinese character recognition between native speakers and CFL learners. For instance, stroke and radical counts have consistent effects on character recognition for native speakers, whereas CFL learners are influenced by additional factors, such as learning stage and task conditions. The word-superiority effect is observed in both native speakers and CFL learners. However, CFL learners lean more towards utilising word-level information for assistance in recognising characters, regardless of their frequency, whereas native speakers predominantly rely on word-level information when dealing with low-frequency characters. Therefore, relevant teaching strategies could be implemented in CFL instruction to enhance learners' Chinese character recognition and utilisation abilities. A summary of the effects reviewed and their possible pedagogical implications is provided in Table 8.1.

However, it is important to recognise certain limitations of the review. Many studies have focused on particular experimental designs and methods, which might not encompass all relevant factors. Moreover, some

Table 8.1 Summary of the impact of orthographic features on Chinese character cognition research

	Research in native speakers	Research in CFL learners	Implications for CFL teaching
Stroke Count Effect	• Stroke count serves as a foundational element in character processing, especially notable among individuals with lower proficiency levels, affecting recognition across both low and high-frequency words.	• CFL learners show a stroke count effect similar to native speakers, but its universality varies with experimental paradigms, affecting its stability; stroke count impact is notable in handwriting tasks.	• In early CFL learning, start with simple characters, emphasising stroke introduction; enhance character recognition through focused stroke teaching in writing courses.
Radical Count Effect	• The number of radicals impacts Chinese character recognition and is linked to character frequency, though results for high- and low-frequency characters vary. Whether characters with more radicals are harder to recognise compared to those with fewer radicals remains uncertain.	• Radical count impact on CFL learners varies with experimental methods and proficiency; they might process high-frequency Chinese characters via strokes and characters, while low-frequency ones involve strokes, radicals and characters; this effect is evident in handwriting tasks.	• Enhancing radical teaching for low-frequency characters is crucial; emphasise radicals in writing courses.
Radical Position Effect	• Radical position information significantly influences character processing; the psychological representation of radicals involves not only their identity but also accurate spatial location.	• CFL learners exhibit a similar pattern to native speakers in terms of the radical position effect.	• Improve CFL learners' radical position awareness; addressing challenges with position-general radicals, especially for novices, is crucial.

(continued)

Table 8.1 (continued)

	Research in native speakers	Research in CFL learners	Implications for CFL teaching
Word Superiority Effect	• Word frequency influences the word-superiority effect, with higher-frequency words exhibiting a more pronounced effect; the word-superiority effect is mainly evident with low-frequency characters.	• Character frequency did not affect the word-superiority effect in CFL learners. Both high- and low-frequency characters showed this effect similarly.	• Vocabulary size is crucial across all proficiency levels; as vocabulary grows, integrate character-level instruction to enhance learning pace.
Neighbourhood Size/ Frequency Effect	• Orthographic neighbourhood effects vary by stroke, radical and character levels. Mixed results occur with stroke neighbour priming, while radical-sharing facilitates naming with larger neighbourhoods but inhibits with higher-frequency neighbours. Larger character neighbourhoods reduce reaction times, while higher-frequency neighbours inhibit.	• Research on orthographic neighbourhood effects in CFL learners primarily focuses on character-level effects; the number of orthographic neighbours influences Chinese character recognition accuracy, which may be influenced by morphemic features and the learners' native language background.	• Limited experimental findings suggest adjusting character repetition in textbooks: in the case of fewer neighbours, increase character repetition; where there are many neighbours, focus on compound words involving the character.

research findings vary across different contexts and learning environments, highlighting the need for more cross-cultural and long-term studies to confirm their general applicability. Lastly, the translation of research findings into tangible teaching strategies and methods requires further practical implementation and validation.

Future research endeavours may need to track the developmental trajectories of CFL learners, particularly in examining whether their character recognition strategies and processing patterns eventually align with those of native speakers. While CFL learners might encounter specific challenges in recognising Chinese characters, such as initial unfamiliarity with the structural and phonetic combinations of characters, their processing approaches could gradually converge with those of native speakers as they accumulate learning experience and enhance their skills. Therefore, upcoming studies could prioritise identifying the specific learning stages and conditions under which CFL learners' character processing abilities begin to mirror those of native speakers, along with investigating the underlying cognitive and neural mechanisms of this progression. Such investigations not only contribute to a more comprehensive understanding of the similarities and differences between native and CFL Chinese character recognition but also offer valuable insights for devising more precise teaching strategies and assessment criteria.

The purpose of this chapter was to identify possible lessons from research in psycholinguistics for pedagogical practice in CFL teaching, specifically relating to character recognition. It is important to keep in mind that most of the research reviewed here was not designed with teaching practice in mind, but rather to deepen our understanding of the cognition of reading. Despite the clear benefits of a broadly scientific approach to reading pedagogy, there is frequently a communication gap between the research community and teachers. This is most clearly demonstrated in the so-called reading wars between advocates of a whole-word versus a phonics approach to teaching English reading (Castles et al. 2018; Seidenberg 2017). Although this is just one example, it is illustrative of the fact that multiple factors—factual and cultural—are often involved in determining what and how of teaching. This is true for the teaching of L1 and L2 reading, right down to the level of teaching character recognition in CFL. With this caveat in mind, we nonetheless hope that we have been able to point to clues in psycholinguistic research that might be of some use to the CFL teacher.

Competing Interests This work was supported by Guangdong Province basic and applied basic research foundation (Grant No.2021A1515111046) and Guangdong Province Philosophy and Social science planning project (GD21CXL05).

References

Carreiras, Manuel, Blair C. Armstrong, Manuel Perea, and Ram Frost. 2014. The What, When, Where, and How of Visual Word Recognition. *Trends in Cognitive Sciences* 18 (2): 90–98.

Castles, Anne, Kathleen Rastle, and Kate Nation. 2018. Ending the Reading Wars: Reading Acquisition from Novice to Expert. *Psychological Science In The Public Interest* 19 (1): 5–51.

Chen, Yuan. 1993. *Analysis of Modern Chinese Character Information*. Shanghai Education Press.

Chen, Lin, Luojin Zhong, and Ying Leng. 2017. Word Superiority Effect for Low Proficiency Korean-Chinese Learners. *Acta Psychologica Sinica* 49 (10): 1277–1286.

Chen, Lin, Charles Perfetti, Ying Leng, and You Li. 2018. Word Superiority Effect For Native Chinese Readers and Low-Proficiency Chinese Learners. *Applied Psycholinguistics* 39 (6): 1097–1115.

Chen, Tianxu, Xu Xintong, Yu Hao, and Sihui Echo Ke. 2023. Connecting the Dots: The Contribution of Orthographic Knowledge to L2 Chinese Reading Comprehension through Serial Mediation of Word Decoding and Listening Comprehension. *Reading and Writing* 36 (5): 1261–1282.

Coltheart, Max, Eileen Davelaar, Jon Torfi Jonasson, and Derek Besner. 2022. Access to the Internal Lexicon. In *Attention and Performance VI*, ed. Stanislav Dornič, 535–555. London: Routledge.

Dictionary of Chinese Character Information [汉字信息字典]. 1988. Shanghai, China: Science Press.

Ding, Guosheng, Danling Peng, and Marcus Taft. 2004. The Nature of the Mental Representation of Radicals in Chinese: A Priming Study. *Journal of Experimental Psychology: Learning, Memory, and Cognition* 30 (2): 530–539.

Feng, Liping. 2002. The Factors Influencing Chinese Character Shape-Phoneme Recognition in Non-Chinese Background International Students. *Chinese Character Culture* 3 (3): 47–49.

Feng, Liping, and Zhiming Song. 2004. The Influence of the Nature and Productivity of Chinese Morphemes on the Morphological Recognition by Foreign Students. *Journal of Yunnan Normal University* 2 (6): 33–38.

Hao, Meiling. 2018. Predictors of Chinese Character Reading: Evidence from Proficient L2 Learners. *Language Teaching and Linguistic Studies* 5: 1–12.

Hao, Meiling, and Youyi Liu. 2007. Occurrence of Character in Textbooks for Learning Chinese as a Second Language: An Experimental Study. *Applied Linguistics* 3 (2): 126–133.

Ho, Connie Suk-Han, Pamela Wing-Yi Yau, and Au. Agnes. 2003. Development of Orthographic Knowledge and Its Relationship with Reading and Spelling among Chinese Kindergarten and Primary School Children. In *Reading Development in Chinese Children*, ed. Catherine McBrideChang and Hsuan-Chih Chen, 51–71. London: Praeger.

Hong, Jon-Chao, Wu Ching-Lin, Hsueh-Chih Chen, Yu-Lin Chang, and Kuo-En Chang. 2016. Effect of Radical-Position Regularity for Chinese Orthographic Skills of Chinese-as-a- Second-Language Learners. *Computers in Human Behavior* 59: 402–410.

Hoover, Wesley A., and Philip B. Gough. 1990. The Simple View of Reading. *Reading and Writing* 2: 127–160.

Jiang, Xin. 2006. The Effects of Frequency and Productivity on Chinese Character Learning by L2 Learners from Alphabetic Language Backgrounds. *Acta Psychologica Sinica* 38 (4): 489–496.

Lei, Linda, and Danping Wang. 2023. Novice Chinese Learners' Character Learning Strategies and Character Skills: A Think-Aloud Study. In *Teaching Chinese in the Anglophone World: Perspectives from New Zealand*, ed. Danping Wang and Martin East, 243–258. Cham: Springer. https://doi.org/10.1007/978-3-031-35475-5_16.

Leong, Che Kan, Shek Kam Tse, Ka Yee Loh, and Wing Wah Ki. 2011. Orthographic Knowledge Important in Comprehending Elementary Chinese Text by Users of Alpha Syllabaries. *Reading Psychology* 32 (3): 237–271.

Li, Qinglin, Hongyan Bi, Tongqi Wei, and Baoguo Chen. 2011. Orthographic Neighborhood Size Effect in Chinese Character Naming: Orthographic and Phonological Activations. *Acta psychologica* 136 (1): 35–41.

Li, Mengfeng, Weichun Lin, Taili Chou, Fuling Yang, and Wu. Jeitun. 2015. The Role of Orthographic Neighborhood Size Effects in Chinese Word Recognition. *Journal of Psycholinguistic Research* 44: 219–236.

Li, Mengfeng, Xinyu Gao, Taili Chou, and Wu. Jeitun. 2017. Neighborhood Frequency Effect In Chinese Word Recognition: Evidence from Naming and Lexical Decision. *Journal of Psycholinguistic Research* 46: 227–245.

Liu, Liping. 2008. The Impacts of the Stroke Number and Structural Way of Chinese Characters on Foreign Students in Learning Chinese Characters. *Language Teaching and Linguistic Studies* 1: 89–96.

Liu, Youyi, Hua Shu, and Ping Li. 2007. Word Naming and Psycholinguistic Norms: Chinese *Behavior Research Methods* 39 (2): 192–198.

Mok, Leh Woon. 2009. Word-Superiority Effect as a Function of Semantic Transparency of Chinese Bimorphemic Compound Words. *Language and Cognitive Processes* 24 (7–8): 1039–1081.

Myers, James. 2019. *The Grammar of Chinese Characters: Productive Knowledge of Formal Patterns in an Orthographic System*. Oxon: Routledge.

Peng, Peng, Kejin Lee, Jie Luo, R. Shuting Li, Malatesha Joshi, and Sha Tao. 2021. Simple View of Reading in Chinese: A One-Stage Meta-Analytic Structural Equation Modeling. *Review of Educational Research* 91 (1): 3–33.

Peng, Danling, and Chunmao Wang. 1997. Basic Processing Unit of Chinese Character Recognition: Evidence from Stroke Number Effect and Radical Number Effect. *Acta Psychologica Sinica* 24 (1): 9–17.

Perfetti, Charles A., and Li Hai Tan. 1998. The Time Course of Graphic, Phonological, and Semantic Activation in Chinese Character Identification. *Journal of Experimental Psychology: Learning, Memory, and Cognition* 24 (1): 101–118.

Perfetti, Charles A., and Sulan Zhang. 1995. Very Early Phonological Activation in Chinese Reading. *Journal of Experimental Psychology: Learning, Memory, and Cognition* 21 (1): 24–33.

Reichle, Erik D. 2021. *Computational Models of Reading: A Handbook*. Oxford University Press.

Seidenberg, Mark. 2017. *Language at the Speed of Sight: How We Read, Why So Many Can't, and What Can Be Done About It*. Basic Books.

Shen, Di, and Kenneth I. Forster. 1999. Masked Phonological Priming in Reading Chinese Words Depends on the Task. *Language and Cognitive Processes* 14 (5–6): 429–459.

Shen, Wei, and Xingshan Li. 2012. The Uniqueness of Word Superiority Effect in Chinese Reading. *Chinese Science Bulletin* 57 (35): 3414–3420.

Su, Yi-Fen, and S. Jay Samuels. 2010. Developmental Changes in Character-Complexity and Word-Length Effects when Reading Chinese Script. *Reading and Writing* 23: 1085–1108.

Tan, Li Hai, Rumjahn Hoosain, and Dan-ling Peng. 1995. Role of Early Presemantic Phonological Code in Chinese Character Identification. *Journal of Experimental Psychology: Learning, Memory, and Cognition* 21 (1): 43–54.

Tong, Xiuli, and Catherine McBride. 2014. Chinese Children's Statistical Learning of Orthographic Regularities: Positional Constraints and Character Structure. *Scientific Studies of Reading* 18 (4): 291–308.

Tong, Xiuli, and Joanna Hew Yan Yip. 2015. Cracking the Chinese character: Radical Sensitivity in Learners of Chinese as a Foreign Language and its Relationship to Chinese Word Reading. *Reading and Writing* 28: 159–181.

Tsang, Yiu-Kei, and Hsuan-Chih Chen. 2009. Do Position-General Radicals have a Role to Play in Processing Chinese Characters? *Language and Cognitive Processes* 24 (7–8): 947–966.

Wang, Jingxin, Jing Tian, Weijin Han, Simon P. Liversedge, and Kevin B. Paterson. 2014. Inhibitory Stroke Neighbour Priming in Character Recognition and Reading in Chinese. *Quarterly Journal of Experimental Psychology* 67 (11): 2149–2171.

Wong, Yu Ka. 2017. Role of Decoding Competence in the Chinese Reading Comprehension Development of Ethnic Minority Students in Hong Kong. *International Journal of Bilingual Education and Bilingualism* 22 (8): 1016–1029.

Wu, Yan, Deyuan Mo, Haiying Wang, Yu Yiyang, Hsuan-Chih Chen, and Ming Zhang. 2016. ERP Effects of Position-Specific Radicals in Chinese Character Recognition: Evidence from Semantic Categorization. *Acta Psychologica Sinica* 48 (6): 599–606.

Yao, Panpan, Adrian Staub, and Xingshan Li. 2022. Predictability Eliminates Neighborhood Effects during Chinese Sentence Reading. *Psychonomic Bulletin & Review* 29: 243–252.

You, Haoji. 2003. How is the Acquisition of Chinese Characters by Learners from the Non-Chinese Character Culture Sphere Affected by Stroke Numbers, Component Numbers and Topological Structural Patterns. *Journal of Chinese Teaching in the World* 2: 72–81.

Yu, Bolin, and Heqi Cao. 1992. A New Exploration on the Effect of Stroke-Number in the Identification of Chinese Characters. *Journal of Psychological Science* 21 (5): 5–10.

Yu, Lili, Qiaoming Zhang, Meiling Ke, Yifei Han, and Sachiko Kinoshita. 2022. Some Neighbors are More Interfering: Asymmetric Priming by Stroke Neighbors in Chinese Character Recognition. *Psychonomic Bulletin & Review* 30 (3): 1065–1073.

Zhang, Jinqiao. 2008. On the Stroke Effect, Word Frequency Effect and Morpheme Frequency Effect in the Recognition of Chinese One-Character Words by Foreign Students. *Journal of College of Chinese Language and Culture of Jinan University* 1: 22–29.

Zhang, Wutian, and Ling Feng. 1992. A Study on the Unit of Processing in Recognition of Chinese Characters. *Acta Psychologica Sinica* 24 (04): 379–385.

Zhang, Qi, and Ronan G. Reilly. 2015. Writing to Read: The Case of Chinese. *Proceedings of the 29th Pacific Asia Conference on Language, Information and Computation*: 341– 350.

Zhang, Jijia, and Hongyan Sheng. 1999. Study on the Influence of the Relationship of the Wholes and Their Parts in the Perceptual Separation of Chinese Characters. *Acta Psychologica Sinica* 31 (04): 369–376.

Zhao, G. 2003. Productivity of Characters in Forming Words and the Acquisition of Characters for CSL Beginners. *Applied Linguistics* 3: 106–112.

Zhu, Zhaoxia, Li Liu, Lei Cui, and Danling Peng. 2019. The Influence of Writing on Reading: Evidence from the Contrast Between Traditional Writing and Typing. *Advances in Psychological Science* 27 (5): 796–803.

Theme IV
Reflective Narrative

9

Reflections on Learning Chinese Characters

Bob Adamson

Introduction

I was delighted to receive an invitation from three leading scholars in the field of Chinese linguistics to contribute a concluding chapter to this book. I will offer some insights from the perspective of a learner of various languages, including Chinese. (I must admit, however, that I have failed miserably to master Chinese characters.) I will also draw on my experiences as a teacher and teacher educator, particularly in the subject areas of English and French. I once designed and taught a brief introduction to conversational Chinese, but I cannot claim any of the specialist pedagogical expertise demonstrated by the chapter authors. I have also worked for many years as a researcher in the area of language policy and curriculum reform, focusing on English language education and, more recently, on multilingual education in China, which has helped me to

---

B. Adamson (✉)
University of Nottingham Ningbo China, Ningbo, China
e-mail: Bob.Adamson@nottingham.edu.cn

understand some of the challenges of teaching and learning languages in complex linguistic settings. In this chapter, I will try to bring together various perspectives to create (I hope) a coherent argument for principled pragmatism in the selection of pedagogical strategies for teaching Chinese characters in different learning contexts.

While my mastery of written Chinese is extremely poor, I do have some competence in spoken Chinese, having lived in mainland China and Hong Kong for more than 30 years—although "some competence" needs elaboration. Without having taken any formal assessments, I estimate that I speak Putonghua at lower intermediate level, and Cantonese at basic level, despite being quite tone-deaf. (My strategy is to talk quickly with plenty of language-teacher gesticulation and to hope that people can decipher my meaning.) I have had very few formal lessons, apart from a ten-day preparatory programme before I left the UK for China in 1983. This programme comprised—to the best of my recollection—long stretches of má-mā-mǎ-mà recitation. Once I arrived at the college in Taiyuan where I was to teach English, I learnt some valuable functional phrases from a kind foreign affairs official (who went on to become a very distinguished professor of Chinese as a foreign language). Otherwise, I picked up spoken Chinese from friends, students, colleagues and people in the community. A local corner shop that stocked strawberry jam became a place for numerous fruitful conversations. Long train journeys in hard-sleeper carriages provided opportunities to develop my conversational skills around the topics of age, salary, family and the cost of consumer items in the UK. Playing for a football team significantly increased my informal vocabulary—and, when asked by teammates for a phrase in English that they could use with impunity against the referee, I taught them "On your bike, ref!", which seemed culturally appropriate at the time. Navigating the intricacies of Chinese bureaucracy became a linguistic opportunity, as I became friendly with officials in travel agencies, visa offices, tax affairs bureaux, banks and police stations. Nonetheless, misunderstandings have always been a feature of my interactions. (I remember trying to buy washing powder and being presented with envelopes.) My listening comprehension is a little better, but I continue to get the wrong end of the stick. Just recently, I was taken from Ningbo to Shanghai by a driver who extolled the virtues of "UberPay", which I took to be a payment mechanism related to car rides. UberPay was quick and robust, he told me. I was intrigued because I thought it was not an available option, so I asked "Is UberPay working in China now?" "No", came the reply. "He plays for Real Madrid now." (It only then clicked with me that we had been discussing the merits of the French footballer, Kylian Mbappé.)

In terms of literacy, I can recognise just a few hundred characters in simplified form and even fewer in full form, being particularly familiar with those used in everyday life and educational contexts. I can write the Chinese version of my name in both forms and can copy unfamiliar characters when needed (such as addressing a package for posting). This very limited stock of knowledge was acquired painfully. My first initiation was in 1983, in Aberystwyth, where I was a student at the University of Wales. Shortly before completing my Postgraduate Certificate of Education there, I received notice from Voluntary Service Overseas that my application to work in China was successful. I eagerly sought the help of a Taiwanese student, who gave me an introduction to a few characters in return for a suitable beverage in a local pub. He wrote some characters, literally on the back of an envelope. Sensibly, he chose pictographs/pictograms for me, and more than 40 years later I can remember that he started with the full-form version of *door* (門), which he likened to the entrance to a saloon bar in a Western film; *person* (人), "a matchstick figure"; and *wood* (木), which resembles a tree. I breezily commented that, based on this evidence, learning Chinese characters seemed to be very straightforward, but he advised me that this was not the case.

Once I had arrived in Taiyuan, the college offered me some Chinese calligraphy lessons, which introduced concepts of stroke order, the balance of characters and aesthetic values. After starting with some easy pictographs, such as *sun* (日) and *mountain* (山), that required just a few strokes, the teacher moved on to common ideographs, including the points of the compass.

I loved the story of the characters that the teacher told me. I discovered that *east* in full form (東) showed the sun rising behind a tree at dawn, and that *west* (西) depicted a bird settling on its nest at sunset. I learnt that the simplified character for *country* (国) had been converted from *king* (王) to *jade* (玉) in an enclosed area to reflect new political realities.

He also told me that the first character in the name for English (英) was in the form of a devil, but the twinkle in his eye revealed that he was pulling my leg. I recall spending endless time practising *eternal* (永), as it comprised all the strokes. This was my first inkling that writing characters was, indeed, far from straightforward and achieving a reasonable degree of mastery would require time, effort and dedication—all of which proved to be deficient in my case. At that time, I did not envisage lifelong engagement with the Chinese language, so I failed to make the requisite investment.

During my four years in Taiyuan, my domains of Chinese language use were mainly oral. What progress I did make with my literacy was largely restricted to public signage and place names. I benefitted significantly from buying a Chinese-English dictionary. Searching for a character involved a fundamental understanding of radicals and strokes, and I enjoyed "character-surfing", beginning with adjacent characters to the one I was seeking to translate and then moving on to characters with the same radical. From this dictionary, I learnt that *cup* (杯) has a wood radical, and that my Chinese name (鲍勃) literally means "prosperous abalone", wherein *abalone* is constructed as "a fish that sounds like *bao*". The dictionary was invaluable when I started conducting research for my master's and doctoral degrees, both of which focused on language policy in China, and I learnt the meaning of a range of characters relating to education and linguistics. I also found a book in French that presented the etymology of numerous characters. I discovered that *no* (不) is a representation of a seed that is unable to penetrate the soil crust, while *exit* (出) comprises two seeds that successfully sprouted. These discoveries fascinated me, but they did little to help my written Chinese.

I briefly flirted with a storytelling approach, whereby the components of a character were transformed into a story that had relevance to the meaning of the character. While this method worked for a few characters, the convoluted nature of some stories presented too much of an information overload for me. A friend then introduced me to another learning method, familiar to many students of Chinese before the advent of computer programs. This approach involved cards with the character (marked with the stroke order) on one side and the *pinyin* and English translation on the other. The method required about 20 minutes per day and suggested that the learner could meet up to ten new characters each time. (I finally settled on three.) On the first day, I looked at the new characters and associated them with their English translation. The cards were placed in Box 1. On the second day, I tested my ability to translate these characters; if successful, I learnt the *pinyin* and tone and moved the relevant card to Box 2; if unsuccessful, the card would remain in Box 1, where they would be joined by three new characters. On the third day, I would look at the characters in Box 2 and, if I could recall the translation, *pinyin* and tone, each card would be promoted to Box 3 but reversed so that the side of the card showing the translation and *pinyin* was visible, while the cards in Boxes 2 and 1 (plus three new characters) would be treated as described above. On the fourth day, I would follow the same procedures and also attempt to write the characters stored in Box 3. I would remove a card from Box 3 once I felt I had mastered the written form of the character as well as its translation, *pinyin* and tone. I enjoyed learning this way, and I estimate that I became confident in recognising and writing some 50 characters, but two factors prevented me from continuing. The first was the random nature of character selection. I drew them from the pile of cards that were provided in the set, but I encountered them without a sense of context. I found it difficult to recognise or reproduce the characters in real life. The second stemmed from this discouragement—I lost confidence in my ability and never resumed any serious attempts to learn characters in a systematic way.

From Taiyuan, I moved to Hong Kong, where I settled for most of my career as a language teacher, teacher educator and academic. I lived and worked in a largely English-speaking environment, though I managed to acquire sufficient spoken Cantonese for everyday interactions. One family activity that we enjoyed was watching TV dramas, and the local stations helpfully provided subtitles in the form of characters for viewers who spoke other varieties of Chinese. I came to recognise a few more characters through this medium. In recent years, translation apps have also helped me to broaden my repertoire. This newly acquired knowledge, however, has not been transferred into the ability to write the characters.

As a somewhat delinquent student, I marvel at the competence of native and non-native writers of Chinese and occasionally wonder (albeit without strong pangs of regret) how I might have done better. Reading the chapters in this book was valuable to me. In Chap. 7, it was reassuring to learn that the various approaches I had stumbled upon, such as using etymological information, visuals or ideographs, storytelling, radicals, and rote-learning were well established and researched in the field, while "chunking" (identifying common non-radical shapes used in characters) opens up new possibilities to me. Chapter 6, meanwhile, made me feel a little better about my incompetence by providing a very good explanation of the challenges I had faced in managing the transition from receptive recognition of characters in reading texts to the active production of them in written output, and also made me realise that I have not explored the opportunities offered by e-learning. Chapter 3 and Chap. 5 developed this thought by conveying the potential for multimodal repertoires that encompass online learning through the judicious use of apps as well as activities that involve face-to-face support from a teacher. Chapter 4 reminded me of the benefits of integration of the learning of oral/aural Chinese with literacy.

Towards a Comprehensive Pedagogy: Principled Pragmatism

The disparate nature of the approaches outlined above leads me to consider how they might be packaged into a personal pedagogy. I would first make a distinction between a personal pedagogy and a methodology. The latter, to my mind, refers to a set of strategies that are derived from a particular theory of language learning, while the former could potentially embrace a range of theories and, by extension, strategies. A personal pedagogy, in this conceptualisation, might be open to criticisms of methodological incompatibility or confusion, because the strategies in the teacher's (or, as in my case, the independent learner's) repertoire might be drawn from different theoretical views of the nature of language, language learning and education in general. For instance, there are methodologies that emphasise the linguistic systems that underpin a language, and promote teaching strategies that mainly focus on the micro-level analysis and mastery of aspects such as morphology, syntax, phonology and—in the case of Chinese—character composition, while other methodologies conceive language as a socio-cultural phenomenon, and encourage the teacher to set up opportunities for students to encounter and develop competence in real-life situations that require appropriate, holistic communication. While not entirely mutually exclusive, these two methodological orientations tend to give rise to learning experiences and materials, teaching points and assessments that are radically different. Similarly, beliefs about language learning can include views that emphasise cognitive, social or whole-person developmental processes.

Languages might be included in an education system for a host of reasons, as there are numerous orientations to education. For instance, *academic rationalism* values established knowledge and cultural traditions. To return to my firsthand experiences, I learnt Latin in secondary school, on the grounds that it was a part of my "classical" heritage of human wisdom and culture and, through engagement with the lexical and grammatical forms, I could also achieve a disciplined sense of how languages are constructed. *Social and economic efficiency* seeks to produce the requisite human resources to satisfy the jobs market and to create a citizenry that is cognisant of its rights and responsibilities. In this respect, the rise of Chinese as an international language can be linked to the emergence of China as an economic power—when the nation was poor, very few schools overseas offered it, especially given the linguistic distance between Chinese and many other languages that complicates the learning process. *Individualism* focuses on personal fulfilment—I also learnt some French, German and Russian at school, with the understanding that these languages provided opportunities for cultural exchanges that could broaden my horizons. (The specific choices seemed pragmatic: French and German are the languages of nearby countries, they use the Roman alphabet, they are reasonably strong international languages; while Russian appeared to be taught because of available expertise among current members of staff.) *Social reconstructionism* views education as a vehicle for societal change. I went to university in Wales at a time when there was a revival in teaching the endangered Welsh language in schools to ensure its survival; I took a course at beginner level taught by the excellent Tedi Millward, who had a fine track record in teaching gauche

Englishmen, as viewers of royal dramas on TV might attest. *Orthodoxy* is concerned with the transmission of a religious or political ideology, which explains why, as a very young altar-boy, I undertook a crash course in Church Latin for use during a Tridentine Mass. (I had only completed the initial pages of this training when a visiting priest came to say a Mass. By the time we reached the Gospel, I had exhausted my knowledge of the Latin version and had to resort to giving the responses in English thereafter, thus pioneering a bilingual approach that sadly did not catch on.) The point I wish to make here is that the pedagogy that we choose to adopt as a teacher needs to take into account the educational purposes that underpin the learning of the particular language, as these affect the content of the curriculum (such as the text types) and the pedagogy (in respect of, for example, the degree of learner autonomy). For instance, a person who wishes to acquire Chinese to live in China would require a different curriculum and pedagogy to a student who wishes to master Chinese calligraphy as an art form.

How languages are to be learnt is another area of complexity. It appears that the search for a supermethod, the one-size-fits-all approach, has been abandoned (despite the occasional burst of overhyping of a methodological fad from excitable proponents, politicians jumping on a bandwagon and commercial publishers looking to corner a market). The days of the zero-sum game, which eliminated tried and trusted methods on the grounds that they were "traditional" (a damning sobriquet) in favour of a new wonder-solution that would predominate until elbowed out by the next whippersnapper, are numbered, although the publication of PISA scores still can elicit a kneejerk pursuit of the elusive silver bullet. Instead (and to continue with the mixed metaphors), language teachers find themselves in a bazaar of shiny baubles for their delectation and delight. Skilful teachers can assess each one for its value, add as many as possible to their collection and produce them on the appropriate pedagogical occasion.

This book also highlights how unexpected circumstances can radically alter the context in which teaching and learning takes place, with implications for the available modes of delivery—which, in turn, impacts on pedagogical approaches. The COVID-19 pandemic brought about major disruption to education on a similar scale to wars, civil turmoil and the

9 Reflections on Learning Chinese Characters 231

aftermath of national disasters. Witnessing and participating in the rapid shift to online delivery of courses, I was reminded of my visit to Sarajevo about 15 years ago. There I met some teachers who had managed to provide schooling to children in the extremely dangerous conditions of the siege of the city in the 1990s. Although schools were closed, makeshift classrooms were set up in the basements of apartment blocks and similar buildings and, as the teachers moved around the various locations, they were exposed to sniper fire. Likewise, I heard a story from a Chinese language teacher about her experiences during the Cultural Revolution (1966–76) in China, when she was kept in the custody of her students as part of their revolutionary action to eradicate traditional education. Despite her ill-treatment—her hair was shaved from half of her head as a sign of disrespect—she continued to act as a mentor to the Red Guards, even pointing out the errors in the characters on their posters and banners. Such traumatic events can bring about a recommitment to fundamental values in education, while also necessitating innovative ideas and practices. The COVID-19 pandemic, for instance, greatly enhanced the use of online learning in places that had access to the requisite technology, while the siege schools of Sarajevo necessitated teachers using whatever resources they could procure under constrained circumstances.

What does all the above mean for the learning and teaching of Chinese characters? Basically, I would argue that the most important fundamental value for a teacher is to teach students. Covering a syllabus is meaningless if the students have not learnt the contents or achieved the set goals. If we take student learning as the main measure of successful teaching, it follows that teachers should select methods that suit the students' needs, interests and abilities. Their needs might be dictated by external forces, such as Chinese being provided as a compulsory subject, the nature of assessments (as discussed in Chap. 2), time constraints (Chap. 6), the requirements of a qualifications framework or the exigencies of a pandemic, but they can also encompass the students' intrinsic motivations. Students' interests can encompass their preferred learning styles and settings, curriculum content and teacher-student relationships. (For instance, in Taiyuan, I enjoyed my informal one-to-one Chinese lessons with the foreign affairs official. She allowed me to select my topics—geography, education, sport and daily life interactions—and displayed patience, encouragement and a capacity for light-touch correction.) Taking students' abilities into consideration can result in successful learning outcomes if the expectations are adjusted to what the students have the potential to achieve. Attending to all three perspectives (needs, interests and abilities) can give rise to greater motivation in students stemming from enjoyment of learning, humanistic pedagogy and a sense of success.

Beyond the students' needs, interests and abilities, the teacher's own training, experience, personality, beliefs and preferred practices can shape pedagogical choices. Available resources and the capacity of the teacher and students to make effective use of them can be important, as vividly illustrated during the pandemic (see Chap. 2). The ethos of the institution in which the learning is taking place (if it is a formal setting) and structures such as promotion criteria, inspection protocols and policy priorities determined by senior management and funding agencies all have a potential impact. Given all the variables facing the teacher, being able to choose from a broad repertoire of pedagogical approaches is invaluable.

Objections to this deployment of an all-encompassing range of approaches can arise as it involves drawing on differing—and even conflicting—theories of language learning. However, it is clear from the fruitless search for the supermethod that there are many valid ways to learn a language and the contexts of learning can change from minute to minute. Pragmatic pedagogical choices can take account of the specific circumstances. The pragmatism should be principled, in that the choices are based on a sound rationale: the selected pedagogy at that given moment should be addressing a particular learning outcome. (This detail is important for professional accountability as well as pedagogical coherence.) When it comes to literacy, the goals are to foster in our students the relevant proficiency in recognising and writing Chinese characters. (Of course, it is highly likely that the students' proficiency in recognising characters will be greater than their proficiency in writing them.)

Figure 9.1 sets out some routes towards achieving these goals. When teaching Chinese characters, the teacher seeks to reach the top-right quadrant through working within and across the other three quadrants. The quadrants are intended to form a reference point for a given learning

9 Reflections on Learning Chinese Characters

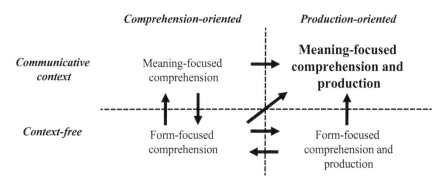

Fig. 9.1 Routes to assist students in comprehending and producing Chinese characters

context. Such contexts could be a very short phase of learning (for instance, a ten- minute sequence in which a new character is presented and de-composed, and then written by the learner for the first time) or cover a longer period—as Chap. 7 notes, the learning styles of novice and experienced learners tend to be different. To allow for flexibility, while the overall progression is from the bottom-left hand quadrant (form-focused comprehension of characters in an uncontextualised setting) to the top- right hand quadrant (meaning-focused comprehension and production of characters in communicative contexts), this is not necessarily a linear progression. There are various routes to the target. There are also various starting points. For instance, the students might be working on a reading comprehension in which a new character appears. They may make an educated guess as to the meaning of the character based on the context, but then the teacher draws their attention to the construction of the character, without making specific reference to its contribution to the reading text. In such a case, the initial encounter with the new character occurred in a communicative context (top- left hand box) but the teaching focus, in which, say, the radical and phonetic components are discussed, might be placed in the bottom-left hand quadrant. Moreover, the quadrants are not rigidly separated—they represent a dominant rather than exclusive focus—and are therefore delineated by dotted lines. (Apart from fleeting moments, it is nearly impossible, for instance, to discuss the form of a character without referring to its meaning.)

The chapters in this volume suggest that teachers require a pedagogical repertoire that could cover all four quadrants. As reported in Chap. 6 and Chap. 7, research suggests that the development of both *perceptual visual* skills and *visual-orthographic* skills is related to character learning success. Such skills can be developed through form-focused as well as meaning-focused learning activities. Any methodology that exists exclusively in individual quadrants might risk denying the learners valuable opportunities either to achieve macro-level communicative competence through Chinese literacy or to develop micro-level strategies that could underpin that competence. As Chap. 8 points out, form and meaning are symbiotic, not mutually exclusive, and reading comprehension and writing production exist in a reciprocal relationship that benefits from an integration of teaching methods across the different quadrants. An argument emerges for presenting new characters within a communicative context rather than isolating them, and to introduce them to the learners in "meaningful" ways, such as by providing both characters in a two-character word, or by selecting characters that are needed for a particular communicative task.

When recounting my personal experiences of learning Chinese characters above, I mentioned that the transition from reading to writing is particularly difficult. This can be explained by the fact that, as a Westerner, I am used to the written form of a language possessing a strong phonetic component—a feature that is far less evident in Chinese writing. Some help is available nowadays with the development of digital software that offers a selection of characters based on the writer's inputting of *pinyin*. This method relies more on receptive recognition than on active production of characters on the part of the learners, to the extent that Linda Lei and Danping Wang in Chap. 2 suggest that learners might not need to learn to write characters themselves in future. If that were the case, they might be missing out on a learning opportunity, as Xi Fan and Ronan Reilly (Chap. 8) set out several ways in which writing characters can reinforce learners' reading comprehension. These are not contradictory messages: they are alternative strategies that are available to the teacher to choose according to the learning context. For instance, if a student is learning the language for purposes that do not require a high level of competence in written Chinese, then the *pinyin*-input method might be

9 Reflections on Learning Chinese Characters 235

appropriate and effective, but if the purposes do require it, then the handwriting approach would enable the behavioural, cognitive and neuroscience advantages to be activated. Chapter 6 offers a syllabus for transitioning from reading to writing with a systematic form-based approach. In the chapter, Andrew Scrimgeour acknowledges the difficulties of mapping such an approach onto a scheme of work that has communicative outcomes as its main goal. In the case of the latter, the requisite vocabulary is determined by the nature of the communication, whereas the former envisages the presentation of characters that have structural similarities rather than lexical associations. Again, though, I would argue that these are not necessarily contradictory. Room can be made in a communicative approach for a strand of learning that is based on character structure—for instance, one character introduced to the students as valuable for a particular communicative setting could also be presented with a few other characters that have a structural connection to it.

Figure 9.1 is presented for the purposes of developing competence in reading and writing Chinese characters. However, it can also apply more generally to receptive (reading and listening) and productive (writing and speaking) skills. So, what is the relationship between oral competence and literacy? The linguistic distance between the oral and written forms of Chinese and the slow pace that is a feature of learning characters have led to arguments for separating the presentation of the two forms to students (see Chap. 6 for a discussion of the pros and cons). A principled pragmatic pedogogy would not rule out making links between teaching oral and written forms. For example, a thematic approach, whereby a topic that matches the students' needs, interests and abilities is selected and explored through relevant text types, offers possibilities for connections to be made across oral and written texts at both the macro- and micro-levels of meaning and form. Likewise, the use of the students' first language might also play a role, both as a linguistic database that they can draw upon or as a medium of instruction. Translanguaging offers potential benefits in this respect.

Given the complexities outlined above, how might a scheme of work be planned? There are several possibilities, such as focusing initially on receptive skills and oral production, while developing understanding of the form of characters, before moving on to a stronger focus on productive skills. I would suggest a thematic approach, which allows for focus on form and meaning, with the theme providing a context that shapes the choice of vocabulary/characters, grammatical points and relevant receptive or productive skills. The sequence of learning design might be as follows:

1. Select a theme.
2. Identify topics within the theme that match the students' needs, interests and abilities.
3. Concoct or select oral and/or written texts.
4. Present and/or elicit key information related to the topic and pre-teach important vocabulary and grammar.
5. Design comprehension activities that focus first on meaning, and then on relevant vocabulary, grammar and skills.
6. Practise character formation in isolation, drawing on examples from the text, but adding characters that share structural similarities as desired.
7. Scaffold student production of oral and written texts on topics related to the theme.

This sequence of learning does not restrict the pedagogical options available to the teachers or students. Principled pragmatism allows for flexibility in this respect, at all stages of the learning process.

To ensure a flexible responsiveness to changing situations of learning, it might be useful to conceptualise some specific choices in terms of continua. The quadrants of Fig. 9.1 are underpinned by a number of polarities. Figure 9.2 sets out some examples. The arrow on each continuum is a slider that can move to the right or to the left according to circumstances. The general direction over time would be to the right, to bring about student autonomous production of meaningful text in authentic communicative situations. However, the learning process may require (as discussed above) phases which are teacher-directed, working on receptive skills, focused on the composition of characters in isolation, handling texts that have been specifically concocted for the needs of the students (and which would not be usually found outside of a learning environment) and restricted to a set time and place. Thus, the arrows might move

9 Reflections on Learning Chinese Characters

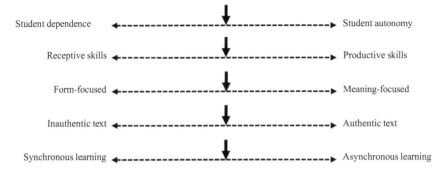

Fig. 9.2 Continua for teacher decision-making

within the course of a brief learning activity as well as over an extended period. Whether the impetus to move the arrows arises from the teacher's and students' beliefs and preferred practices, or from the impositions of external factors, principled pragmatism offers a flexible and coherent response to complex challenges. Pedagogy that encompasses both poles on the continua is valid, and even essential for effective learning.

Concluding Comments

In this chapter, I have picked out several ideas that I have gleaned from this excellent book. Those that I have selected resonated with aspects of my own experiences as a language teacher, and I have sought to devise a pedagogical approach that is coherent in my own mind. It is underpinned by my view that the purpose in learning Chinese characters is to be able to use the knowledge and skills autonomously for written communication in real-life situations. Others may have different goals, but I surmise that the purpose I set out chimes with most learners. A major concern for me in constructing my approach has been to address the problems that I have encountered in learning Chinese characters—again, others may have different problems—but, without making any false claims to be a definitive approach, I believe it can be flexible enough to incorporate changes. For instance, the transition from a focus on reading to writing characters can be facilitated—as this book argues—by online resources, which also have the merit of fostering autonomous learning, but students in low-tech environments might not have access to these programmes; instead, they can be supported by more "traditional" or time- honoured pedagogies that serve the same function.

I also appreciate that my lack of expertise in mastering characters—let alone teaching them—might stimulate some (very reasonable) scepticism among readers who have been highly successful in these endeavours when they engage with my opinions on the subject. Such scepticism is healthy and welcome—it is an important skill for any teacher to sift through pedagogical suggestions in order to separate the recyclable from the landfill. There are many ideas in the chapters that readers will find more valuable and inspiring, and which I have overlooked, so I would recommend that readers undertake, individually or collectively, their own process of synthesising the insights afforded by this book and their own pedagogical beliefs. If that happens, this book will have achieved its purpose.

Index

C

Character structure, 143, 148, 149, 151
Chinese character, 12, 23, 24, 26, 30–32, 34, 36, 39, 51, 197, 199–202, 204, 207, 208
Chinese writing system, 135–137, 139–141, 143, 144, 148, 150, 151, 153, 157, 158
  routine writing practice, 135, 139, 146, 147, 156
Chunking, 163, 164, 167, 172–175, 178–180, 185, 188, 189
Components, 135, 137, 140–145, 147–149, 152–158
  configurations, 149, 153, 154
Curriculum, 4, 7, 10, 14

E

Embodied, 106, 109, 110, 123–128
Embodiment, 106, 109, 127, 128
Emergency remote teaching (ERT), 13, 23, 27, 33, 39
E-writing, 81–85, 87, 88, 90, 96, 97

H

Handwriting, 5–8, 47, 48, 53, 61, 64–66, 68, 71–73, 105–130

L

Learning strategies, 61, 62, 65, 71

M

Memorisation, 139, 145, 147

O

Orthographic awareness, 163, 165, 169, 172, 189, 190

P

Psycholinguistics, 197

R

Radicals, 135–137, 140, 141, 147, 149, 152, 156, 197, 199, 200, 203, 205, 210
  phonetic radical, 135, 137–141, 150
  semantic radical, 137–140, 142, 149, 152

Reading, 135, 139, 145–148, 153

S

Strokes, 137, 139–141, 144, 147, 149, 151, 152, 154, 155
Stroke sequences, 139, 151

T

Technology, 5, 14, 50, 52, 54, 61, 63, 64, 71–73
Typing, 6, 7, 47, 48, 54, 61, 64, 66, 68, 71, 72, 105–111, 113, 114, 116–121, 123–128

V

Visual skills, 163–167, 169, 170

Printed in the USA
CPSIA information can be obtained
at www.ICGtesting.com
CBHW062112131024
15794CB00006B/349